Better Homes and Gardens

ENCYCLOPEDIA
of
COOKING

Volume 14

Perk up your pickle and olive relish plate with Carrot-Olive Slaw. It's simple to make. Just combine shredded carrots and sliced, ripe olives with a vinegar-oil dressing.

On the cover: Whether it's by the link and accompanied with potato salad or sliced for a sandwich, sausage is an all-time favorite. Popular accompaniments are mustard and pickles.

BETTER HOMES AND GARDENS BOOKS
NEW YORK • DES MOINES

©Meredith Corporation, 1971. All Rights Reserved.
Printed in the United States of America.
First Printing.
Library of Congress Catalog Card Number: 73-129265
SBN 696-02014-9

RELISH—A food served as an accompaniment to add color and flavor to a meal. Popular relishes include crisp, raw vegetables—carrot sticks, celery strips, cauliflowerets, pickles, olives—and succulent mixtures of chopped fruits or vegetables such as cranberry relish and corn relish. A piquantly dressed salad, pickled or spiced fruits and vegetables, and applesauce also fall into the relish category. Even catsup and mustard are sometimes considered relishes.

Red Pepper Relish

  20 sweet red peppers
   6 medium onions
   3 cups vinegar
   3 cups sugar
   2 tablespoons salt
   2 tablespoons mustard seed

Halve peppers; discard stems and seeds. Grind peppers through food chopper, using coarse blade to make 2 quarts ground peppers. Coarsely grind onions to make 3 cups ground onion. Combine undrained vegetables with vinegar, sugar, salt, and mustard seed. Simmer, uncovered, 45 minutes. Seal at once in hot, sterilized jars. Chill. Makes six ½-pints.

Pickled Apricots

   1 cup dried apricots
   1 cup brown sugar
  ¼ cup vinegar
   2 inches stick cinnamon
   6 whole cloves
  24 to 30 walnut halves

Rinse apricots. In saucepan cover apricots with 1 inch water. Cover and simmer gently for 15 minutes. Drain, reserving ¾ cup apricot liquid. In saucepan combine reserved apricot liquid, brown sugar, vinegar, stick cinnamon, and whole cloves. Stir in apricots; return to boiling and simmer, covered, till the apricots are tender, about 10 minutes more.

    Cool apricots in syrup. Refrigerate till ready to serve. At serving time, remove the apricots from the syrup. Fill each apricot half with a walnut half. Makes 2 to 2½ dozen.

Bean Relish

   1 16-ounce can whole green beans
  ⅓ cup vinegar
   2 tablespoons sugar
   1 teaspoon salt
   1 teaspoon dillseed
   1 teaspoon mixed pickling spices
        • • •
   1 medium onion, sliced and
      separated in rings
   1 tablespoon salad oil

Drain beans, reserving liquid. In saucepan combine reserved liquid with vinegar, sugar, salt, dillseed, and mixed pickling spices; simmer 5 minutes. Add beans; heat the mixture through. Cool mixture. Then, drain off excess liquid. Toss beans with onion rings and salad oil. Chill before serving. Makes about 2 cups.

Apple-Pickle Relish

Combine 2 unpeeled tart apples, chopped; ¼ cup chopped onion; and ¼ cup chopped dill pickle. Combine ¼ cup sugar and 2 tablespoons vinegar. Toss with apple mixture; chill the mixture thoroughly. Makes about 3 cups relish.

Confetti Relish

   1 16-ounce can French-style green
      beans, drained
   1 12-ounce can whole kernel corn,
      drained
   1 8½-ounce can peas, drained
   1 6-ounce can sliced mushrooms,
      drained
  ¼ cup chopped onion
  ¼ cup diced canned pimiento
  ⅓ cup white wine vinegar
  ¼ cup sugar
   1 teaspoon salt
  ½ cup salad oil

Combine the first 6 ingredients in a large bowl. In screw-top jar combine vinegar, sugar, and salt; cover and shake till the sugar is dissolved. Add oil and shake the mixture well. Pour oil mixture over vegetable mixture. Chill several hours, stirring occasionally. Drain well before serving. Makes about 5 cups.

Fresh Corn Relish

A summertime favorite—

>   4 cups fresh, cut corn (6 to 8
>   medium ears)
>   2 cups chopped cabbage
>   2 tablespoons chopped onion
>   ¾ cup vinegar
>   ½ cup water
>   ½ cup sugar
>   ½ envelope French salad dressing
>   mix (1 tablespoon)
>   ½ cup chopped green pepper
>   2 tablespoons chopped canned
>   pimiento

In saucepan combine corn, cabbage, onion, vinegar, water, sugar, and salad dressing mix. Simmer about 20 minutes, stirring occasionally. Cool; add chopped green pepper and pimiento. Chill thoroughly. Makes 5 cups relish.

Cranberry-Orange Relish is perfect for holiday gift giving. Tuck a jar inside a grater, and trim with ribbons and stars.

Cranberry-Orange Relish

>   1 pound fresh cranberries
>   2 cups sugar
>   ½ cup water
>   1 teaspoon grated orange peel
>   ½ cup orange juice
>   ½ cup slivered almonds

In saucepan combine cranberries, sugar, water, orange peel, and orange juice. Cook, uncovered, till cranberry skins pop, about 10 minutes, stirring once or twice. Remove mixture from heat. Stir in the almonds. Cool. Store relish in covered container in the refrigerator till ready to serve. Makes about 4 cups relish.

Carrot-Olive Slaw

>   ¼ cup salad oil
>   2 tablespoons vinegar
>   2 tablespoons sugar
>   ½ teaspoon salt
>   Dash pepper
>   3 cups shredded carrots
>   ¼ cup sliced pitted ripe olives

Combine salad oil, vinegar, sugar, salt, and pepper. Toss lightly with shredded carrots and sliced olives. Chill. Makes about 2½ cups.

Salsa

Serve this delicious Mexican-style sauce as a relish with meats or omelets—

>   4 medium firm, ripe tomatoes,
>   peeled and finely chopped
>   ½ cup finely chopped onion
>   ½ cup finely chopped celery
>   ¼ cup finely chopped green pepper
>   ¼ cup olive oil or salad oil
>   2 tablespoons red wine vinegar
>   1 tablespoon mustard seed
>   1 teaspoon coriander seed, crushed
>   2 to 3 tablespoons drained, canned,
>   finely chopped green chilies
>   1 teaspoon salt
>   Dash pepper

Mix all ingredients together in a bowl. Chill several hours or overnight. Makes 3 cups.

Oriental Relish

 2 cups paper-thin cucumber slices
 ½ teaspoon salt
 2 cups shredded carrots
 ¼ teaspoon salt
 ½ cup sugar
 ½ cup white vinegar
  Lettuce

Sprinkle cucumber slices with ½ teaspoon salt; chill. Drain in sieve, pressing with paper toweling to remove excess moisture. Sprinkle shredded carrots with ¼ teaspoon salt. Dissolve sugar in vinegar. Place cucumber slices and carrots in separate dishes. Pour vinegar mixture over. Chill at least 1 hour. Before serving, drain. Heap cucumbers in center of lettuce cup; circle with carrots. Makes 3½ cups.

Peppy Beet Salad

 1 16-ounce can sliced or diced
  beets
 ⅓ cup vinegar
 1 tablespoon sugar
 ½ teaspoon ground cinnamon
 ¼ teaspoon ground allspice
  Dash ground cloves
 ¼ cup pickle relish
 2 tablespoons chopped onion

Drain beets, reserving liquid. Add enough water to liquid to make 1 cup; add vinegar, sugar, cinnamon, allspice, and cloves. Bring the mixture to boiling. Stir in beets; bring the mixture to boiling again. Remove from heat. Chill beets in liquid. Drain; stir in pickle relish and onion. Mix well. Makes 2 cups.

Applesauce Relish

Quick fix-up for applesauce—

 1 16-ounce can applesauce
 ¼ cup red cinnamon candies
 1 teaspoon prepared horseradish

In saucepan combine applesauce, candies, and horseradish. Cook and stir over medium heat till candies are dissolved. Cool; refrigerate till ready to serve. Makes 2 cups relish.

Gifts from the kitchen include trimmed jars of Elegant Pickled Mushrooms, and Corn and Tomato Relish (see *Turmeric* for recipe).

Elegant Pickled Mushrooms

 ⅓ cup dry white wine
 ⅓ cup white wine vinegar
 ⅓ cup salad oil
 ¼ cup finely chopped onion
 2 tablespoons snipped parsley
 1 small clove garlic
 1 bay leaf
 1 teaspoon salt
 ¼ teaspoon dried thyme leaves,
  crushed
  Dash freshly ground pepper
 2 6-ounce cans mushroom crowns

In saucepan combine all ingredients except mushrooms. Bring to boiling. Drain mushrooms; add to hot mixture and return to boiling. Simmer, uncovered, 8 to 10 minutes. Ladle into hot, scalded jars. Or cool and store, covered, in refrigerator. Makes two ½-pints.

RELLENO *(rāl yā' nō)*—A Spanish word meaning to stuff or fill. The popular Mexican dish Chilies Rellenos con Queso consists of stuffed chili peppers with cheese.

RÉMOULADE SAUCE *(rā' muh läd')*—A sharp-flavored sauce based on mayonnaise, anchovies or anchovy paste, capers, gherkins, and chopped herbs. The sauce is often used as an accompaniment.

Artichoke and Crab Rémoulade

      4 artichokes
        Lemon juice
        Vinegar
      ¾ teaspoon dried tarragon leaves,
        crushed
      ½ teaspoon dried chervil leaves,
        crushed
      1 cup mayonnaise
      1 tablespoon drained, mashed
        capers
      2 teaspoons prepared mustard
      ½ teaspoon anchovy paste
        Medium-thick tomato slices
        Lettuce cups
      1 cup drained flaked crab meat

With a sharp knife cut off stems of artichokes; dip bases in lemon juice to prevent darkening. Remove fuzzy chokes and all leaves. Trim artichoke bottoms to make them sit flat; cut around the outside edges with a circular motion (as if peeling an apple) till light-colored meat is visible. Rub with lemon juice and vinegar.

Cook artichoke bottoms, covered, in a small amount of boiling, salted water till just tender. Chill thoroughly. Meanwhile, combine 1 tablespoon warm water, tarragon, and chervil. Let stand 10 minutes. Blend herbs, mayonnaise, capers, mustard, and anchovy paste. Chill.

To assemble the salads place tomato slices in lettuce cups. Top each salad with a cooked, chilled artichoke bottom, then with about ¼ cup crab meat. Top with sauce; garnish with capers, if desired. Makes 4 servings.

RENDER—To melt down a solid fat. Animal fat is so treated to separate the fat from the meat tissue. This treatment is also known as "trying out" the fat.

RENNET—A natural substance extracted from the lining of the fourth stomach of calves that is used to coagulate milk in cheesemaking. Rennet extract is also used in preparing delicate milk desserts and as an ingredient in ice cream.

Refrigerator Vanilla Ice Cream

      1 rennet tablet
      1 cup light cream
      ½ cup sugar
      1¼ teaspoons vanilla
          . . .
      1 cup whipping cream

Crush rennet tablet in 1 tablespoon cold water; dissolve. Combine the cream and sugar; heat slowly till *warm* (110°), not hot. Stir in rennet mixture. Add vanilla; stir quickly for a few seconds. Pour into refrigerator tray. Let stand at room temperature for 10 minutes.

Freeze till firm. Break in chunks with wooden spoon; turn into chilled bowl. Beat smooth with electric mixer. Whip cream; fold into whipped mixture. Return quickly to *cold* tray; freeze firm. Makes 4 to 6 servings.

RHUBARB—A perennial plant belonging to the buckwheat family that has edible pink- to red-tinged leaf stalks and quite large, green, inedible leaves. An old-fashioned name for rhubarb is pieplant. By technical standards, rhubarb is a vegetable, but because of the ways in which it is used in cooking, homemakers usually associate rhubarb with fruits.

No one knows for sure where rhubarb originated. One theory is that it probably first grew in the southern part of Siberia, then was brought to the western world via Italy. However, Chinese writings from 2700 B.C. indicate that certain species of rhubarb have long been used for medicinal purposes in that country.

How rhubarb is produced: The rhubarb plant is very hearty and grows well in northern and southern climates. Most often, rhubarb is propagated by dividing the roots, but occasionally seeds are employed. With either method, the stalks are not ready for use until two years after they have been planted. A crop can be harvested early in the year if the plants are subjected to hothouse procedures.

Nutritional value: Raw rhubarb has very few calories (16 calories to 3½ ounces), but the caloric value soars when enough sugar is added to make the rhubarb taste good (143 calories to ⅜ cup of cooked, sweetened rhubarb). Although it is not a significant contributor of any one nutrient, rhubarb contains an assortment of important vitamins and minerals.

How to select and store: Both fresh and frozen rhubarb can be purchased. The largest share of fresh rhubarb is available between February and June.

When buying rhubarb, choose stalks that are fresh-looking, firm, bright, and glossy, and that contain a fairly large amount of pink or red color. Avoid extremely thick stems, as these will usually be tough and stringy, and wilted or flabby ones, which will lack freshness. Store rhubarb in the vegetable crisper of the refrigerator. Since it is perishable, be sure to use rhubarb within a few days.

A fluted tube mold makes Ruby Rhubarb Salad, served with tangy, whipped cream dressing, party-special. And there's a surprise inside, too—cream cheese cubes and sliced banana.

Serve generous portions of rosy Rhubarb Ice Cream by itself as shown, or add a topping of slightly sweetened and mashed strawberries.

How to prepare and use: The flavor of raw rhubarb stalks is strongly acidic, but when it is cooked and sweetened, rhubarb has a lingering tartness that is very pleasing to many people. Avoid eating the leaves, as they may be poisonous due to their high oxalic acid content. However, the stalks are perfectly safe to eat.

Rhubarb preparation is an agreeably simple operation. Cut off the leaves and the stalk ends of the rhubarb, then wash the stalks carefully in cold water. For speedier top-of-the-range or in-the-oven cooking, cube or dice the stalks.

Rhubarb Sauce, one of the easiest rhubarb recipes to make, has multiple uses. It is popularly served as a side dish, as a dessert by itself, or as a dessert topping for cake, ice cream, or pudding.

Rhubarb Sauce

> 3 cups rhubarb, cut in 1-inch pieces
> ½ to ¾ cup sugar

In saucepan combine rhubarb, sugar, and ¼ cup water. Bring to boiling. Cover; cook over low heat till tender, 5 minutes. Makes 2 cups.

Rhubarb is often used as a pie filling. This being the case, it is easy to see why it has long been called pieplant.

Rhubarb Pie

> 1 pound rhubarb, cut in 1-inch slices (4 cups)
> 1⅔ cups sugar
> ⅓ cup all-purpose flour
> Dash salt
> Pastry for 2-crust 9-inch pie (See *Pastry*)
> 2 tablespoons butter or margarine

Combine the first 4 ingredients. Let stand 15 minutes. Prepare pastry. Line 9-inch pie plate with half of pastry. Fill with rhubarb mixture. Dot with butter. Adjust the top crust, cutting slits for the escape of steam. Seal and flute. Bake at 400° for 50 minutes.

Strawberry-Rhubarb Pie

Combine 1½ cups sugar, 3 tablespoons quick-cooking tapioca, ¼ teaspoon salt, and ¼ teaspoon ground nutmeg. Mix in 1 pound rhubarb, cut in ½-inch pieces, and 1 cup sliced fresh strawberries. Let stand 20 minutes.

Prepare pastry for one 9-inch lattice-top pie (See *Pastry*). Line 9-inch pie plate with pastry. Fill with fruit mixture. Dot with 1 tablespoon butter or margarine. Adjust lattice top; seal. Bake at 400° for 35 to 40 minutes.

The flavor of rhubarb stands on its own merits and also blends well with many fruits – strawberries, pineapples, bananas, and cherries. Such perky combos produce invigorating jams, salads, pies, and baked desserts. (See also *Vegetable*.)

Gingered-Rhubarb Jam

In large saucepan combine 4 cups diced fresh rhubarb, 3 cups sugar, 3 tablespoons finely snipped candied ginger, and 2 tablespoons lemon juice. Let stand till sugar is moistened by juices, 15 minutes. Cook over medium-high heat, stirring often, till thickened and clear, 12 to 15 minutes. Skim off foam; add few drops red food coloring, if desired. Ladle into hot, scalded jars; seal. Makes three ½-pints.

Ruby Rhubarb Salad

 2 cups diced fresh rhubarb
 ½ cup sugar
 ¼ cup water
 2 3-ounce packages strawberry
    flavored gelatin
1¾ cups cold water
 1 tablespoon lemon juice
 2 3-ounce packages cream cheese,
    chilled and diced
 1 banana, sliced
    Lemon-Orange Dressing

In saucepan combine rhubarb, sugar, and the ¼ cup water. Cover and cook over medium heat till rhubarb is barely tender, about 3 minutes, stirring occasionally. Cool. Drain, reserving syrup. Add enough water to syrup to make 2 cups; return to saucepan. Bring to boiling. Stir in gelatin till dissolved. Add cold water and lemon juice. Chill till partially set.

Stir rhubarb, cream cheese, and banana into gelatin mixture. Turn into 6½-cup mold. Chill till firm. To serve, unmold gelatin onto plate. Pass Lemon-Orange Dressing. Serves 8 to 10.

Lemon-Orange Dressing: In saucepan beat 1 egg. Add 1 teaspoon grated lemon peel, 1 teaspoon grated orange peel, 2 tablespoons lemon juice, and ⅓ cup sugar. Cook and stir over low heat till thickened, about 5 minutes. Cool to room temperature. Whip 1 cup whipping cream; fold into citrus mixture. Chill.

Rhubarb-Strawberry Compote

For garnish, top with a dollop of whipped cream—

 3 cups fresh rhubarb, cut in
    1-inch slices (¾ pound)
 ⅓ cup sugar
 1 cup water

         • • •

 1 tablespoon cornstarch
    Dash salt
 ¼ cup cold water
 1 teaspoon lemon juice
    Few drops red food coloring
 2 cups fresh strawberries,
    sliced

In saucepan combine rhubarb, sugar, and water; bring to boiling. Reduce heat; simmer till almost tender, about 2 minutes. Remove from heat; drain rhubarb, reserving syrup. Add water to syrup, if necessary, to make 1¼ cups.

Combine cornstarch and salt with cold water; blend into the rhubarb-syrup mixture. Cook, stirring constantly, till thickened and bubbly. Cook 2 minutes longer. Remove from heat; cool slightly. Stir in lemon juice and food coloring. Gently stir in rhubarb and strawberries. Chill thoroughly. Makes 8 servings.

Rhubarb spiked with ginger cooks to a satisfyingly tart Gingered-Rhubarb Jam. It's perfect for fresh-from-the-oven biscuits.

Strawberry-Rhubarb Rolls

¾ cup sugar
1 cup water
2 cups sifted all-purpose flour
1 tablespoon sugar
3 teaspoons baking powder
½ teaspoon salt
6 tablespoons butter or margarine
⅔ cup milk
1 beaten egg
1 tablespoon butter or margarine, melted
1 cup sliced fresh strawberries
2 cups finely diced rhubarb
⅓ cup sugar

Add ¾ cup sugar to water; simmer 5 minutes. Pour into 9x9x2-inch pan. Sift together flour, the 1 tablespoon sugar, baking powder, and salt; cut in the 6 tablespoons butter till like coarse crumbs. Mix milk and egg; add all at once, stirring just to moisten. Roll to 12x8-inch rectangle. Brush with melted butter.

Top with strawberries and rhubarb. Sprinkle with sugar. Roll jelly-roll fashion, starting at long side; seal edge. Cut in 12 slices; place atop syrup, cut side down. Bake at 450° for 25 to 30 minutes. Serve warm. Serves 12.

Flavorful juices stay in Strawberry-Rhubarb Pie when you flute the edges high. Top with vanilla ice cream for an à la mode treat.

Rhubarb Whip

This dessert is as light as a cloud—

1 pound rhubarb, cut in 1-inch pieces (4 cups)
½ cup sugar
¼ cup water
1 3-ounce package strawberry-flavored gelatin
½ cup cold water
. . .
½ cup whipping cream
Fresh strawberries, halved

In saucepan combine rhubarb, sugar, and the ¼ cup water. Bring to boiling, stirring occasionally. Cover and cook over medium-high heat 8 to 10 minutes. Add strawberry-flavored gelatin; continue to cook and stir till gelatin dissolves. Stir in the ½ cup cold water. Chill gelatin mixture till partially set.

Whip cream. With electric or rotary beater whip gelatin till fluffy; fold in cream. Spoon into sherbets; chill till serving time. Garnish with strawberries. Makes 5 to 6 servings.

Rhubarb Crunch

Best served warm—

1 pound rhubarb, cut in 1-inch pieces (4 cups)
½ cup granulated sugar
1 tablespoon all-purpose flour
1 teaspoon shredded orange peel
. . .
¾ cup all-purpose flour
¾ cup brown sugar
Dash salt
¼ cup butter or margarine
½ cup dairy sour cream
2 tablespoons confectioners' sugar
½ teaspoon vanilla

Combine rhubarb, granulated sugar, the 1 tablespoon flour, and orange peel; turn mixture into an 8¼x1¾-inch round baking dish.

For topping combine flour, brown sugar, and salt. Cut in butter till crumbly. Sprinkle over rhubarb. Bake at 350° for 40 to 45 minutes. Combine sour cream, confectioners' sugar, and vanilla; spoon atop. Serves 6.

Rhubarb Ice Cream

        3 cups diced fresh rhubarb
        ¾ cup sugar
        1 cup water
        2 tablespoons lemon juice
        ¼ teaspoon salt
        ¼ teaspoon red food coloring
        2 egg whites
        ¼ cup sugar

In saucepan combine rhubarb, the ¾ cup sugar, and water. Cook, covered, till tender, 10 to 15 minutes. Cool slightly; add lemon juice, salt, and food coloring. Pour into an 8-cup refrigerator tray; freeze till firm.

Break frozen mixture into chunks; place in *chilled* bowl and beat smooth with electric mixer. Beat egg whites till soft peaks form. Gradually add the ¼ cup sugar, beating till stiff peaks form. Whip cream; fold egg white mixture and whipped cream into rhubarb mixture. Freeze till firm. Makes ½ gallon.

Rhubarb Cake

        3 tablespoons butter or margarine,
            melted
        ½ cup sugar
            Few drops red food coloring
        1 pound rhubarb, finely diced
            (about 3 cups)
        1 package 1-layer-size white
            cake mix

Combine butter, the ½ cup sugar, and food coloring. Add rhubarb; toss mixture lightly. Spread in an 8x8x2-inch pan. Prepare cake mix using package directions; pour over fruit. Bake at 375° till done, about 35 minutes.

Immediately run spatula around edge of pan and invert onto serving plate. Before lifting off pan, let syrup drain onto cake for 3 to 5 minutes. Cut while warm. Pass whipped cream, if desired. Makes 6 to 8 servings.

RIB—A portion of a meat carcass containing rib bones and meat that make excellent eating. Meat cuts identified as rib roasts, short ribs, spareribs, and riblets are all taken from various portions of the rib section. (See also *Meat.*)

RIBBON CAKE—A novelty cake for special occasions. It takes its name from the four different-colored layers that give it a ribbon appearance when sliced.

Ribbon Cake

Prepare 1 package 1-layer-size white cake mix according to package directions; divide batter in half. To *half* add 2 drops red food coloring; leave other half white. Pour each batter into paper-lined 8x1½-inch round pan. Bake at 350° till done, 12 to 15 minutes. Cool.

Prepare 1 package 1-layer-size yellow cake mix according to package directions; divide batter in half. To *half* add one 1-ounce square unsweetened chocolate, melted and cooled, and 1 tablespoon milk. Add 5 drops yellow food coloring to other half. Pour each batter into paper-lined 8x1½-inch round pan. Bake at 350°, about 15 minutes. Cool. Fill and frost with Seven Minute Frosting. (See *Frosting.*)

RIBOFLAVIN *(rī′ bō flā′ vin)*—A water-soluble B vitamin once known as vitamin B2 and as vitamin G. Riboflavin is fairly stable to heat and acids, but it is destroyed by light or alkalies.

Although nutritional research on riboflavin began in 1879, it was not until the 1930s that its function began to be understood. Riboflavin plays a role in the proper functioning of the eyes and nervous system, and in reproduction and lactation. Riboflavin helps the cells use oxygen and combines with body proteins in the formation of important enzymes.

A riboflavin deficiency affects the corneas of the eyes and produces sores around lips and reddening and scaling of the skin around nose, ears, and mouth.

Although not stored by the body, generous amounts of riboflavin are available in many of the foods consumed daily—milk, cheese, meats (especially liver), eggs, dark green leafy vegetables, whole and enriched cereal grains, and legumes. Cooking methods that retain riboflavin best are those that use a minimum of cooking liquid, have a short cooking time, and expose a minimum of the food's surface area. (See also *Nutrition.*)

RICE—The starchy seed of a cereal grass. Rice is native to the delta areas of the major Asiatic rivers: Tigris, Euphrates, Ganges, and Yangtze. Wild rice, although often thought to be a member of the rice family, is the seed of a marsh grass.

Primitive man depended heavily on rice for survival, just as much of the world's population does today. Even before crops were cultivated or history was recorded, he gathered rice and the seeds of other wild grasses for his food.

As civilization developed and man began to keep records, surviving writings show that rice continued to play an important role in the diet. From these writings we know that around 3000 B.C., a plant called *newaree* in India was an early form of rice and that a Chinese ruler started a rice-planting feast.

The migration of rice from the Orient to the Middle East to Europe occurred via the usual method of traders or invaders introducing it to an area where it was later cultivated. For example, the Saracens took rice home with them, to what is now Europe, during medieval times.

Its arrival into the United States, however, was most unusual. In 1694 a ship bound for England from the island of Madagascar was blown off course and onto the east coast of South Carolina. It landed at Charleston, where the natives took care of the captain and his crew. In appreciation, the captain presented the governor of the colony with a handful of rough rice grains. From these grains stem the cereal crop that now is a staple of many "deep south" states. That rice is able to grow in the deep south states, extending from the Carolinas to Louisiana and Texas, is a testament of the high productivity and adaptability of this cereal.

Today, rice is a major crop in the southern rice belt (Arkansas, Louisiana, Mississippi, and Texas) and in California.

Buffet entertaining

← Use burners to keep Shrimp Elegante with Rice warm on the buffet table. Complete the menu with a bread, salad, and dessert.

However, on the world scale, the American crop is not large, as 95 percent of the world crop is grown in Asiatic countries.

How rice is produced: For best growth, rice needs temperatures that are tropical to temperate and an abundant supply of fresh water that will cover the land. The two main types of rice are aquatic, which is grown in marshy or flooded lands, and hill rice, grown where the rainfall is steady and the growing season is long.

The harvesting of rice, done primarily by man and animal power in the Orient, is a mechanized process in the United States. Tractors, threshers, and loading machinery all lighten the work of rice farmers. Airplanes are also used in seeding, fertilizing, and for pest control.

Rice is harvested with a thresher. The kernel of rice, as it leaves the thresher, is enclosed by a hull or husk and is known as paddy or rough rice. Before this rice is processed, it is mechanically dried to bring the moisture content down to about 13 to 14 percent, which is low enough to prevent the grain from spoiling while in storage. During commercial drying, a coarse cleaning removes foreign materials. After drying, the rice is either stored for use as seed or animal feed or taken to the milling and processing plant.

At the processing plant, the first step in rice milling is removing the husk from each grain of rice. After this has been done, the rice is called *brown rice.* Only a small amount is marketed in this form. Brown rice is the most nutritious of the rice forms and has a nutlike flavor and a chewy texture.

The form of rice that is most familiar to the housewife is *white milled rice,* from which several layers of bran have been removed. The process of removing the bran to reveal the familiar white rice kernel takes several steps and two or three types of machines. After the removal of the bran, the rice is ready for further optional processing or grading.

One of the optional processing steps involves adding vitamins to the grain to produce *enriched rice.* Another process that increases the nutritional value of rice is parboiling. *Parboiled rice* results from a soaking and steaming process that forces the water-soluble B vitamins from the outer layers and the germ into the center of the grain. This process also gelatinizes the starch, which produces grains that stay separate when cooked.

Precooking is a process in which the rice is cooked after milling. The moisture is then removed by dehydration. *Precooked rice* is a "convenience food" because restoring the water content takes only a few minutes of heating in water.

Nutritional value: All rice has high energy value due to the high carbohydrate content. Rice is also a source of calcium, iron, and the B vitamins (thiamine, niacin, and riboflavin). It even contributes a small amount of protein to the diet.

The different forms of rice, however, vary greatly in vitamin and mineral content. Brown rice makes the biggest nutritive contribution to the diet, followed by parboiled, enriched, and regular milled white rice. A ½-cup serving of plain cooked rice yields about 90 calories.

The low fiber content of rice makes it easy to digest, and the chemical structure of rice enables the body to use it effectively. While polished rice does lack some nutrients, the accompaniments with

To test for doneness, squeeze grains of rice between your thumb and forefinger. The rice is done if there is no hard core.

How much rice to cook

When figuring how much rice to prepare, it is helpful to know the proportion of uncooked rice to cooked rice. The following measurements will be helpful to you. Count on ½ cup of cooked rice per serving.

Uncooked	Cooked
1 cup regular milled white rice	3 cups
1 cup parboiled rice	4 cups
1 cup brown rice	3 cups
1 cup precooked rice	2 to 3 cups

---

which it is generally served, often meat and vegetable sauces, make up for its shortcomings. In any case, rice provides an economical source of energy.

Rice classifications: Although there are thousands of rice varieties, they are generally classified into three main groups — long-, medium-, and short-grain rice.

The grains of long-grain rice are four or five times as long as they are wide. The cooked grains are light and fluffy, and they tend to separate well. This type of rice is preferred for salads and meat dishes such as curries and stews.

Plump, fairly short kernels identify short- and medium-grain rice. When they are cooked, these types produce moist, tender rice that is easily molded, such as croquettes and rice rings.

How to buy and store: Whether you buy long-, medium-, or short-grain rice as brown rice, regular rice, parboiled rice, precooked rice, or rice mixed with seasonings depends on personal preference and on how you are going to use the rice. If the rice is to be a side dish, any kind of rice is suitable. However, if the rice is to be combined with other ingredients, use the kind specified in the recipe.

Rice usually is purchased packaged in either cardboard cartons or see-through packages. For storage, it is best to transfer rice from its package into a container with a tight lid. This will deter insect invaders. Rice keeps on the pantry shelf for up to six months, so it's easy to keep a supply of this grain on hand.

How to prepare: One of the advantages of serving rice is that it takes only a minimum of effort to prepare. Simply combine the rice, water, and seasonings, such as salt, and then cook the mixture either on top of the range or in the oven. To test the rice for doneness, pinch a grain between your fingers. It is done if there is no hard core. When preparing precooked rice or other specially processed rice, follow the label directions carefully. For flavor and color variation, brown the rice before cooking it.

Since rice combines well with so many foods, leftovers are more of a bonus than a problem. Tightly covered rice keeps in the refrigerator for up to a week and in the freezer for up to eight months. To reheat cooked rice, put one tablespoon water per cup of rice in a saucepan, then cover and simmer until the rice is heated.

Fluffy Rice

    1 cup uncooked rice
    2 cups cold water
    ½ to 1 teaspoon salt

Put uncooked rice, water, and salt in a 2-quart saucepan; cover with a tight-fitting lid. Bring to a vigorous boil; then, turn heat as low as possible. Continue to cook for 14 minutes. Do not stir or lift cover. Remove from heat; allow rice to steam, covered, for an additional 10 minutes. Makes about 3 cups.

Browned Rice

Toast 1 cup uncooked long-grain rice in *ungreased* skillet over medium heat, shaking often, till rice is golden brown, about 20 minutes. Turn into 1-quart casserole; add 2½ cups hot water and ¼ teaspoon salt, stirring to separate rice. Cover and bake at 350° till rice is tender and all water is absorbed, about 1 hour. Fluff rice with fork. Garnish with chopped pimiento, if desired. Serves 6.

How to use: A bowlful of hot, fluffy rice is a delicious substitute for potatoes or other vegetables. Although butter alone is a popular seasoning, you can vary the flavor of rice by adding seasonings such as cumin, cinnamon, curry powder, parsley, onion, saffron, green pepper, and chives. Another easy way to flavor rice is to cook the rice in liquids such as chicken broth or tomato juice rather than in water.

Remember, however, that rice has many places in the menu other than as a side dish. For a flavorful first course try a soup containing rice. Rice also has a place in the salad course. It is delicious in vegetable, gelatin, and meat salads.

One of the most frequent uses for rice is in main dishes. A bed of hot rice is an excellent base for saucy main dishes such as beef stroganoff, chicken à la king, and pork chow mein. To make the main course fancier, mold the hot rice into a ring shape. Casseroles are another popular use for rice. It's easy to make an enticing casserole with rice and any of a variety of meats, seafoods, and vegetables.

Rice is even used in desserts. Custardy rice pudding is probably the most popular dessert made with rice, but rice is also used in various other puddings, and in fruit dessert recipes. (See also *Grain.*)

Delight guests with tasty Rice and Tuna Pie, which uses a subtly herbed rice shell as the base for the tuna, egg, and cheese filling.

Confetti Rice Ring

Cook one 10-ounce package frozen peas according to package directions; drain. Combine 4 cups hot cooked rice, peas, 3 tablespoons chopped canned pimiento, and 2 tablespoons butter or margarine, melted. Press lightly into greased 5½-cup ring mold. Unmold at once.

Butter-Baked Rice

> 1 cup parboiled rice
> Dash garlic salt
> ¼ cup butter or margarine
> 1 13¾-ounce can chicken broth
> *or* 2 chicken bouillon cubes
> dissolved in 1¾ cups boiling
> water
> 2 tablespoons finely snipped
> parsley
> ¼ cup toasted, slivered
> almonds (optional)

Place uncooked rice in 1-quart casserole; sprinkle with ¼ teaspoon salt and garlic salt. Add butter and hot bouillon; stir to combine. Cover tightly. Bake at 325° for 35 minutes. Stir occasionally. Remove cover. Stir in parsley. Sprinkle with almonds, if desired. Bake, uncovered, 10 minutes longer. Makes 6 servings.

For an unusual vegetable dish, serve Green Rice Bake. This tasty blend of rice, spinach, and cheese goes well with most meats.

Green Rice Bake

In mixing bowl combine 2 slightly beaten eggs and 2 cups milk. Add ¾ cup uncooked packaged precooked rice; ⅓ cup finely chopped onion; one 10-ounce package frozen chopped spinach, cooked and drained; 4 ounces sharp process American cheese, shredded (1 cup); and ½ teaspoon garlic salt. Pour into a 10x6x 1¾-inch baking dish. Bake at 325° till firm, about 35 to 40 minutes. Makes 4 to 6 servings.

Shrimp Elegante with Rice

> 3 pounds fresh or frozen shrimp
> in shells (50 large)
> Boiling water
> 2 7-ounce packages frozen Chinese
> pea pods
> 3 chicken bouillon cubes
> 2½ cups boiling water
> ½ cup chopped green onion
> 3 tablespoons soy sauce
> 1 teaspoon salt
> 4 tablespoons cornstarch
> ¼ cup cold water
> 4 medium tomatoes, cut into
> eighths
> Saucepan Rice

Thaw shrimp, if frozen; peel and devein. Set aside. Pour boiling water over pea pods and carefully break apart with fork; drain immediately. In large saucepan or Dutch oven dissolve bouillon cubes in 2½ cups boiling water; add shrimp, onion, soy sauce, and salt. Return to boiling; cook, uncovered, for 3 minutes, stirring the shrimp mixture occasionally.

In small bowl blend together cornstarch and cold water; stir into shrimp mixture. Cook, stirring constantly, till mixture thickens and bubbles. Add tomato wedges and drained pea pods. Cook the mixture till the tomatoes are heated through, about 3 minutes longer. Spoon over hot Saucepan Rice. Makes 12 servings.

Saucepan Rice: In a large saucepan combine 2 cups uncooked long-grain rice, 4 cups cold water, and 1 teaspoon salt; cover the mixture tightly. Bring to a vigorous boil, then turn heat low. Continue cooking 14 minutes (do not lift cover). Remove from heat; let rice stand, covered, for 10 minutes. Garnish cooked rice with parsley sprigs, if desired.

Rice and Tuna Pie

    2 cups cooked rice
    2 tablespoons butter or margarine,
        melted
    1 tablespoon chopped onion
    ¼ teaspoon dried marjoram leaves,
        crushed
    1 slightly beaten egg
    1 9-ounce can tuna, drained and
        flaked
    3 beaten eggs
    1 cup milk
    4 ounces process Swiss cheese,
        shredded (1 cup)
    1 tablespoon chopped onion
    ¼ teaspoon salt
        Dash pepper
    ¼ teaspoon dried marjoram leaves,
        crushed
        Canned pimiento (optional)

For rice shell, combine cooked rice, melted butter or margarine, the 1 tablespoon chopped onion, ¼ teaspoon crushed marjoram, and 1 slightly beaten egg. Press into bottom and sides of a lightly buttered 10-inch pie plate or a 10x6x1¾-inch baking dish. Layer flaked tuna evenly over rice shell.

Combine 3 beaten eggs, milk, shredded cheese, 1 tablespoon chopped onion, salt, pepper, and dried marjoram. Pour over tuna.

Bake at 350° till knife inserted just off-center comes out clean, about 50 to 55 minutes. Garnish with pimiento, if desired. Serves 6.

Pork Chops on Amber Rice

    6 pork chops, ¾ inch thick
        Salt
        Pepper
    1⅓ cups packaged precooked rice
    1 cup orange juice
    1 10½-ounce can condensed
        chicken-rice soup

Brown pork chops in heavy skillet; season with salt and pepper. Place uncooked rice in an 11¾x7½x1¾-inch baking dish; pour orange juice over rice. Arrange browned pork chops on rice. Pour condensed chicken-rice soup over all. Cover; bake at 350° for 45 minutes. Uncover and bake 10 minutes longer. Serves 6.

Calico Rice Salad

    3 cups cooked rice
    6 hard-cooked eggs, coarsely
        chopped
    ½ cup chopped onion
    ¼ cup chopped canned pimiento
    ¼ cup chopped green pepper
    ¼ cup chopped celery
    ¼ cup chopped dill pickle
    ⅓ cup mayonnaise or salad
        dressing
    ¼ cup French salad dressing
    2 tablespoons prepared mustard
        Lettuce

Combine cooked rice, eggs, onion, pimiento, green pepper, celery, dill pickle, 1 teaspoon salt, and dash pepper. Blend together mayonnaise, French salad dressing, and prepared mustard; add to rice mixture and toss. Chill thoroughly. Lightly pack rice mixture into five 5-ounce custard cups; immediately turn out on lettuce-lined plates. Makes 5 servings.

Baked Rice Pudding

Combine 2 cups milk, 3 slightly beaten eggs, ½ cup sugar, 1 teaspoon vanilla, and ½ teaspoon salt; mix well. Add 1¾ to 2 cups cooked long-grain rice and ⅓ to ½ cup raisins (optional). Turn into 10x6x1¾-inch baking dish. Bake, uncovered, at 325° for 30 minutes; stir. Sprinkle with ground nutmeg. Continue baking till knife inserted halfway between center and edge of dish comes out clean, about 30 minutes more. Makes 6 servings.

Saucepan Rice Pudding

In a 2-quart saucepan combine 2½ cups milk, ⅔ cup uncooked packaged precooked rice, ⅓ cup sugar, 1 teaspoon vanilla, ½ teaspoon salt, and ⅓ cup raisins (optional). Bring just to boiling. Reduce heat and cook, uncovered, over low heat 20 minutes, stirring often.

Combine 1 slightly beaten egg and 2 tablespoons milk. Stir a small amount of hot rice mixture into egg; return to saucepan. Cook and stir over low heat till mixture thickens slightly, about 3 to 4 minutes. Serve warm or chilled with light cream. Makes 4 servings.

For pudding with a difference, serve Rice Pudding Royale. Coriander, fruit peel, and cottage cheese are the unusual ingredients.

Rice Pudding Royale

    3 cups milk
    ½ cup long-grain rice
    ½ cup sugar
    ¼ teaspoon salt
    ½ teaspoon grated lemon peel
    ¼ teaspoon grated orange peel
    ½ teaspoon ground coriander
    1 teaspoon vanilla
    ¾ cup cream-style cottage
        cheese

Scald milk in top of double boiler. Add uncooked rice, sugar, and salt. Cook, covered, over boiling water for 1 hour, stirring frequently. Uncover; cook till thickened, 30 to 40 minutes. Remove from heat; stir in lemon and orange peels, coriander, and vanilla. Chill.

Beat cottage cheese; stir into rice mixture. Spoon into dessert dishes. Garnish with a little shredded orange peel or ground coriander, if desired. Makes 6 to 8 servings.

Rice Pudding

    2½ cups milk
    ½ cup long-grain rice
    ⅓ cup sugar
    ⅓ cup raisins (optional)
    1 teaspoon vanilla

In a heavy 1½-quart saucepan combine milk, uncooked rice, sugar, raisins (if desired), vanilla, and ½ teaspoon salt. Bring to boiling. Reduce heat and cook, covered, over very low heat till rice is tender and milk is absorbed, about 45 to 50 minutes; stir frequently. Serve with light cream. Makes 4 servings.

Glorified Rice

Drain one 8¾-ounce can crushed pineapple, reserving syrup. Combine ⅔ cup uncooked packaged precooked rice, ⅔ cup water, syrup, and ½ teaspoon salt. Stir to moisten. Bring to boil. Cover; simmer 5 minutes.

Remove from heat; let stand 5 minutes. Add pineapple and 2 teaspoons lemon juice; cool. Stir in 1½ cups miniature marshmallows and 1 ripe banana, sliced. Whip 1 cup whipping cream. Fold cream and 2 tablespoons chopped maraschino cherries into rice mixture. Chill mixture thoroughly. Makes 8 servings.

Blueberry-Rice Bavarian

    1 envelope unflavored gelatin
        (1 tablespoon)
    ⅓ cup sugar
    1 7-ounce bottle lemon-lime
        carbonated beverage
    1 tablespoon lemon juice
    1½ cups cooked long-grain rice
    1 cup whipping cream
    2 cups fresh blueberries *or well-
        drained* frozen blueberries

In saucepan combine gelatin, sugar, and dash salt. Add ½ cup water. Heat and stir till gelatin dissolves; remove from heat. Cool. Stir in carbonated beverage, lemon juice, and cooked rice. Chill till partially set. Whip cream; carefully fold cream and blueberries into gelatin mixture. Spoon into sherbet glasses; chill till set. Makes 8 servings.

RICE CEREAL—Rice processed into puffed kernels, flakes, or granules for use as a breakfast cereal. (See also *Cereal*.)

Flowerpot Cookie Cups

    6 cups puffed rice cereal
    ½ pound large marshmallows (32)
    ¼ cup butter or margarine
    ¼ teaspoon peppermint flavoring
      Chocolate ice cream
      Flowers made from gumdrops
        and pipe cleaners

Place puffed rice cereal in shallow pan. Heat at 350° for 10 minutes. Turn into a large, greased bowl. Melt marshmallows and butter over very low heat, stirring till mixture is smooth; add peppermint flavoring.

Pour marshmallow mixture over cereal, mixing till all the cereal is coated. Press into bottom and sides of 10 greased custard cups. (If mixture cools too fast, return to oven and heat slightly.) Cool; remove from cups. Fill with chocolate ice cream (or a combination of your favorite flavors). Insert gumdrop flowers in ice cream. Makes 10.

Meatball Casserole

    ½ cup chopped onion
    1 tablespoon butter or margarine
    2 15¼-ounce cans meatballs in
      gravy
    1 16-ounce can sliced carrots,
      drained
    2 tablespoons snipped parsley
    2 teaspoons Worcestershire sauce
    ¼ cup crushed, crisp rice cereal
    ½ teaspoon sesame seed
    1 package refrigerated biscuits
      Milk

In large skillet cook onion in butter till tender but not brown. Add meatballs and gravy, carrots, parsley, and Worcestershire sauce. Heat till bubbling. Pour into 2-quart casserole. Mix cereal, sesame seed, and ⅛ teaspoon salt. Brush tops of biscuits with milk; then dip in cereal mixture. Arrange biscuits atop *hot* meat mixture. Bake at 425° till biscuits are done, 10 to 12 minutes. Serves 6.

Creamy white ricotta cheese has a nutlike flavor.

Eggs Au Gratin

In skillet melt 2 tablespoons butter or margarine. Add 2 cups crisp rice cereal and mix gently. Spoon *half* the cereal mixture into bottoms of four 10-ounce casseroles.

In saucepan combine one 11-ounce can condensed Cheddar cheese soup, ¼ cup milk, and ¼ cup sliced ripe olives; heat through. Slice 6 hard-cooked eggs (reserve 8 slices for garnish). Fold eggs into soup mixture. Spoon into prepared casseroles. Top each with 2 egg slices; wreathe with remaining cereal. Bake at 400° about 15 minutes. Makes 4 servings.

RICE FLOUR—Finely milled flour that is made from white rice. This flour is used most frequently as a substitute for all-purpose flour in wheat-free diets.

RICER—A kitchen utensil that consists of a perforated cylinder and a plunger. Foods, such as cooked potatoes, are placed in the cylinder and then forced through the holes by the plunger. This gives particles that resemble grains of rice.

RICOTTA CHEESE (*ri kot'uh, -kô'tuh*)—A creamy smooth, almost satiny, uncured cheese traditionally made from the whey left from the manufacture of other cheeses. Ricotta, first made in Italy and still very popular in Europe, resembles cottage cheese in appearance and flavor.

Although European ricotta is made almost exclusively from whey, that of the United States is usually made from whole milk or a mixture of whey and whole milk. This cheese is an ingredient in many Italian dishes. (See also *Cheese*.)

Cheese-Filled Manicotti

          ¾ **pound ground beef**
          ¼ **pound fresh pork sausage**
          2 **6-ounce cans tomato paste**
          ½ **cup chopped onion**
          1 **3-ounce can sliced mushrooms,
               drained**
          2 **teaspoons dried oregano leaves,
               crushed**
          1 **teaspoon sugar**
          1 **large clove garlic, minced**
       1½ **cups ricotta *or* cream-style
               cottage cheese, drained**
          ¼ **cup Parmesan cheese**
          1 **slightly beaten egg**
          2 **tablespoons snipped parsley**
          6 **to 8 manicotti**

In large saucepan brown meats; drain off excess fat. Add 2 cups water, tomato paste, onion, mushrooms, oregano, 1½ teaspoons salt, sugar, and garlic. Simmer, uncovered, for 30 minutes, stirring occasionally. Meanwhile, combine ricotta *or* cottage cheese, Parmesan cheese, egg, parsley, and ½ teaspoon salt.

Cook manicotti in boiling salted water just till tender, about 20 minutes; drain. Rinse in cold water; drain. Using small spoon, stuff each shell with about 3 tablespoons cheese mixture. Pour *half* the meat sauce into 11¾x7½x1¾-inch baking dish. Arrange stuffed manicotti in a row. Spoon remaining sauce over. Bake, covered, at 350° for 30 to 35 minutes. Pass Parmesan, if desired. Serves 4 to 6.

Blonde Lasagne

Cook 3 ounces wide noodles (2⅓ cups) in boiling, salted water till tender; drain. Cook one 10-ounce package frozen peas according to package directions; drain. Cook 12 slices bacon till crisp; drain and crumble. Tear 6 ounces provolone cheese into pieces. In greased 10x6x1¾-inch baking dish, arrange *half* the noodles; top with bacon, 1 cup ricotta or cream-style cottage cheese, peas, *half* the provolone cheese, and *half* of a 10½-ounce can white sauce. Top with remaining noodles, remaining provolone cheese, and remaining white sauce.

Combine 1 cup bread crumbs and 2 tablespoons butter, melted; sprinkle over casserole. Bake at 350° for 25 minutes. Serves 4 or 5.

Peppy Lasagne

In skillet cook 1 pound bulk Italian sausage, ½ cup chopped onion, ½ cup chopped celery, and ½ cup chopped carrot till meat is lightly browned. Drain off excess fat. Stir in one 16-ounce can tomatoes, cut up; one 6-ounce can tomato paste; 1 teaspoon salt; ½ teaspoon dried oregano leaves, crushed; and ¼ teaspoon pepper. Simmer, uncovered, for 30 minutes, stirring mixture occasionally.

Cook 10 ounces lasagne noodles according to package directions; drain well. Combine 3 cups ricotta or cream-style cottage cheese, ½ cup grated Parmesan cheese, 2 beaten eggs, 2 tablespoons parsley, and ¼ teaspoon pepper.

Place *half* the noodles in a greased 13½x8¾x1¾-inch baking dish. Spread with *half* the cheese filling; add 8 ounces mozzarella cheese, thinly sliced, and *half* the meat sauce. Repeat layers using another 8 ounces mozzarella cheese. Bake, uncovered, at 375° for 30 minutes. Let stand 10 to 15 minutes before serving. Cut into squares to serve. Serves 10 to 12.

RIGATI—A word meaning grooved that often is applied to hollow forms of pasta that have a ridged surface.

RIGATONI *(rig′uh tō′nē)*—A popular type of pasta that is tube-shaped and has a ridged surface. (See also *Pasta.*)

RIJSTTAFEL *(ri stä′fuhl)*—A type of Indonesian banquet, which was adopted by the Dutch settlers and is now popular in the Netherlands as well as in Indonesia. At a typical presentation, many dishes are served by a steady stream of waiters.

As is indicated by the word rijsttafel, which literally means rice table, rice is an important part of this meal. Traditionally, rice is placed in the center of the guest's plate, and around it is heaped a selection of food from a large assortment of dishes. This array often includes pork, chicken, duck, goose, beef, lamb, fish, crab, shrimp, lobster, vegetables, and fruits prepared in various ways.

Although the size of a traditional rijsttafel limits it to special restaurants, you can serve a mini-rijsttafel to your guests by using the following recipes.

Rijsttafel Rice

1½ cups long-grain rice
2¼ cups cold water

Wash uncooked rice 3 to 4 times alternately in cold and warm water. Soak the rice 15 minutes in cold water; then drain. Add rice to the 2¼ cups cold water; bring to a boil. Stir once. Then, cover the kettle tightly and turn heat down as low as possible. Cook rice for 15 minutes without removing the cover.

Lift cover and test rice for doneness, but do not stir it. If the rice is not sufficiently cooked, sprinkle a little hot water over it. Replace the cover and steam for 3 to 5 minutes longer. Turn off heat and let kettle of rice stand for 5 minutes. Serve cooked rice without stirring. It should be soft, yet grainy, fluffy, and entirely dry. Any small amount of rice that adheres to the kettle should be discarded rather than used. Serve the hot rice with Pork Sate and Peanut Sauce. Makes 8 servings.

Pork Sate (Pork Kabobs)

Use the blender to mix the marinade—

  3 cups onion pieces
  ¼ cup peanut butter
  1 clove garlic
  3 tablespoons soy sauce
  1 tablespoon brown sugar
  1½ teaspoons ground coriander
  1½ teaspoons salt
  1 teaspoon grated lemon peel
  1½ teaspoons lemon juice
  1 teaspoon ground cumin
  ½ teaspoon ground red pepper
  ½ teaspoon black pepper
  2 pounds boneless lean pork,
    cut in ¾-inch cubes

In blender container combine onion, peanut butter, garlic, soy sauce, brown sugar, coriander, salt, lemon peel, lemon juice, cumin, red pepper, and black pepper. Cover and blend for 30 seconds. Marinate pork cubes in this mixture overnight in the refrigerator.

Thread pork cubes on skewers and broil 3 to 4 inches from heat till pork is cooked through and very tender, about 15 to 18 minutes, turning once. Makes 8 servings.

Peanut Sauce

In a saucepan combine ½ cup coconut milk (milk drained from fresh coconut, with water added, if necessary, to make ½ cup liquid), 2 tablespoons peanut butter, 1 tablespoon minced green pepper, 1½ teaspoons lemon juice, 1 teaspoon brown sugar, and 1 teaspoon soy sauce. Simmer over low heat for 5 minutes. Use as a dip for Pork Sate. Makes ⅔ cup.

RILLETTE *(ri let′)*—A French hors d'oeuvre specialty consisting of spiced or well-seasoned ground pork or pork pâté.

RIND—**1.** The rather thick outer coating of certain vegetables and fruits, especially citrus fruits. **2.** The pig skin on smoked bacon or ham. **3.** The crust on cheese.

RING MOLD—A circular mold, usually of metal, with a hole in the center. It is most commonly used for molding gelatin in the form of a ring. However, cooked rice may be pressed into a ring mold to take its shape, and spinach or carrot mixtures are sometimes baked in such a mold.

Foods molded in a ring mold are attractively served by filling the hollow center with a complementary food. For example, try fruits, vegetables, or a dressing with gelatin molds, creamed chicken or seafood with rice, and peas with carrots, diced carrots, or beets with a spinach ring.

RIPEN—To allow foods such as fruits, vegetables, and fruitcakes to attain full maturity, best texture, and richest flavor.

Fruits that must be picked before the last stage of ripeness to withstand the rigors of shipping and handling (peaches, tomatoes, and avocados, for example) or to have best eating texture (pears) often need a day or two of ripening at room temperature before they are ready to use.

To hasten the ripening of bananas and tomatoes, enclose them in a paper bag. Don't put ripening fruits on a sunny windowsill because they will wrinkle and shrivel rather than ripen properly.

RISOTTO *(ri sô′ tō, -sot′ ō)*—The Italian name for various rice dishes.

RISSOLE *(ri sōl', ris' ōl)* — A small, fried pastry of French origin that has a meat or a sweet filling. Rissoles are generally served as appetizers and light main dishes; however, smaller versions are used as garnishes on meat dishes.

Rissoles are shaped into small balls like fritters or folded like turnovers. They are usually fried in deep fat. However, some are panfried or ovenfried. Rissoles are served with lemon or a sauce.

RISSOLE POTATOES — Small pieces of potato cooked in the rissole manner. The potatoes are either fried in deep fat or browned in a skillet till golden and crisp.

RIVVEL — A Pennsylvania Dutch word meaning lump or flake. Rivvel soup is made by dropping a flour mixture into boiling broth. This is done by rubbing the dough through the hands, by pushing it through the holes in a colander, or by simply dropping in chunks of the dough. As the dough hits the boiling soup, it forms irregular-shaped lumps and flakes.

ROAST *(noun)* — A thick, tender cut of beef, pork, lamb, or veal. Roasts are usually cooked by dry heat in an oven or over coals. However, some roasts such as chuck are less tender and require a moist-heat cooking method such as pot-roasting.

A roast differs from a steak or a chop in thickness. Roasts are usually over two inches thick, while steaks and chops are less than two inches. Steaks and chops are often made by slicing a roast into pieces of the desired thickness.

Horseradish–Stuffed Rib Roast

Combine ¼ cup prepared horseradish and 2 cloves garlic, minced. Unroll one 5- to 6-pound rolled rib roast; spread with horseradish. Reroll roast and tie securely. Balance roast on rotisserie spit, fastening with holding forks. Rub outside of roast with additional clove of garlic. Insert meat thermometer. Attach spit and turn on motor. Roast over *medium* coals till meat thermometer registers 150° for medium-rare, about 2½ to 3 hours, or till preferred doneness. Let stand 15 minutes. Serves 10 to 12.

ROAST *(verb)* — A dry-heat method of cooking. Roasting includes cooking on a spit over a fire; embedding in coals; heating in order to brown and dry out; and baking, uncovered, in an oven.

Cooking meats over fire is probably one of the oldest methods of roasting and may even be the oldest way of cooking. The modern adaptation is rotisserie cooking.

Roast Pork Chops

1 cup chopped onion
1 clove garlic, minced
¼ cup salad oil
¾ cup catsup
⅓ cup lemon juice
3 tablespoons sugar
2 tablespoons Worcestershire sauce
1 tablespoon prepared mustard
2 teaspoons salt
¼ teaspoon bottled hot pepper sauce
6 pork rib or loin chops, 1 to 1¼ inches thick

Cook onion and garlic in hot oil till tender but not brown. Add 1 cup water and remaining ingredients *except* chops; simmer, uncovered, for 15 minutes. Lock chops in a spit basket. Rotate over *slow* coals till done, about 45 minutes. Baste with sauce during the last 20 minutes of cooking. Makes 6 servings.

Roasting by embedding foods in coals or ashes is another ancient procedure that is still used at cookouts. Potatoes and ears of corn are cooked in this way.

Fresh Corn on the Cob

Remove husks from fresh corn. Remove silks with stiff brush. Place each ear on a sheet of foil. Spread corn liberally with softened butter or margarine and sprinkle with salt and pepper.

Wrap foil securely around each ear of corn—don't seal seam, but fold or twist foil around ends. Place on grill and roast over *hot* coals till corn is tender, 15 to 20 minutes, turning ears frequently. Pass extra butter.

Roasting versus pot-roasting

Roasted foods are cooked without moisture; pot-roasted foods, with moisture. If pan is covered, the food wrapped in foil, or moisture added, you are pot-roasting.

Chestnuts, peanuts, and coffee beans are examples of foods that are heated to brown and dry them out. This roasting develops the flavor and color of the food.

Cooking meats in an oven is the most common type of roasting. Tender cuts of beef, veal, pork, and lamb are suitable.

When roasting meats, place the meat, fat side up, on a rack in a shallow pan. This allows the meat to baste itself and holds it up and out of the drippings. The rack also provides even heat circulation. You may season the meat any time during cooking according to personal preference. Cook the meat at about 300° to 350°.

Roasting charts give you the approximate length of cooking time. Frozen meats may be roasted, but allow extra time if not indicated on the chart. A meat thermometer inserted into the meat indicates when the exact degree of doneness is reached. Roast should rest for 15 to 20 minutes before carving. (See also *Meat*.)

Savory-Stuffed Rolled Rib Roast

A sophisticated roast that pleases the men—

> 4 ounces thinly sliced ham, chopped (1 cup)
> 3 slices bacon, snipped
> ¼ cup chopped onion
> 2 tablespoons chopped pimiento-stuffed green olives
> 1 clove garlic, minced
> 1 beaten egg
> 1 4- to 5-pound rolled rib roast

Combine ham, bacon, onion, olives, garlic, and egg. Unroll roast; spread ham mixture over meat. Reroll and tie roast; place on rack in shallow roasting pan. Roast at 325° till tender, about 2½ to 3 hours. Makes 12 to 14 servings.

ROASTER—An animal, such as a chicken or a pig, that is the appropriate size for roasting. Chickens classified as roasters range between three and five pounds, and their flesh is quite tender.

Roast Chicken with Stuffing

Stuffed with sweet potato and apple for holiday or year-round menus—

> 1 17-ounce can vacuum-packed sweet potatoes
> 1 medium apple, peeled, cored, and diced (1 cup)
> ⅓ cup chopped onion
> 6 tablespoons butter or margarine
> • • •
> 1 tablespoon sugar
> 1 teaspoon salt
> ¼ teaspoon ground nutmeg
> 2 cups soft bread cubes (about 2½ slices bread)
> • • •
> 1 3-pound whole, ready-to-cook, roasting chicken
> Salt
> Salad oil

Drain sweet potatoes; mash. In skillet cook apple and onion in butter till tender. Stir in the 1 tablespoon sugar, the 1 teaspoon salt, and the ¼ teaspoon nutmeg. Combine with sweet potatoes and bread cubes; mix well.

Rinse bird; pat dry. Lightly salt inside; stuff with sweet potato mixture. Truss bird and place, breast side up, on rack in shallow roasting pan. Rub skin with salad oil. (If meat thermometer is used, insert in center of inside thigh muscle, making sure bulb does not touch bone.) Roast, uncovered, at 375° for 1 hour, brushing dry areas of skin occasionally with pan drippings. Cut band of skin or string between legs and tail. Continue roasting till tender, about 15 to 30 minutes longer. (Meat thermometer should register 185°.) Serves 6.

ROASTER OVEN—An electrical appliance that cooks by roasting or baking. Roaster ovens resemble large baking pans. They include an inner, removable pan and a lid usually having a glass window. A cabinet to set the roaster oven on may be bought. Some have automatic timers.

Roaster ovens hold several dishes at a time, so you can cook a complete oven meal in them. You can also roast a turkey or cook a large dish, such as baked beans for 50 people. Roaster ovens are used as warmers, too. They keep dishes hot.

ROASTING EAR – Corn in the husks cooked on an open fire. These are placed on a rack over the fire or directly on hot coals.

ROASTING PAN – A shallow, oblong pan designed for cooking meats. Roasting pans may come with racks, handles, and lids. They are constructed of metal or glass.

ROBERT SAUCE (*rô bêr'*) – A brown sauce flavored with onions and mustard. Robert sauce is named after Robert Vinot, who is credited with having developed the sauce in the seventeenth century. Today, bottles of Robert sauce are available in most supermarkets. Robert sauce goes quite well with beef, pork, and poultry.

ROB ROY – An alcoholic drink made of scotch, sweet vermouth, and bitters. Also popular is a Rob Roy made with scotch, dry vermouth, and a dash of bitters, and one in which the bitters are not added.

ROCAMBOLE (*rok' uhm bōl*) – A plant of the lily family that resembles a large garlic. Often called giant garlic, it has cloves, which are used like garlic, and leaves, which are used like chives. Rocambole is more common to Europe than to America.

ROCK – **1.** A rich drop cookie flavored with spices and filled with nuts and fruits and popularly made at Christmastime. (See also *Cookie.*) **2.** A word that is used for ice. For instance, beverages served on the rocks are poured over ice cubes.

ROCK AND RYE – An alcoholic beverage made of rye whiskey, rock candy or syrup, and lemon or orange juice. Bottles of rock and rye that include all the ingredients are available at many supermarkets.

ROCK CANDY – Large, clear, hard crystals of sugar that are stuck together. Rock candy is available in either light or dark colors. It comes in thin strings and on the ends of swizzle sticks. Rock candy is used in making various kinds of alcoholic drinks such as rock and rye.

ROCK CORNISH GAME HEN – Another name for Cornish game hen. The bird is a cross of English Cornish and White Rock breeds. Thus, the word rock is sometimes added to the name of this bird. (See also *Cornish Game Hen.*)

ROCK CRAB – A small crab found along the California and New England coasts. Rock crabs resemble Dungeness crabs, but weigh only one-third to one-half pound.

Rock crabs are sold alive. The brownish-colored meat also is available fresh cooked and canned. (See also *Crab.*)

ROCKET – A plant with a strong odor and a flavor similar to horseradish. Rocket leaves are used in Europe and in the Middle East to give sharp flavor to salads.

ROCKFISH – A food fish found on the Pacific coast from California to Alaska. There are over 50 types of rockfish including the orange, yellowtail, red, and bocaccio. Rockfish coloring ranges from a black or gray to a bright orange or red. White or pink flesh has a mild flavor.

Fresh rockfish are sold whole, dressed, and filleted. In markets outside northwestern coastal areas, frozen fillets are more commonly available. Cook rockfish as you would other fat fish by baking, broiling, frying, steaming, and boiling. Cooking increases the calorie count of this fish: a 3½-ounce uncooked portion of rockfish contains 97 calories, while a 3½-ounce serving that has been oven-steamed has about 107 calories. (See also *Fish.*)

ROCK LOBSTER TAIL – A section of the rock or spiny lobster commonly sold in American supermarkets. Unlike the true lobster, whose meat is located in the claws, the majority of the meat in a rock or spiny lobster is in the tail portion.

Rock lobster tails, ranging from tiny hors d'oeuvre size to large ones for entrées, are found in the frozen foods department of most supermarkets.

Cook lobster tails by boiling or by cutting in butterfly-style and broiling. Serve the tails hot with melted butter and lemon or chill and use in salads and casseroles. Allow about one 8-ounce tail for each person. (See also *Lobster*.)

ROCK SALT — Large, coarse crystals of salt. Rock salt is sold in large bags for freezing ice cream. The salt hastens freezing by lowering the melting point of the ice around the outside of the ice cream freezer. It helps to cool beverages when poured on the ice surrounding bottles, too.

Rock salt also acts as a conductor of heat when cooking oysters or clams on the half shell. It speeds up cooking by transferring heat so that the seafoods do not become tough by cooking slowly. In addition, rock salt helps to balance small shells. (See also *Salt*.)

Clams Casino

Use oysters another time in this appetizer—

>   24 small hard-shell clams
>   in shells
>   Salt
>   • • •
>   ¼ cup butter or margarine,
>   softened
>   ¼ cup chopped green onion
>   ¼ cup chopped green pepper
>   ¼ cup finely chopped celery
>   2 tablespoons chopped canned
>   pimiento
>   1 teaspoon lemon juice
>   4 slices bacon, crisp-cooked and
>   crumbled
>   Rock salt

Open clams. With knife remove clams from the shells. Wash shells. Place each clam in deep half of shell. Sprinkle clams with table salt. Blend remaining ingredients. Top each clam with a scant tablespoon of mixture. Arrange half-shells on rock salt in a shallow pan. Bake at 425° for 10 to 12 minutes. Serves 8.

ROE *(rō)* — The eggs of female fish and shellfish or the milt (sperm or reproductive glands filled with sperm) of male fish. The eggs of some fish, especially the sturgeon and salmon, are made into caviar. The shellfish roe are taken from crustaceans, such as the lobster. Their roe are sometimes called coral.

Roe consist of the eggs or sperm enclosed in a membrane. The size of the membrane varies with the type of fish. Those from the shad, the one most commonly used, average about five inches long, three inches wide, and one inch thick. These are available in canned, frozen, or fresh forms in supermarkets.

There are various methods used for cooking roe — boiling, baking, and broiling. Regardless of the method used, first simmer the roe in salted or seasoned water for about 15 minutes. The membrane should be punctured before boiling so that it will not burst. After precooking, roe are used in entrées or appetizers.

Roe supply protein, B vitamins, and vitamin C in the diet. A 3½-ounce portion has 130 calories before other ingredients are added to the dish.

Fried Shad Roe

A change of pace for brunch or lunch—

>   2 pairs fresh shad roe*
>   2 cups water
>   1 tablespoon vinegar
>   1 teaspoon salt
>   1 beaten egg
>   1 tablespoon lemon juice
>   ½ cup crushed saltine crackers
>   ¼ cup butter or margarine
>   Paprika

Rinse roe. In saucepan combine water, vinegar, and salt. Bring to boiling. Add roe. Cover and simmer till done, 5 to 10 minutes; drain.

Cut roe into serving-sized pieces. Combine egg and lemon juice. Dip roe into egg mixture and roll in cracker crumbs. Fry in butter till browned, turning carefully. Sprinkle roe with paprika, if desired. Makes 4 servings.

*Or substitute one 7½-ounce can shad roe and omit precooking roe in salted water.

ROLL *(noun)*– **1.** A small, individual-sized bread. **2.** A thin sweet bread with a jam or sweet filling that is often called a sweet roll. **3.** A cut of meat that is boned and wrapped around itself.

Rolls in the first and most used sense are popular as dinner breads. Served hot from the oven, homemade rolls have an enticing aroma and flavor. They add a special, personal touch to the meal.

Making rolls for your family is similar to making breads. Rolls are usually made of yeastlike breads but consist of a richer, softer dough than breads. The basic techniques of mixing breads apply to rolls. The dough is kneaded, then allowed to rise in the bowl. The dough is proofed (rises a second time) after being shaped.

Roll recipes give the temperature and approximate length of baking time for the dough. Additional tests for doneness are the golden brown color and the hollow sound when you tap the bottom or side of a roll. Remove rolls from pan immediately and serve hot or cool on a rack.

If you do not want to mix and bake the rolls at the same time, rolls from recipes such as the following one keep well in the freezer or refrigerator. You can freeze completely or partially baked rolls (cooked 30 minutes at 350°) for two months. Partially baked rolls need to be thawed 15 minutes and baked at 450° for 5 to 10 minutes. If you plan to serve the rolls within five days, refrigerate according to the recipe for Refrigerator Rolls.

Bring out an elegant, late-evening snack of Coffeetime Twists and Cappuccino (see *Cappuccino* for recipe). The glazed hot rolls boast a filling of brown sugar and cinnamon.

How to make crisp or tender crusts

How to make crisp or tender crusts

If you like a crisp crust on rolls, brush them with a mixture of one beaten egg and one tablespoon milk before baking.

If you like a more tender crust, use salad oil or melted butter or margarine instead.

Basic Roll Dough

Shape into cloverleaf, butter fan, bowknot, or Parker House rolls—

   1 **package active dry yeast**
3½ **cups sifted all-purpose flour**

      •   •   •

1¼ **cups milk**
 ¼ **cup sugar**
 ¼ **cup shortening**
  1 **teaspoon salt**
  1 **egg**

In large mixer bowl combine yeast and *2 cups* flour. Heat milk, sugar, shortening, and salt just till warm, stirring occasionally to melt shortening. Add to dry mixture in mixing bowl; add egg. Beat at low speed with electric mixer for ½ minute, scraping sides of bowl constantly. Beat 3 minutes at high speed. By hand, gradually stir in remaining flour to make a soft dough, beating well. Place in greased bowl; turn once to grease surface. Cover and let rise till double, 1½ to 2 hours.

Turn dough out on lightly floured surface and shape as desired (see page 1900 and individual entries). Cover and let rolls rise till double, 30 to 45 minutes. Bake on greased baking sheet or in greased muffin pans at 400° for 12 to 15 minutes. Makes 2 dozen rolls.

Refrigerator Rolls

Prepare Basic Roll Dough. *Do not let rise.* Place dough in greased bowl, turning once to grease surface. Cover tightly; chill at least 2 hours, or up to 4 or 5 days.

About 2 hours before serving, shape the dough as desired on floured surface. Cover; let rise till double, about 1¼ hours. Follow the baking times for Basic Roll Dough.

How to shape rolls: Using Basic Roll Dough, you can make rolls in many shapes. The most common ones are Parker House; butter fan or fantan; pan rolls; cloverleaf; bowknot and rosette; twist and corkscrew; butterhorn; and crescent or croissant.

Parker House rolls are flat circles of dough folded off-center. Butter fan or fantan rolls are made by stacking about six strips of dough and slicing these in short lengths. They are placed in a muffin tin with the cut side down. Round pan rolls are small balls of dough baked separately in muffin tins or side by side in a pan. The following recipes and pictures illustrate some of these shapes.

Manna Rolls

Onion, bacon, and beer flavor these large rolls—

  2 **packages active dry yeast**
3¾ **to 4 cups sifted all-purpose flour**
 ¼ **cup dry onion soup mix**
  8 **slices bacon**
  1 **12-ounce can beer (1½ cups)**
 ¼ **cup milk**
  1 **tablespoon sugar**
   Melted butter or margarine
  2 **tablespoons yellow cornmeal**

In large mixer bowl combine yeast, *1¾ cups* flour, and onion soup mix. Cook bacon till crisp; drain, reserving 2 tablespoons drippings. Crumble bacon; set aside. Heat together beer, milk, sugar, and reserved drippings just till warm (mixture will appear curdled). Add to dry ingredients in mixer bowl. Beat at low speed on electric mixer for ½ minute, scraping bowl constantly. Beat 3 minutes at high speed. Stir in crumbled bacon and enough of the remaining flour to make a moderately stiff dough.

Knead till smooth and elastic. Place in greased bowl, turning once to grease surface. Cover; let rise till almost double, 40 to 45 minutes. Punch down. Shape into 16 balls. Place in two 9x1½-inch round baking pans. Brush tops of rolls with melted butter or margarine and sprinkle with cornmeal. Cover lightly. Let rise till almost double, 25 minutes. Bake at 375° till golden, 20 minutes. Makes 16.

Cloverleaf rolls are made by placing three small balls of dough into each muffin tin. Shape balls by pulling under edges of dough.

Clothespin Rolls

        1 package active dry yeast
    2½ to 3 cups sifted all-purpose
            flour
        ½ cup cornmeal
        ¾ cup milk
        ½ cup shortening
        ¼ cup sugar
        1 teaspoon salt
        2 eggs

In large mixer bowl combine yeast, *1½ cups* flour, and cornmeal. Heat milk, shortening, sugar, and salt just till warm, stirring occasionally to melt shortening. Add to dry ingredients in bowl; add eggs. Beat at low speed with electric mixer for ½ minute, scraping sides of bowl constantly. Beat at high speed for 3 minutes. By hand, stir in enough of the remaining flour to make a soft dough. Turn out on lightly floured surface; knead till smooth. Place in greased bowl, turning dough once to grease surface. Cover; let rise in a warm place till double, about 1¼ hours.

Punch down; turn out on lightly floured surface. Shape pieces of dough into ropes about 8 inches long and ¼ inch in diameter. Wrap around greased peg clothespins, pressing gently to seal ends. Place on greased baking sheet; cover. Let rise till double, about 45 minutes. Bake at 375° till done, about 10 minutes. Immediately remove clothespins by twisting gently. Makes 24. *Note:* Dough may be formed into 20 pan rolls. Bake 15 minutes.

Orange Rosettes

        1 package active dry yeast
    5 to 5½ cups sifted all-purpose
            flour
    1¼ cups milk
        ½ cup shortening
        ⅓ cup sugar
        2 beaten eggs
        2 tablespoons grated orange peel
        ¼ cup orange juice

In mixer bowl combine yeast and *3 cups* flour. Heat milk, shortening, sugar, and 1 teaspoon salt just till warm, stirring to melt shortening. Add to dry mixture; add eggs, orange peel, and juice. Beat at low speed with electric mixer ½ minute, scraping sides of bowl. Beat 3 minutes at high speed. By hand stir in enough of the remaining flour to make a soft dough.

Knead dough on lightly floured surface till smooth and elastic, about 8 to 10 minutes. Place in greased bowl, turning to grease surface. Cover; let rise in warm place till double, 2 hours. Punch down; cover and let rest 10 minutes. Roll dough in 18x10-inch rectangle, ½ inch thick. Cut strips 10 inches long and ¾ inch wide. Shape into rosettes (see picture below). Place on greased baking sheets. Cover; let rise till almost double, 45 minutes. Bake at 400° for 12 minutes. Cool on rack. Frost with Orange Icing, if desired. Makes 2 dozen.

Orange Icing: Blend 1 teaspoon grated orange peel, 2 tablespoons orange juice, and 1 cup sifted confectioners' sugar.

Bowknots are formed by rolling strips of dough lightly under fingers and tying in loose knot. Tuck under ends for rosettes.

Coffeetime Twists

  1 package active dry yeast
¼ teaspoon baking soda
  3 cups sifted all-purpose flour
  1 cup buttermilk
  3 tablespoons sugar
  2 tablespoons shortening
  1 teaspoon salt
  1 slightly beaten egg
  2 tablespoons butter, softened
⅓ cup brown sugar
  1 teaspoon ground cinnamon
    Icing

In mixer bowl combine yeast, soda, and *1½ cups* flour. Heat buttermilk, sugar, shortening, and salt just till warm, stirring to melt shortening. Add to dry mixture; add egg. Beat at low speed with electric mixer for ½ minute, scraping sides of bowl. Beat 3 minutes at high speed. By hand, stir in remaining flour. Turn out on lightly floured surface; knead till smooth.

Roll the dough into a 24x6-inch rectangle, about ¼ inch thick. Spread with butter. Combine brown sugar and cinnamon; sprinkle over lengthwise half of the dough. Fold other half over. Cut dough into 1-inch strips.

To form rolls, hold strip at both ends and twist in opposite directions. Place on greased baking sheet; let rise in warm place till light, about 1 hour. Bake at 375° for 12 to 15 minutes. Frost with Icing while warm. Makes 24.

Icing: Blend 1 cup confectioners' sugar, 2 tablespoons milk, and ¼ teaspoon vanilla.

Twists are made by folding dough in half and cutting into one-inch strips. Grasp each end and twist in opposite directions.

Shape butterhorns by cutting a circle of dough into wedges. Roll each wedge toward the point. Curve rolls to make crescents.

Double Butterscotch Crescents

1½ cups milk
  1 4-ounce package *regular* butterscotch pudding mix
½ cup butter or margarine
  2 envelopes active dry yeast
  2 eggs
  2 teaspoons salt
  5 to 5½ cups sifted all-purpose flour
    Butterscotch Filling

Using the 1½ cups milk, prepare pudding according to package directions. Remove from heat; stir in butter. Cool to lukewarm, stirring once or twice. Dissolve yeast in ½ cup warm water; stir into cooled pudding. Beat in eggs and salt. Gradually add just enough flour to make a moderately soft dough. Turn out onto floured surface and knead till dough is smooth and elastic, 5 to 10 minutes. Place in greased bowl; turn to grease surface. Let rise till double, 1 to 1½ hours. Punch down; divide into 4 parts. Cover and let rest 10 minutes.

Roll out one part of dough to a 12-inch circle. Spread with ¼ of the Butterscotch Filling. Cut into 12 triangles. Roll into crescents; place, points down, on greased baking sheet. Repeat with remaining dough and filling. Let rise till almost double, 45 minutes. Bake at 375° for 12 to 15 minutes. Cool. Makes 48.

Butterscotch Filling: Stir together ¼ cup melted butter, ⅔ cup brown sugar, ⅔ cup flaked coconut, and ⅓ cup chopped pecans.

Raisin-Cinnamon Rolls

Spread dough with a sweet filling and roll jelly-roll fashion for a pinwheel effect—

½ recipe Basic Roll Dough
¼ cup granulated sugar
2 tablespoons butter or margarine, melted
1 teaspoon ground cinnamon
¼ cup raisins
1 cup sifted confectioners' sugar
2 tablespoons milk
½ teaspoon vanilla
Dash salt

Prepare ½ recipe Basic Roll Dough as directed, rolling dough on lightly floured surface to 16x8-inch rectangle. Combine sugar, butter, and cinnamon; spread over dough. Sprinkle with raisins. Roll lengthwise as for jelly roll. Seal edge; cut in 1-inch slices. Place, cut side down, in greased 9x9x2-inch baking pan. Cover. Let rise till double, 30 to 40 minutes.

Bake rolls at 375° till done, 20 to 25 minutes. Remove rolls from pan. Combine confectioners' sugar, milk, vanilla, and salt. Frost rolls with confectioners' icing. Makes 16.

Caramel Rolls

½ recipe Basic Roll Dough
¼ cup butter or margarine, melted
¼ cup brown sugar
1 teaspoon ground cinnamon
½ cup brown sugar
¼ cup butter or margarine
1 tablespoon light corn syrup

Prepare ½ recipe Basic Roll Dough as directed, rolling on lightly floured surface to 12x8-inch rectangle. Brush with ¼ cup melted butter; sprinkle with the ¼ cup brown sugar and cinnamon. Roll lengthwise as for jelly roll; seal edge. Cut roll in 1-inch slices.

In saucepan combine the ½ cup brown sugar, ¼ cup butter or margarine, and corn syrup. Heat slowly, stirring often. Pour into 8x8x2-inch baking pan. Place rolls, cut side down, over mixture. Cover; let rise in warm place till double, 35 to 45 minutes. Bake at 375° about 20 minutes. Cool 2 to 3 minutes. Invert on rack; remove pan. Makes 1 dozen rolls.

Hard Rolls

Form dough into ovals or rounds for miniature loaves of thick-crusted French bread—

Prepare ½ recipe French Bread Dough. (See *French Bread.*) Knead dough 10 to 15 minutes or till very elastic, kneading in remaining ¼ cup flour. Place dough in lightly greased bowl, turning once to grease the surface. Cover dough; let rise in warm place till double, about 45 to 60 minutes. Punch down. Let the dough rise till double again, about 30 to 45 minutes.

Turn out on lightly floured surface and divide into 2 portions. Cover and let rest 10 minutes. Divide each half into 9 portions. Shape each in oval or round roll. Place about 2 inches apart on greased baking sheets that have been sprinkled with cornmeal.

Add 1 tablespoon water to 1 slightly beaten egg white; brush over tops and sides of rolls. For crisp crusts, just brush the rolls with some water. Cover with a damp cloth, not touching dough. Let rise in warm place till double, about 45 to 60 minutes.

Place large, shallow pan on lower rack of oven; fill with boiling water. Bake rolls at 400° for 15 minutes. Brush again with egg white mixture or water. Bake till nicely browned, 10 to 15 minutes longer. For crackly crust, cool in draft. Makes 18 hard rolls.

Convenience products: If you don't have time to bake homemade rolls, look for convenience product substitutes at the supermarket. The shelves contain a wide array of brown-and-serve rolls, ready-to-serve rolls, hot roll mixes, and refrigerated rolls. These come in a variety of styles—crescent, Parker House, butterflake, French, and pan or dinner rolls.

You can serve your family an interesting selection of breads just by using these products as they are. Or, if you want more variety, try dressing up the convenience products with additional ingredients. Spread rolls with a blend of softened butter and an herb, such as thyme, dill, sage, or basil. Cheese spreads, bits of crisp bacon, onion, and garlic also add flavor to the rolls, which, in turn, complement the entire meal and arouse the family's interest. (See also *Bread.*)

Add fragrant, orange-flavored rolls to the brunch menu to make a hit with the crowd. Make either rosettes or bowknots (shown here) from the Orange Rosette dough — the only difference is tucking under the loose ends of the knots for rosettes.

Croissants Elegante

    1 13¾-ounce package hot roll mix
   ¾ cup warm water
    1 egg
    1 tablespoon sugar
   ¾ cup *cold* butter or margarine

In large bowl dissolve yeast from hot roll mix in warm water. Stir in egg and sugar. Add roll mix; beat well. Turn out onto lightly floured surface; knead till smooth, about 3 to 5 minutes. Let dough rest for 20 minutes.

Roll *cold* butter between two sheets of waxed paper to 9x7-inch rectangle; chill. Roll dough out to 16x10-inch rectangle. Place butter rectangle on one end of dough; fold other end of dough over and seal edges. Roll dough out to a 16x10-inch rectangle; fold in thirds. Wrap in waxed paper; chill 20 minutes. Roll, fold, and chill 2 more times. After final chilling, roll chilled dough out to 20x16-inch rectangle.

Cut crosswise into 4 strips; cut each strip crosswise into 4 rectangles. Cut each rectangle diagonally into 2 triangles. Starting with long side, roll each piece of dough toward point.

Place, point down, on *ungreased* baking sheet; curve ends to form crescent. Let rise in warm place till light, about 30 to 45 minutes. Bake at 400° till the rolls are golden brown, about 12 to 15 minutes. Makes 32 rolls.

Thyme-Buttered Crescents

Try the herb butter on English muffins, too—

  ½ cup butter or margarine,
       softened
   1 teaspoon lemon juice
  ½ teaspoon dried thyme leaves,
       crushed
      • • •
   1 package refrigerated crescent
       rolls (8 rolls)

Cream butter or margarine till fluffy. Stir in lemon juice and thyme. Keep herb butter at room temperature for 1 hour to mellow before using. Unroll crescents; spread *2 teaspoons* herb butter on each crescent. Roll up and bake according to package directions. Makes 8 rolls.

ROLL *(verb)*—**1.** To coat with crumbs or chopped nuts by moving the food around in a dish of the pieces. **2.** To shape food.

Foods are rolled into many different shapes. Doughs are spread out flat with a rolling pin; jelly rolls are rolled into long, round shapes; refrigerated cookie doughs are formed into long cylinders; various mixtures are shaped into balls.

ROLLED COOKIE—A type of cookie that is spread flat and cut into shapes before baking. Rolled cookies are made from stiff doughs. If the dough is rolled very thin, the cookies will be crisp; if the dough is thicker, they will be soft.

Rolled cookies serve a dual purpose when there are children in the house. Not only are the cookies good to eat, but they are also fun to shape. Children enjoy cutting rolled cookies into designs ranging from simple triangles cut with a knife to elaborate ones made with cookie cutters. You can experiment with additional decorations by topping with sugar, small decorative candies, or icings.

Another decorative variation is to stack two cookies with or without a filling between them. Attractive combinations of colors and shapes carry out a holiday or party theme. The following recipes might be varied to suit the occasion.

Be creative with rolled cookies—it's not complicated. Try cutting tiny holes off-center with a thimble for an unusual design.

Delight children and adults with this pair of cookies. The center cutout for Cameo Cutouts (left) is made with hors d'oeuvre cutters. Mincemeat Marvels (right) are decorated with a glacé candy apple topknot.

Mincemeat Marvels

1⅓ cups shortening
1½ cups sugar
  2 eggs
  1 teaspoon vanilla
  1 teaspoon grated orange peel
  4 cups sifted all-purpose flour
  3 teaspoons baking powder
½ teaspoon salt
  2 to 3 tablespoons milk
    Mincemeat Filling

Thoroughly cream shortening, sugar, eggs, and vanilla. Stir in orange peel. Sift together flour, baking powder, and salt. Add to creamed mixture alternately with milk. Divide dough in half; chill. On lightly floured surface, roll to ⅛-inch thickness. Cut with 2¾-inch round cutter. Make small round cutout in centers of *half* the cookies.

Place 1 heaping teaspoon Mincemeat Filling on each plain cookie; top with a cutout cookie. Press edges with fork or tip of hook-type opener to seal. Place on greased cookie sheet; bake at 375° for 12 minutes. Garnish with Glacé Candy Apples, if desired. Makes 30.

Mincemeat Filling: Break one 9-ounce package mincemeat into pieces. Add 2 tablespoons sugar, 2 teaspoons grated orange peel, 1 teaspoon grated lemon peel, ½ cup orange juice, and ¼ cup lemon juice. Heat, stirring till mincemeat pieces are broken; simmer 1 minute. Cool; stir in ¼ cup chopped walnuts.

Cameo Cutouts

    ¾ cup butter or margarine
    ⅔ cup sugar
    ½ cup dark corn syrup
    1 egg
    1½ teaspoons vanilla
    3 cups sifted all-purpose flour
    1 teaspoon baking powder
    ½ teaspoon salt
    1 1-ounce square unsweetened
        chocolate, melted and cooled

Cream butter, sugar, and syrup till fluffy. Beat in egg and vanilla. Sift together flour, baking powder, and salt; stir into creamed mixture. Divide dough in half. To one half add melted chocolate; blend. Leave other half plain. Chill both doughs thoroughly.

On well-floured surface, roll chocolate dough to ⅛-inch thickness. (Keep plain dough chilled.) Cut in 2½-inch scalloped rounds. Place on *ungreased* cookie sheet. Repeat with vanilla dough. With floured tiny cutter or thimble, make center cutouts. Place chocolate cutouts on plain cookies and vice versa. Bake at 350° for 8 to 10 minutes. Cool slightly; remove the cookies to rack.

Nut-Butter Rounds

    1 cup sifted all-purpose flour
    ⅓ cup granulated sugar
    ½ cup ground pecans
    ½ cup butter or margarine, softened
    ⅔ cup sifted confectioners' sugar
    ¼ cup butter or margarine
    2 1-ounce squares unsweetened
        chocolate, melted and cooled
    Apricot preserves

Sift together flour and granulated sugar; stir in ground pecans. Blend in the ½ cup butter or margarine with spoon. On floured surface, roll to ⅛-inch thickness. Cut in 2-inch rounds and place on *ungreased* cookie sheet. Bake at 375° till lightly browned, 8 to 10 minutes. Cool slightly before removing to rack.

Cream confectioners' sugar, ¼ cup butter, and melted chocolate till well combined. Spread chocolate filling on *half* the cookies. Top chocolate-covered cookies with plain cookies. Spread tops lightly with preserves. Makes 1½ dozen.

Refrigerator cookies are a slightly different kind of rolled cookie. These are shaped into long, round cylinders and then sliced. (See also *Cookie.*)

Sugar-Pecan Crisps

    ¾ cup butter or margarine
    ⅔ cup sugar
    1 egg
    1 teaspoon vanilla
    ¼ teaspoon salt
    1¾ cups sifted all-purpose flour
    ½ cup finely chopped pecans

Cream together butter or margarine and sugar till light. Beat in egg, vanilla, and salt. Gradually stir in flour. Shape dough into 2 rolls, each about 6 inches long and 1½ inches in diameter; roll each in ¼ cup of the pecans to coat outside. Wrap in waxed paper; chill thoroughly. Cut into slices ¼ inch thick. Place on *ungreased* cookie sheet. Bake at 350° for 15 to 17 minutes. Makes 4 dozen cookies.

ROLLED OATS—A cereal product that is made by pressing oat grains into flat flakes. Rolled oats are often called oatmeal. (See also *Oatmeal.*)

Oatmeal Crunchies

    1 cup sifted all-purpose flour
    ½ cup granulated sugar
    ½ teaspoon baking powder
    ½ teaspoon baking soda
    ¼ teaspoon salt
    ½ cup brown sugar
    ½ cup shortening
    1 egg
    ¼ teaspoon vanilla
    ¾ cup quick-cooking rolled oats
    ¼ cup chopped walnuts

Sift together first 5 ingredients. Add the ½ cup brown sugar, shortening, egg, and vanilla; beat well. Stir in rolled oats and walnuts. Form into small balls. Dip tops in a little additional granulated sugar. Place on *ungreased* cookie sheet. Bake at 375° for about 10 to 12 minutes. Makes about 3½ dozen.

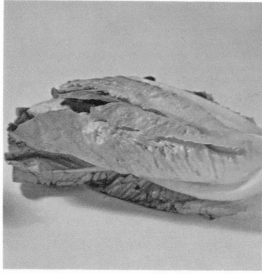

The rich green color of romaine makes a pleasing contrast in a salad greens mixture. The elongated heads and leaves are easily recognizable at the supermarket when compared to other heading lettuce varieties.

Romaine leaves are prepared in the French style by cutting out the leaf ribs with a knife. For a garnish, snip the edges of the leaves into points. Then, insert them, pointed ends out, around the salad.

ROLLING PIN—A cylindrical roller, usually with handles, used to flatten dough for pastries, cookies, and biscuits.

When rolling dough, take care not to pinch dough at the edges. Roll with even pressure, from center outward. Lift the rolling pin when it reaches the edge.

ROLLMOP—A herring fillet rolled around a piece of pickle or small onion and marinated in a seasoned, white wine solution.

ROLY-POLY—A dessert of sweet biscuit dough spread with jam or fruit filling and folded up like a jelly roll. Roly-poly can be baked, steamed, or boiled.

ROMAINE—Also called cos, this lettuce variety has a pronounced cylindrical head shape. Its coarse, dark green leaves, stronger in flavor than iceberg lettuce, overlap closely around the heart.

As is indicative of dark green vegetables, romaine is higher in vitamin A than the lighter lettuce varieties. Nonetheless, romaine is low in calories like other members of the lettuce family.

Fresh-looking, crisp romaine leaves with a minimum of blemishes should be selected. Wrapped in foil, cellophane, or a plastic bag, romaine can be stored in a vegetable crisper for up to one week.

Although much depends on other flavorings in a recipe, romaine is usually utilized with a mixture of greens. However, some classic recipes, like Caesar salad, use romaine as the only green. Stronger seasonings mute the bitter romaine flavor. (See also *Lettuce*.)

Modern Caesar Salad

Shake together ½ cup salad oil; ¼ cup red wine vinegar; 1 large clove garlic, crushed; 2 teaspoons Worcestershire sauce; ¼ teaspoon salt; and dash pepper in screw-top jar. Refrigerate a few hours or overnight to blend flavors.

Toast 3 slices bread, cubed, slowly at 225° for 2 hours. To serve, sprinkle ½ cup shredded Parmesan cheese and 1 ounce blue cheese, crumbled (¼ cup), over 8 cups torn romaine (about 1 medium head). Shake 1 egg well with dressing; toss lightly with salad. Serves 6 to 8.

ROMANO CHEESE—A very hard Italian cheese with sharp, pungent flavor and solid, granular texture. Most romano cheese is made in various regions of Italy, although some is made in America.

When first produced in Latium, Italy, romano was made solely from ewe's milk, but in recent years, cow's and goat's milk have been utilized. The milk is partly skimmed and may be pasteurized. After processing, the cheese is cured for at least five months, and, in most cases, for over one year. If short-term cured (five to eight months), romano may be eaten as a table cheese. Longer curing increases the cheese's hardness, making it suitable for grating only. Grated cheese is used with soups, spaghetti, and other dishes.

Romano is often named according to the type of milk from which it is made. When ewe's milk is used, it is called Pecorino romano; when cow's milk, Vacchino romano; when goat's milk, Caprino romano.

Since most romano available in the United States has a long-term cure, the cheese is shredded or grated and used in cooking like Parmesan cheese. Its flavor, however, is stronger than Parmesan. Thus, use it sparingly. Add a little and then increase until of the desired flavor level.

Hard romano cheese is just right for grating.

Noodles Romano

Combine ¼ cup softened butter; 2 tablespoons parsley flakes; and 1 teaspoon dried basil leaves, crushed. Blend in one 8-ounce package softened cream cheese and dash pepper; stir in ⅔ cup boiling water. Blend well. Keep warm.

Cook one 8-ounce package fettucini, thin noodles, *or* spaghetti in large amount of boiling, salted water till tender; drain. Cook 1 clove garlic, minced, in ¼ cup butter for 1 to 2 minutes; pour over noodles. Toss lightly. Sprinkle with ½ cup shredded or grated romano cheese; toss again. Pile noodles on warm platter; spoon sauce over. Sprinkle with ¼ cup shredded or grated romano cheese. Toss lightly. Garnish with parsley. Makes 6 servings.

The robust flavor of romano cheese stars in this Italian-style Noodles Romano. A smooth, cream cheese sauce moistens the thin fettucini, while fluffy parsley sprigs serve as garnish.

ROME BEAUTY APPLE—A firm, mild-flavored apple variety that is most often used for cooking and baking. (See also *Apple*.)

ROOT BEER—A nonalcoholic, caramel-colored, carbonated beverage. This sweetened, yeast-flavored drink is made with a syrup of herb, bark, and root juices.

Root beer, a popular soft drink, is sold in bottles and in jugs. If you are so inclined, you can make your own root beer. (See also *Carbonated Beverage*.)

ROQUEFORT CHEESE (*rōk' fuhrt*)—A cheese made in Roquefort, France. Roquefort is a semisoft to hard cheese with a chalky white color and blue veins. It is made of sheep's milk.

This gourmet cheese has been made for centuries. Supposedly, it was first made by a shepherd boy who left his lunch, including curds, in a cave. When he returned sometime later, the curds had changed. Of course, his curiosity demanded that he sample this blue-streaked wonder. Whether or not this story is true is not known, but Roquefort cheese has achieved a kingly status since that time.

Today, there is a worldwide demand for this sharp, piquant cheese. However, Roquefort cannot be made any place other than in Roquefort, France. Only cheeses ripened in Roquefort caves can be labeled Roquefort and identified by the red sheep emblem on the package. There are regional dairies in France that begin the processing of the ewe's milk. Then, the curds are sent to Roquefort to be ripened in the caves. These caves have a special mold and atmospheric conditions that produce the flavor of Roquefort.

Blue, Gorgonzola, and Stilton are kin to Roquefort.

You can find Roquefort in most American supermarkets and cheese stores. How you use it will depend on your particular preference. Cheese lovers enjoy Roquefort in many types of dishes. One of the most popular uses is in salad dressing.

Roquefort Dressing

½ cup mayonnaise
½ cup light cream
1½ teaspoons lemon juice
4 ounces Roquefort cheese (1 cup)

Combine mayonnaise, light cream, and lemon juice. Crumble cheese into mayonnaise mixture; mix well. Chill. Serve with lettuce or tomato wedges, as desired. Makes 1½ cups.

Other uses for Roquefort range from appetizers of dips, canapés, and spreads to accents in meat dishes to desserts.

Roquefort Dessert Spread

8 ounces Roquefort cheese (2 cups)
1 tablespoon sauterne
3 tablespoons diced almonds, toasted
Fresh fruit

With electric or rotary beater, whip together cheese and sauterne till light and fluffy. Stir in almonds. Form mixture into a bar; chill. Slice and serve with fresh fruit.

Besides adding interesting flavor, Roquefort contributes nutrients to the diet. It contains protein, fat, calcium, phosphorus, the B vitamins, and some vitamin A. A one-ounce serving has about 110 calories. (See also *Cheese*.)

ROSÉ (*rō zā'*)—A pink table wine. Rosé is made in most wine-producing countries from black or red grapes. After a few days of fermenting, the grapes' skins are removed to control the wine's delicate color. Rosé ranges from dry to sweet and is served well chilled, about 45° to 50°. This light-bodied wine goes with most foods, especially chicken, seafood, veal, and lamb. (See also *Wines and Spirits*.)

ROSEFISH—A bright red or reddish orange, saltwater fish. The rosefish is also called redfish, blackbelly rosefish, and ocean perch. It inhabits deep waters of the northern Atlantic Ocean. The firm, rich-flavored rosefish is prepared like other fat fish. (See also *Perch*.)

ROSE GERANIUM—A fragrant member of the geranium family. The narrow, light green leaves are used in cooking.

Fresh leaves are used to give flavor to jam or jelly and to baked custards. They also make an attractive, sweetly aromatic garnish for fruit cups, fruit salads, and cakes. Dried rose geranium leaves are included in some herb-tea mixtures.

Most homemakers who like to use rose geranium leaves grow them at home, but you can get them at greenhouses and specialty food stores. (See also *Herb*.)

Rose Geranium Cake

```
 24 fresh rose geranium leaves
  1 cup butter or margarine
       (2 sticks)
1¾ cups sugar
  6 egg whites
  3 cups sifted cake flour
  4 teaspoons baking powder
 ½ teaspoon salt
 ¾ cup milk
 ½ cup water
  1 teaspoon vanilla
    Rose Geranium Frosting (See
       page 1910)
    Frosted Rose Geranium Leaves
       (See page 1910)
```

Rinse rose geranium leaves; wrap 5 or 6 leaves around each stick of butter. Wrap butter in foil or plastic wrap; refrigerate overnight. Remove leaves; rinse and save leaves.

Cream butter; gradually add sugar, creaming till light and fluffy. Add egg whites, two at a time, beating well after each addition. Sift together flour, baking powder, and salt. Combine milk, water, and vanilla.

Alternately add dry ingredients and milk mixture to creamed mixture, beginning and ending with dry ingredients; beat smooth after each addition. Grease and flour two 9x1½-inch layer cake pans. Arrange 10 to 12 rose geranium leaves (including those saved from the butter) on bottom of each cake pan. Spoon batter over leaves. Bake at 350° till cake tests done, about 30 to 35 minutes. Cool in pans for 10 minutes. Remove cake layers from pans; cool on racks. Remove rose geranium leaves from cake bottoms; discard leaves. Frost cooled cake with Rose Geranium Frosting and garnish with Frosted Rose Geranium Leaves.

Capture garden-fresh flavor and beauty in Rose Geranium Cake. The leaves accent the cake and frosting, and add a garnish.

Rose Geranium Frosting

1½ cups sugar
3 or 4 fresh rose geranium leaves
2 egg whites
⅓ cup cold water
¼ teaspoon cream of tartar
Dash salt
5 drops red food coloring

Pour *half* the sugar into a container with a tight-fitting cover. Wash leaves; add to sugar container. Cover with second half of sugar. Cover container. Let stand overnight. Remove rose geranium leaves before using sugar.

Place rose geranium sugar, egg whites, water, cream of tartar, and salt in top of double boiler (not over heat). Beat 1 minute with electric or rotary beater. Place over, but not touching boiling water. Cook, beating constantly, till frosting forms stiff peaks, about 7 minutes (do not overcook). Remove from boiling water. Add food coloring; beat till of spreading consistency. Frost cake.

Frosted Rose Geranium Leaves

Wash fresh rose geranium leaves; *thoroughly* pat dry. Carefully brush with 1 slightly beaten egg white; sprinkle with granulated sugar till well coated. Allow to dry and harden on wire rack. Store in airtight container.

ROSE HIP—The ripened fruit of a rose. Rose hip is the round, red part on the bush after the petals have fallen from the blossom. The cleaned and seeded rose hips are sold dried whole, cut, and powdered. They are used primarily in making jams and jellies.

ROSEMARY—An herb of the mint family. Rosemary has a warm, mintlike flavor and a spicy bouquet. The leaves resemble curved pine needles. They are about one inch long and are dark green in color.

Rosemary has been used in many ways since at least 500 B.C. It has been esteemed as a perfume, decoration, symbol of remembrance, and as a seasoning.

Legend says rosemary grows only in the gardens of the righteous. If you do not want to test the legend, you can purchase dried rosemary leaves at the supermarket. Use rosemary sparingly so it does not overwhelm the flavor of the food. Crushing the leaves and simmering or soaking them in a dish for at least 15 minutes helps to develop the full flavor.

Use rosemary with lamb, chicken, soups, stews, marinades, potatoes, cauliflower, turnips, peas, citrus fruits, spinach, and squash. (See also *Herb*.)

Turkey Timbales

2 beaten eggs
1 cup milk
½ cup quick-cooking rolled oats
1 cup chopped celery
1 tablespoon finely chopped onion
½ teaspoon salt
¼ teaspoon dried rosemary
leaves, crushed
Dash pepper
2 cups ground cooked turkey
1 10½-ounce can condensed
cream of mushroom soup
⅓ cup milk

Combine first 8 ingredients; add turkey and mix well. Pour into 4 greased 6-ounce custard cups. Bake at 350° for 45 to 50 minutes. Run spatula around timbales. Let stand 5 minutes before removing from cups. Combine mushroom soup and ⅓ cup milk in saucepan. Heat. Serve with timbales. Makes 4 servings.

Rosemary, an evergreen of the mint family, is native to the Mediterranean area. It grows as a tree or bush in warm climates.

Broiled Salmon Epicurean

    2 pounds fresh or frozen salmon
        steaks
  1/4 cup salad oil
    2 tablespoons lemon juice
  1/2 teaspoon dried rosemary
        leaves, crushed
      Salt and pepper

Thaw frozen fish. Combine next 3 ingredients; shake well. Let stand at room temperature 1 hour; strain. Cut fish into 6 portions. Dip into oil mixture; sprinkle with salt and pepper. Place in a greased wire broiler basket. Grill over *medium-hot* coals about 5 to 8 minutes. Baste and turn. Brush other side; broil till fish flakes easily when tested with a fork, about 5 to 8 minutes longer. Makes 6 servings.

ROSETTE–1. Food formed into a shape similar to a rose. **2.** A thin pastry used as a dessert or as a shell for a main dish.

Tomatoes and radishes are good examples of foods formed into rosettes. By cutting through the skin four or five times, petals are formed. These make attractive relishes and garnishes for plates.

Pastry rosettes also are attractively shaped. They are made into elaborate designs by the mold on the rosette iron. These irons are heated, dipped into the thin batter, and placed into deep, hot fat for a short time. The crisp rosette is formed in the design of the iron.

Pastry rosettes become exotic desserts when sprinkled with confectioners' sugar, topped with a sauce, or served with fruit. They can also form the base for the main dish when used as a shell for a creamed meat mixture, such as chicken à la king.

Rosettes

    2 eggs
    1 tablespoon granulated sugar
  1/4 teaspoon salt
    1 cup sifted all-purpose flour
    1 cup milk
    1 teaspoon vanilla
          • • •
      Confectioners' sugar

Combine eggs, granulated sugar, and salt; beat well. Add flour, milk, and vanilla; beat smooth. Heat rosette iron in deep, hot fat (375°) for 2 minutes. Remove; drain off excess fat.

Then, dip hot iron into batter to 1/4 inch from top of iron. Dip at once into hot fat (375°). Fry the rosette till golden, about 1/2 minute. Lift the iron out; tip it slightly to drain off any excess fat. With a fork push the rosette off the iron onto paper toweling placed on rack. Reheat iron for 1 minute; make next rosette. Sift confectioners' sugar over cooled rosettes. Makes 3 1/2 dozen.

ROSETTE IRON–A long-handled metal utensil with a decorative disk screwed onto the handle. Most rosette irons come packaged with a wide variety of disks in elaborate designs, such as butterflies.

ROSE WATER–A liquid flavored and scented with roses. It is available at pharmacies and some specialty food stores.

You can use rose water to add a delightful, delicate flavor to cakes, pound cakes, jellies, custards, and confections. If you want to experiment with the flavor of rose water, substitute it in recipes calling for vanilla and almond extracts.

ROTARY BEATER–A kitchen utensil consisting of interlocking blades that are turned by a geared handle. Rotary beaters are used to whip eggs and other foods.

Mold crisp Rosettes into a variety of shapes simply by changing the disks that screw onto the end of the rosette iron.

ROTE – A pasta shaped like a wheel. Rote has a disk in the center with spokes running to the outside rim. (See also *Pasta*.)

ROTISSERIE *(rō tis' uh rē)* – An appliance with a motor-driven spit that is used for broiling foods. The spit rotates the food over, under, or in front of the heat, thus, ensuring even cooking and self-basting.

Rotisseries come in several forms. Some are portable appliances, which double as ovens and broilers. Other rotisseries are a special attachment on a barbecue grill or in the oven of a range. Depending on the appliance, the heat may be an electric heating unit, gas flame, or hot coals.

Rotisserie cooking is a dry-heat method that produces food with a delicious, crisp, brown exterior and a tender, moist interior. This method is suitable for tender cuts of meat, poultry, fruits, and vegetables. Some of the foods adapted to the rotisserie are chicken, duck, turkey, rolled roast, kabob assortments, crookneck squash, eggplant, pineapple, cherry tomatoes, and button mushrooms.

Mounting poultry correctly on the spit

Pull neck skin to back; fold under. Secure skin to bird with a nail or skewer. Tie with a cord to hold the nail in place.

Place holding fork on rod, tines toward point; insert rod through bird (pinch tines together and push firmly into breast meat).

Using 24 inches of cord, start cord at back and loop around each wing. Make slipknots to secure wings. Tie in center; leave ends.

Using 18 inches of cord, loop around tail and then around crossed legs. Tie tightly to hold bird securely onto rod; leave ends.

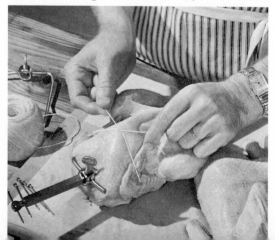

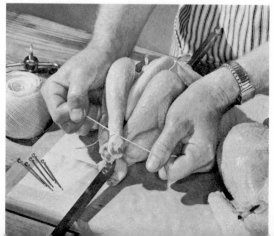

The instructions that come with your rotisserie will give explicit directions for operating the appliance. One of the important points is to be sure that the food is balanced on the spit. If it is not balanced, the food will flop on the spit and some parts, such as wings and legs of chickens, may char. Test the balance according to manufacturer's directions in the beginning and adjust the food until the spit turns smoothly.

When time is important, use your rotisserie to cook meals for the family and company. Foods cooked this way generally take less time than when they are roasted, so it helps to speed up meal preparation. It also gives a distinctive broiled or barbecued flavor to the food, which is as popular today as it was when the cavemen hung pieces of meat over a campfire.

Today, however, rotisserie cooking is surrounded with more glamour than in the past. People enjoy the special treat of watching while the food slowly turns and browns. You might take advantage of this by arranging for a party to be in the area of the rotisserie so that aroma and sight of the food cooking will whet the appetite of the guests. (See *Appliance, Barbecue* for additional information.)

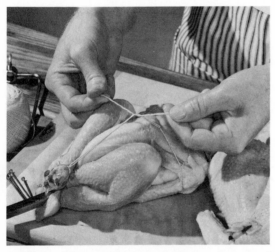

Pull together cords attached to wings and legs; tie tightly. Truss the bird neatly to avoid flying drumsticks or wings.

If cooking more than one bird, fasten others on spit in same way, using holding fork for each. Tighten thumbscrews with pliers.

Brush the birds well with salad oil for even browning and to hold the seasonings. Sprinkle well with salt, pepper, and paprika.

Brush the birds with a glaze or sauce several times during the last 30 minutes of cooking time on the rotisserie, if desired.

Spinning Chicken

Glaze chicken with a tangy basting sauce—

> 1 3- to 4-pound ready-to-cook
>   whole broiler-fryer chicken
> 1 teaspoon salt
>   Dash pepper
>   • • •
> ½ cup chopped celery leaves
> ¼ cup snipped parsley
> ¼ cup chopped onion
> 2 tablespoons butter or
>   margarine, melted
>   • • •
> ¼ cup catsup
> ¼ cup corn syrup
> 2 tablespoons lemon juice
> 2 tablespoons salad oil
> 2 tablespoons prepared
>   mustard

Rinse chicken and pat dry with paper toweling. Rub body cavity with salt and pepper. Combine celery leaves, parsley, onion, and melted butter; place in body cavity. Fasten neck skin to back with nail or skewer. Tie with cord to hold nail. To mount the chicken on the spit, place holding fork on rod, tines toward point; insert rod through the chicken (press tines firmly into the breast meat).

To tie wings, use 24 inches of cord. Start cord at back; loop around each wing tip. Make slipknots so wings can't straighten. Tie in center, leaving equal ends. Now, take an 18-inch piece of cord. Loop around tail, then around crossed legs. Tie very tightly to hold bird securely onto rod, leaving cord ends. Pull together cords attached to wings and legs; tie tightly. (If barbecuing more than one bird, fasten others on spit in same way, using holding fork for each; place birds close together.) Adjust holding forks and fasten screws tightly.

Test balance. Place chicken on the rotisserie, having *medium* coals at back and front of chicken and a drip pan under the revolving bird. Roast the chicken for about 2 hours without the barbecue hood or about 1¾ hours with the barbecue hood down.

Combine catsup, corn syrup, lemon juice, salad oil, and prepared mustard to make the basting sauce. Use the sauce to baste the chicken occasionally during the last 30 minutes of cooking. Makes 3 or 4 servings.

Spinning Ham

Begin the barbecue season early in the spring with fruit-flavored ham—

> 1 boneless, fully cooked ham
>   *or* canned ham
>   • • •
> 1 8¾-ounce can crushed
>   pineapple
> 1 cup brown sugar
> 2 tablespoons prepared mustard
> 2 tablespoons lemon juice

Score ham, if desired. Tie ham at intervals with cord. Center ham lengthwise on rotisserie spit; fasten with holding forks. Adjust for balance. Let ham rotate over coals till heated through, allowing 10 minutes per pound.

Drain pineapple, reserving 2 tablespoons syrup. Mix crushed pineapple, reserved syrup, brown sugar, prepared mustard, and lemon juice. Brush pineapple glaze on ham occasionally during the last 20 minutes of cooking.

Grilled Rib Eye Roast

Herb butter complements an all-time favorite—

> 1 5- to 6-pound beef rib eye
>   roast
> ½ cup butter or margarine,
>   softened
> 2 teaspoons seasoned salt
> 1 teaspoon fines herbes
> ¼ teaspoon freshly ground
>   pepper
>   Few drops bottled hot pepper
>   sauce

Tie rib eye roast with string at 1½-inch intervals. Center meat on spit; fasten with holding forks. Attach spit; turn on motor. Have *hot* coals at back of firebox and drip pan under roast. Roast 2 to 2½ hours for medium-rare or to your liking. Meat thermometer will register 140° for rare, 160° for medium, and 170° for well-done. Let roast stand 15 minutes to firm up before carving.

Meanwhile, blend softened butter, seasoned salt, fines herbes, pepper, and bottled hot pepper sauce. Dab a little of the herb butter on each serving—it's potent.

ROULADE *(roo läd')*—A slice of meat spread with a filling, rolled up, and cooked. Roulade is made with various ingredients. Slices of beef, veal, pork, or fish are wrapped around a minced mixture such as ham, sausage, or cheese. The rolls are browned and simmered in wine or broth.

ROUND—The portion of the hind leg of a beef animal below the rump and above the shank. The corresponding section of pork, lamb, and veal is called the leg.

The round is cut into steaks and roasts or pot roast, or it is ground. These cuts may be divided into the top round (the inside portion) and the bottom round (the outside portion), which usually includes the eye of the round. The top round, within the same cut, is more tender than the bottom round. Most cuts from the round are best when braised. (See also *Beef*.)

ROUX *(roo)*—A blend of flour and fat that is cooked and used for thickening in sauces and gravies. Roux is used extensively in French and Creole cookery as the base for a variety of sauces. In mixing roux, butter, margarine, salad oil, or meat drippings and flour are mixed in equal parts. While the roux is cooking, stir it constantly so that it does not scorch, as this causes an unpleasant flavor and decreases the thickening power of the roux.

Roux can be cooked to three different shades, depending on its use. If the mixture is cooked for only a few minutes, it remains light. This type of roux is used in making light-colored sauces such as velouté. Heating the roux a few minutes longer gives it a light golden color. This blond roux is used in lightly colored sauces. Still longer cooking makes a rich, nut-colored sauce. The brown roux is used in making brown sauces. (See also *Sauce*.)

Steak Marchand De Vin

    2 teaspoons butter or margarine
    2 teaspoons all-purpose flour
    1 cup beef broth *or* consommé
            •   •   •
    1 tablespoon chopped mushrooms
    3 tablespoons Burgundy

    ⅓ cup cognac
    1 teaspoon finely chopped
        shallots
    ½ bay leaf
        Dash dried thyme leaves,
        crushed
    2 peppercorns
    1½ pounds sirloin steak,
        cut 1 inch thick

In a saucepan melt butter and blend in flour. Cook and stir over low heat till mixture browns. Add beef broth and bring mixture to boiling; cook 3 minutes, stirring constantly. Lower heat and simmer for about 20 minutes.

In another saucepan combine mushrooms and Burgundy; simmer the mixture till the liquid is reduced to half, about 5 minutes. Stir in brown sauce and remove from heat.

In a third saucepan combine cognac, shallots, bay leaf, thyme, and peppercorns. Cook till all liquid evaporates. Remove bay leaf and peppercorns. Add mushroom mixture; stir. Place steak in heavy skillet; cook 6 minutes on each side. Add 2 tablespoons cognac, if desired; set aflame. Pour sauce over. Serves 2.

RUE *(roo)*—A bitter herb. Rue has grayish green leaves, yellow flowers, a strong odor, and acrid flavor. Because of the strong, bitter flavor, use the leaves sparingly in chicken dishes, stews, salads, and cottage cheese. (See also *Herb*.)

RUM—An alcoholic liquor distilled from fermented sugar cane products. Rum ranges in color from a clear white to amber to mahogany. It varies from light to heavy in body and has a molasses flavor.

Rum was first made over 300 years ago in the West Indies. It soon became an important article of trade between the American colonies, West Indies, and Africa. Not all of the rum was traded to other countries, however. The colonists kept a lot for their own consumption— about four gallons per person each year.

Due to its widespread popularity, rum played a part in early American history. Because so much illicit rum was brought into the colonies, the British levied a tax on all rum imports. This tax was a major cause of the American Revolution.

How rum is produced: Rum is made from sugarcane—its juice, syrup, or molasses. The process is similar to the distilling of other liquors, except that rum does not need to be malted (changed from starch to sugar) since it is already a sugar. The sugarcane is fermented from 12 to 36 hours for light-bodied rums and up to 12 days for heavy-bodied rums. The liquor is then aged for one to four years in charred oak barrels. Caramel is added for color, but its flavor is so similar to molasses that it does not distort the taste. Then, the rum is aged in vats until ready for bottling. Most rum is bottled with the alcoholic content at about 80 proof.

Types of rum: Basically, there are three different types of rum. The first type is heavy, full-bodied, and dark. Jamaican rum, an example of this type, has a rich, full-molasses flavor. The second type is light-bodied and pungent. An example of this type, Bataria Arak, is made in the East Indies. The third type of rum is light, dry, and brandylike. There is a faint molasses taste. This rum is made in Puerto Rico and the Virgin Islands and accounts for about 70 percent of the rum sold in the United States.

The name on a rum bottle tells you its place of origin rather than its type. Cuban, Demerara, Martinique, and Haitian are

Please the most sophisticated tastes with a combination of rum and chocolate. Marble-Top Chocolate-Rum Pie will please the cook, too, since it is made ahead and refrigerated till later.

each from that respective area. Generally, certain types of rum are identified with certain areas—Cuban rums are light, while Jamaican rums are heavy. However, rums in *each area* are different primarily because of the variation in climate, water, and method of making liquor. Cubans also make a heavy rum.

Uses of rum: Rum is primarily used as a beverage. White liquor is often drunk straight in rum-producing countries, while people in the United States usually like it mixed with a fruit juice for use in punches and cocktails. Some of the more popular rum drinks are planters' punch, rum swizzle, daiquiri, bacardi, and the cold weather favorite, hot buttered rum.

Hot Buttered Rum

    1 piece stick cinnamon
    1 teaspoon sugar
    1 slice lemon peel
    2 jiggers rum (3 ounces)
      Boiling water
      Butter

In an old-fashioned glass combine cinnamon, sugar, lemon peel, and rum. Fill glass with boiling water; float butter pat atop. Serves 1.

The cooks of the world have also discovered uses for rum. It gives food a unique flavor when added to sauces, ice cream, candies, pies, and various desserts. The alcohol evaporates when the food is cooked, leaving only the molasses flavor. (See also *Wines and Spirits*.)

Rum-Eggnog Pie

In a bowl combine one 3¾- or 3⅝-ounce package *instant* vanilla pudding mix, 1¾ cups eggnog, and 1 tablespoon rum. Beat 1 minute. Pour into cooled, *baked* 9-inch pastry shell (see *Pastry*); chill till filling sets. Prepare one 2-ounce package dessert topping mix according to package directions. Beat in 1 teaspoon rum. Pile over pudding. Chill. Top with chopped candied fruit and toasted almonds.

Marble-Top Chocolate-Rum Pie

    ½ cup sugar
    1 envelope unflavored
      gelatin (1 tablespoon)
      Dash salt
    1 cup milk
    2 beaten egg yolks
    1 6-ounce package semisweet
      chocolate pieces (1 cup)
    ⅓ cup rum
    2 egg whites
    ¼ cup sugar
    1 cup whipping cream
    1 teaspoon vanilla
    1 *baked* 9-inch pastry shell,
      cooked (See *Pastry*)

In heavy saucepan combine the ½ cup sugar, gelatin, and salt. Stir in milk and egg yolks. Cook and stir over low heat till slightly thickened. Remove from heat. Add chocolate pieces; stir till melted. Add rum. Chill the mixture till it is partially set.

Beat egg whites till soft peaks form. Gradually add the ¼ cup sugar, beating till stiff peaks form. Fold into partially set chocolate mixture. Whip cream with vanilla. Layer whipped cream and chocolate mixture in pastry shell, ending with the whipped cream. Swirl the top to marble. Chill till firm. Garnish with additional whipped cream and semisweet chocolate pieces, if desired.

Peaches à la Rum

    3 tablespoons rum
    1 29-ounce can peach halves,
      drained
        •   •   •
    1 2-ounce package dessert
      topping mix
      Slivered, toasted almonds

Drizzle *2 tablespoons* rum over drained peach halves. Cover and chill for several hours. When ready to serve, prepare topping mix according to package directions. Stir in 1 tablespoon rum. Spoon some topping into 8 sherbet glasses. Top with peach half, rounded side down. Spoon additional topping in each peach cavity and sprinkle with slivered, toasted almonds. Serve cold. Makes 8 servings.

RUM FLAVORING—A commercially bottled liquid that has an imitation rum flavor. It is popular in desserts, frostings, and cakes. (See also *Flavoring*.)

RUMP—A cut of beef from the hindquarter. A rump roast is usually marketed as a rolled roast (bone removed, rolled, and tied) and seldom as a standing rump roast (bone in). This flavorful cut may be roasted if of top grade. However, if the roast is of a lower grade, braise it.

Plan on two servings from rump roast with bone and three servings from a roast without bone. (See also *Beef*.)

RUSK—A crisp, dry slice of bread. Rusks are made from a sweet or plain raised bread. The baked bread is sliced and baked again to dry it out and to brown it.

Rusks are available in packages in many supermarkets. Rusks are excellent bases for eggs Benedict and creamed meat, seafood, and poultry mixtures. Use rusk crumbs when making desserts.

RUSSET POTATO—An oblong potato with heavily netted skin, shallow eyes, and white flesh. Russet potatoes are so named because of their russet brown skin coloring. This potato category includes both the Norgold Russet and Russet Burbank species. The latter is known as the Idaho potato. (See also *Potato*.)

RUSSIAN COOKERY—Foods of Russia that are tinged with the grand cuisine of the days of the czars and with the individuality of the many geographical areas included in the vast nation, the United Soviet Socialist Republic. The national dishes range from elaborate desserts to simple soups and from the fare of a frozen land to that of a sub-tropical area.

Just how the Russian food pattern began to emerge is obscure. During the sixteenth century, Ivan the Terrible brought Italian workmen to Russia. They introduced Italian-styled pastries and frozen desserts, which became a favorite in Russia. German and French influences began to be felt late in the eighteenth century during the reign of Catherine the Great. The influence of Near East cookery

is evident in the southern parts of Russia. Regardless of whether Polish foods were adopted by Russia or vice versa, there is a similarity between some of the dishes.

Out of these foreign influences, the conditions imposed by the weather, and the economics of the land, typical Russian foods have been developed.

Typical Russian appetizers: *Zakouska*, the Russian appetizer, consists of small portions of hot and cold foods. These are fork foods to be eaten while seated. An elaborate array, set out on a separate table at an occasion, might include a dozen varieties to be taken at will with small squares of thin white or dark bread.

An appetizer might include caviar, marinated herring, smoked sturgeon or eel, eggs with anchovies, shellfish in mayonnaise, patés, cucumbers or mushrooms in sour cream, vegetable salads, hot chicken livers, meatballs, and fish balls. Appetizers are usually accompanied by chilled vodka. At a simple home dinner, the array is not so lavish. Individual plates with an assortment of four appetizers are placed before each person.

Typical Russian soups: Soups are an important part of the Russian diet. At an elaborate Russian dinner, soup follows the zakouska. This course might include as many as three soups with a variety of both hot and cold soups.

For everyday meals, however, hearty soups are often the mainstay of the diet. Consequently, soups are frequently served as the main dish of the meal.

Vegetable soups are frequently found on the table. These are made with or without meat. Sometimes, a piece of meat that is cooked with the soup for flavor is removed and served at another meal. *Shchi*, cabbage soup, is made with fresh cabbage or sauerkraut as the base, and other vegetables are added if they are available.

Borsch, a classic soup of Russia, is always made with beets or with other vegetables accompanying the beets. *Smetana* (sour cream) is served with both shchi and borsch. *Rassolnik*, a tart meat soup, is flavored with pickles, olives, pickled mushrooms, and pickled cherries.

The Russians also prepare many cold soups. These usually are made with a base of *kvass*, a slightly fermented brew that is made from black or white bread.

Accompaniments for the soup are an important food in Russia, too. *Kasha* is one of the most commonly served accompaniments. In fact, it's considered one of the basic foods in the peasants' diets. Kasha is made by frying grain till browned and then baking it with a little water. A variety of grains are used. In the northern areas of Russia it is made of buckwheat groats. In some other areas, wheat or rice is used. But in the south it is made of corn.

Piroshki, a small, individual pastry pocket, is also served with soup. These are filled with minced meat, mushrooms, eggs, or cheese to blend with the flavor of the soup. Then, there are *pelmeri*, small dumplings, which are also filled and boiled in broth before being served.

Typical Russian meats: Russia has a variety of meats. The Ukraine and southern Russia provide pork, turkey, and smoked goose. The Caucasus have excellent lamb and mutton and some beef. Siberia has smoked bear. Throughout Russia, chickens, ducks, and furred and feathered game are available.

Russian meats are cooked many ways. Steaks are fried; beef filets, roasted. Cossack steaks are meat patties crumbed, fried, and served in a sour cream gravy with dill. Russian stew is made of crumbed and fried meat chunks, cooked with carrot, onion, and cubes of black bread.

The Russians often boil ham or bake it in a crust. Goose is stuffed with buckwheat groats. Instead of using apples in the filling, Russian cooks bake apples around the goose. Lamb is cooked in a pilaf, Turkish-style. Pork is cooked with sauerkraut with a piece of garlic-flavored sausage added. Game is roasted or braised. Some meats, especially lamb, are broiled on skewers.

Probably the two most famous Russian meat dishes are Beef Stroganoff, named for the Stroganov family of imperial Russia, and the excellent Chicken Kiev. The following recipe is a simplified version of the latter classic meat dish.

Chicken Kiev

    4 large chicken breasts, boned,
      skinned, and halved
      lengthwise
    2 tablespoons snipped parsley
    ¼ pound stick butter, chilled
      All-purpose flour
    1 beaten egg
    1 tablespoon water
    ½ cup fine dry bread crumbs

Place chicken breasts, boned side up, between two pieces of clear plastic wrap. Pound from center out to form cutlets not quite ¼ inch thick. Peel off wrap; season with salt.

Sprinkle parsley over cutlets. Cut cold butter into 8 sticks; place a stick at end of each cutlet. Roll meat as for jelly roll, tucking in sides. Press seam to seal well. Coat each roll with flour and dip in mixture of the egg and water. Then, roll in crumbs. Chill thoroughly, at least 1 hour. Fry chicken rolls in deep, hot fat (375°) till golden brown, about 5 minutes. Makes 4 to 8 servings.

Typical Russian fish: Fish and shellfish hold an important place in Russian cookery. Among the many species available throughout Russia are salmon, sturgeon, trout, pike, smelts, herring, and crayfish. These different varieties are enjoyed smoked and pickled as well as fresh.

One of the favorite fish products in Russia and also one of the most widely known is caviar. This roe from sturgeons and salmons is a delight that Russians savor on toast or crackers. It is included on the well-stacked zakouska table.

In Russian cookery, fish are often boiled and served either hot or cold. A horseradish cream or mustard sauce usually complements the fish. Other ways of cooking fish include poaching in wine, baking in pastry cases, frying, and steaming. Crabs are cooked in white wine, while crayfish are cooked in thyme-flavored sour cream and a wine sauce.

Kulebiaka is one of the classic fish dishes. Salmon is used for a filling inside the flaky pastry. For an authentic Russian meal, try serving sour cream with the recipe on the following page.

Kulebiaka

2 tablespoons chopped onion
3 tablespoons butter or
   margarine
2¼ cups sifted all-purpose flour
¼ teaspoon dried dillweed
1 cup milk
2 tablespoons dry white wine
1 16-ounce can red salmon,
   drained and flaked
2 cups cooked rice
1 3-ounce can sliced mushrooms,
   drained
2 tablespoons snipped parsley
⅔ cup shortening
1 beaten egg

In saucepan cook onion in butter till tender. Blend in ¼ *cup* flour, ½ teaspoon salt, and dillweed. Add milk. Cook and stir till thickened and bubbly; cook 1 minute more. Stir in wine, salmon, rice, mushrooms, and parsley. Sift together 2 cups flour and ½ teaspoon salt; cut in shortening till mixture resembles coarse crumbs. Gradually add ⅓ to ½ cup cold water, tossing with fork. Form into ball.

Roll dough between 2 pieces of waxed paper to a 20x10-inch rectangle. Remove top paper. Mound salmon mixture lengthwise down center third of rectangle. Fold one side of dough over salmon; peel paper back. Repeat with second side. Moisten edges with water; seal. Fold ends up; moisten and seal. Lifting paper, transfer to large greased baking sheet, seam side down. Peel off paper. Form into horseshoe shape; brush with egg. Prick top. Bake at 400° for 25 to 30 minutes. Serves 6 to 8.

Typical Russian breads: Breads are a basic food in Russia. The types and kinds are astoundingly numerous, with dark bread being the predominant variety. Added to this variety are whole grain and white breads baked in every shape.

One of the most popular types of bread is the Russian pancake, *blini.* These are not ordinary pancakes, but yeast-raised cakes made from buckwheat flour or a mixture of buckwheat and white flour. Blini are eaten with melted butter and fish, mushrooms with onions, or jam. Special occasions call for caviar filling.

Typical Russian desserts: Some of the most spectacular desserts appear during the Easter season. *Kulich* and *paskha* are the traditional Easter desserts.

Kulich is a special form of the tall Russian cake called a *baba.* The kulich, raised with yeast and rich with eggs, contains almonds, raisins, liqueur, and candied fruit peel. It is baked in a tall, round mold and comes out of the oven measuring about 12 inches. It is sometimes cut in horizontal slices to serve.

Paskha is served with the kulich. Paskha is made of cottage cheese, butter, sugar, eggs, cream, raisins, candied fruits, and almonds. The mixture is heated, then stirred to a velvety smoothness as it cools. It is then pressed into the traditional, wooden, pyramid-shaped mold, or into a gauze-lined flowerpot and left to drain off any excess liquid.

Other magnificent desserts include the charlotte and elaborate ice cream desserts. *Gureu Kasha*, a caramel-glazed farina pudding, is regarded by some to be the supreme Russian dessert.

Not all Russian desserts are as elaborate as these or as time consuming to make. Simplest and one of the most popular is the *kissel.* This pudding dessert is frequently served at family meals. It is made of puréed berries or other fruit and thickened with cornstarch. The berries commonly used are strawberries, apples, apricots, and rhubarb.

Vatruskhi, an individual pastry filled with cheese or fruit, is served with melted butter and sour cream. This is similar to American cheesecake. Fresh fruits in season are made into cooked compotes. Care is taken to keep the fruit pieces whole during cooking, and hot syrup is poured over uncooked fruit to preserve the shape. Sometimes, berries are served with sugar and wine for a simple dessert.

RUSSIAN DRESSING—A sharp-flavored salad dressing often containing chili sauce, peppers, chopped pimiento, chopped pickle, or caviar. Originally, this dressing was made with mayonnaise; however, today's dressing sometimes has a cooked base. Recipes for Russian dressing vary. (See also *Salad Dressing.*)

Russian Dressing

        ¼ cup sugar
        3 tablespoons water
    1½ teaspoons celery seed
        ½ teaspoon salt
        ½ teaspoon paprika
    2½ tablespoons lemon juice
        1 tablespoon Worcestershire
            sauce
        1 tablespoon vinegar
        1 cup salad oil
        ½ cup catsup
        ¼ cup grated onion

Cook sugar and water till mixture spins a thread (232°). Cool. Mix the remaining ingredients; beat in the sugar syrup. Chill thoroughly. Makes 2 cups salad dressing.

RUTABAGA—A root vegetable, relative of the turnip and member of the mustard family. Unlike turnips, rutabagas were developed fairly recently. It's believed they originated in Scandinavian regions during the seventeenth century. Some credence is given to this by the long-time use of the name Swede or Swede turnip for this vegetable. They are still grown widely in northern Europe, but in the Western Hemisphere production is limited to Canada and the United States.

Although rutabagas and turnips are used similarly, the yellow and white rutabaga varieties differ from turnips in size, shape, and color. They are larger and have a characteristic neck at the top. Yellow-fleshed rutabagas are usually bronze-skinned, but they can be green or purple; white-fleshed ones have a green skin.

Nutritionally, rutabagas are low in calories, only 35 to 1 cup cooked and cubed. They are a good source of vitamin C, while other vitamins and minerals are more sparingly represented.

When you buy rutabagas, look for roots that are heavy for size, firm and smooth, and free of cuts and blemishes. Select small or medium-sized ones in preference to large, overgrown rutabagas that tend to be woody and tough. Rutabagas are primarily a fall and late-winter crop and should be refrigerator-stored.

The flavor of rutabagas resembles that of turnip, except that it may be stronger. To prepare them for cooking, peel away the wax-coated skin down to the inner flesh of the root. To cook, peel and slice or cube. Add them to a saucepan with a small amount of boiling, salted water and cook, covered, for 25 to 40 minutes.

Try rutabagas and apples together for a blend of flavors with a slightly sweet taste. Or combine rutabagas and potatoes in a fluffy whip. (See *Turnip, Vegetable* for additional information.)

Rutabaga Whip

    3 cups peeled, cubed rutabaga
    3 cups peeled, cubed potato
    2 tablespoons chopped onion
        Light cream
        Butter or margarine
        Salt and pepper

Cook rutabaga, potatoes, and onion in boiling, salted water till tender, about 20 minutes. Drain and mash with cream and butter till light and fluffy. Season to taste with salt and pepper. Makes 4 to 6 servings.

Try a new vegetable dish to spruce up family meals. Rutabaga Whip combines potatoes and rutabaga for a tasty combination.

RYE—A cereal grain used for making flour and whiskey. Rye can be grown almost anywhere, but it is cultivated mainly in cold, damp climates. In the United States, rye is grown in North and South Dakota, Nebraska, Kansas, and Minnesota.

Rye flour: Rye is milled into flour for making breads, rolls, muffins, and crackers. The flour has a darker color than wheat flour. Bleaching during milling does not affect the color but does improve the baking qualities. Rye flour produces bread that has less volume and a more compact texture than wheat bread.

Light, medium, and dark rye flours are available on the market. These should be stored in the refrigerator or freezer. The maximum recommended storage time for rye flour is six months. When used, rye flour should be stirred with a spoon rather than sifted like wheat flour.

Pumpernickel is an example of a bread made entirely of rye flour. Most breads, however, are made with a combination of rye flour and another flour, such as wheat, for better volume and a milder flavor.

Light Rye Mixer Bread

>   1 package active dry yeast
> 1½ cups stirred rye flour
> 2¼ cups sifted all-purpose flour
>   1 tablespoon caraway seed
>   1 teaspoon salt
> 1¼ cups warm water
>   2 tablespoons salad oil
>   2 tablespoons honey

In large mixer bowl combine yeast, rye flour, ½ *cup* all-purpose flour, caraway, and salt. Mix together water, oil, and honey. Add to dry mixture in bowl. Beat ½ minute at low speed of electric mixer, scraping bowl constantly. Beat 3 minutes at high speed. Stir in the remaining all-purpose flour. Place the dough in greased bowl, turning once to grease surface. Cover; let dough rise till double, about 1 hour.

Punch down. Spread evenly in well-greased 9x5x3-inch loaf pan. Let rise till nearly double, about 30 to 35 minutes. Bake at 375° for 45 to 50 minutes. If bread browns too quickly, cover top loosely with foil.

Quick Swedish Rye Bread

> 2 eggs
> 1 13¾-ounce package hot roll mix
> ¾ cup medium rye flour
> 1 tablespoon brown sugar
> 2 tablespoons molasses
> 1 to 2 teaspoons caraway seed

Using 2 eggs, prepare hot roll mix according to package directions. Stir in rye flour, brown sugar, molasses, and caraway seed. Let rise according to package directions. Turn out on floured surface, tossing lightly to cover dough with flour. Divide the dough in half; shape in loaves. Place the dough in two greased 8½x 4½x2⅝-inch baking dishes. Let rise according to package directions. Bake at 350° about 30 minutes. Makes 2 rye loaves.

Rye bread: Rye breads come in a variety of shapes and colors. They are molded into loaves, ovals with pointed ends, and rounds. The color varies from the almost-black pumpernickel to a light brown color.

Caraway seeds are a natural combination with rye breads. The seeds are usually included in commercial breads, and you can add them to suit your taste in homemade products. Another good flavor accent is orange. In Swedish cookery, a touch of orange peel is typical in rye bread.

The heavy texture, chewy crust, and distinctive flavor of rye bread makes it an appealing food. Appetizers made with rye bread are stimulating to the eye and the appetite. Rounds and triangles of rye or the party-sized bread are good for canapés and hors d'oeuvres, and with dips.

Toasty Rye Curls

> 1 loaf tiny dark rye bread
> ½ cup butter or margarine,
>   melted
>   Dash garlic powder

With a very sharp knife, slice bread paper-thin. Place the bread in a single layer on baking sheet. Dry in a 300° oven till crisp, about 20 minutes. Combine butter and garlic powder; use mixture as a dip for rye slices.

Rye bread goes well with lunches and dinners, especially those including European foods. Try it spread with butter or margarine or even with sour cream in the European fashion. The flavor of rye bread is equally good as the base for a stuffing in the meat dish.

Ham with Rye Stuffing

  ¼ **cup finely chopped onion**
   3 **tablespoons butter or margarine**

      •   •   •

   1 **beaten egg**
   2 **teaspoons prepared mustard**
  ½ **teaspoon caraway seed**
   9 **slices light rye bread,**
      cubed (6 cups)
   1 **fully cooked ham slice, cut 1½**
      inches thick (2¼ pounds)

In a small saucepan cook onion in butter or margarine till tender but not brown. In a large bowl combine egg, mustard, caraway seed, and onion mixture. Add bread cubes; toss till thoroughly mixed. Shape the mixture into balls, using about ½ cup bread mixture for each ball. Place ham slice on rack in a shallow roasting pan. Bake at 325° for 20 minutes. Then, place the stuffing balls on rack around ham and bake 20 minutes more. Makes 6 servings.

Another popular use for rye bread is in sandwiches. The distinctive flavor of rye bread goes well with ham and cheese, braunschweiger, cold cuts, and other full-flavored fillings. Rye bread spread with cream cheese and topped with slices of smoked salmon makes an elegant lunch.

Nutritionally, rye bread contributes carbohydrates, minerals, and the B vitamins thiamine and riboflavin. There are 56 calories in a slice of rye bread and 40 calories in a slice of party rye measuring about 3 x 2 x ½ inches.

Rye whiskey: Rye is used in making rye whiskey and sometimes in making vodka. Rye whiskey must be made with at least 51 percent rye mash and be not more than 160° proof according to government regulations. Most of this liquor is made in the states of Pennsylvania and Maryland.

Rye whiskey comes in a variety of forms. Straight rye is heavier than bourbon, and it is not mixed with any other rye or liquor. Blended straight rye contains a combination of straight rye whiskeys. Blended rye contains other whiskeys and is lighter than straight rye.

In drinks, rye whiskey is used in making highballs, Manhattans, old-fashioneds, and whiskey sours. (See *Grain, Whiskey* for additional information.)

Slice Light Rye Mixer Bread into thin pieces. This full-flavored rye accented with honey and caraway seeds makes great sandwiches.

S

SABAYON (sa ba yôn') – The French version of zabaglione, an Italian sauce. Sabayon is made of egg yolks, sugar, and wine. The sauce is served hot over desserts, such as fruitcake, and cold over fruits. It also serves as a custardlike dessert when eaten alone. (See also *Zabaglione.*)

SACCHARINE (sak'uh rin, -rīn') – A white, crystalline compound that is approximately 500 times sweeter than sugar. Saccharine is a synthetic compound discovered at Johns Hopkins University in 1879. Since that time, it has been used as a sugar substitute for low-calorie diets, and in products such as tobacco.

A little saccharine goes a long way. It comes in powder, tablet, and liquid forms, which dissolve and blend easily in liquids. However, saccharine cannot be substituted as easily in baked products. You should select a recipe designed for a sugar substitute if you want to cut down on sugar in baked foods.

SABLEFISH – A saltwater flatfish found along the Pacific coast. Sablefish, often mislabeled Alaska black cod or butterfish, has a buttery texture and delicate flavor.

Sablefish, sold smoked and kippered, is used like smoked salmon in appetizers and sandwiches. Fresh fillets and steaks are best broiled, fried, or baked.

Nutritionally, sablefish contributes protein and the B vitamins thiamine and riboflavin. One 3½ ounce uncooked portion has 190 calories. (See also *Fish.*)

SACHER TORTE (sä'kuhr tôr'tuh) – A rich chocolate cake with an apricot filling, a chocolate frosting, and usually a garnish of whipped cream. This elegant dessert was created many years ago in Vienna, Austria, by a member of the Sacher family for whom the famous Sacher Hotel in that city was named. (See also *Torte.*)

Chocolate Torte Frosting

Frosting for the Sacher Torte—

> 2 1-ounce squares unsweetened chocolate
> 3 tablespoons butter or margarine
> 3 cups sifted confectioners' sugar
> Dash salt
> 1½ teaspoons vanilla
> 5 to 6 tablespoons boiling water

Melt chocolate and butter over hot water. Remove from heat. Stir in confectioners' sugar, salt, and vanilla. Gradually stir in enough boiling water to make thin frosting. (If frosting begins to thicken, add additional water.) Fill and frost Sacher Torte as directed.

Sacher Torte

   3 1-ounce squares unsweetened
     chocolate
  ⅔ cup sugar
  ½ cup milk
   1 beaten egg

     • • •

  ½ cup shortening
   1 cup sugar
   1 teaspoon vanilla
   2 eggs

     • • •

   2 cups sifted cake flour
   1 teaspoon baking soda
  ¼ teaspoon salt
  ⅔ cup milk

     • • •

   1 12-ounce jar apricot preserves,
     sieved
     Chocolate Torte Frosting
     Whipped cream

Combine unsweetened chocolate, the ⅔ cup sugar, ½ cup milk, and 1 beaten egg in a saucepan. Cook and stir over low heat till the chocolate melts and the mixture thickens; cool the mixture. Beat the ½ cup shortening to soften. Gradually add the 1 cup sugar, creaming till it is light and fluffy. Add the 1 teaspoon vanilla. Add the 2 eggs, one at a time, beating well after each addition.

Sift together flour, soda, and salt. Add to creamed mixture alternately with the ⅔ cup milk, beginning and ending with the flour mixture; beat well after each addition. Blend in chocolate mixture. Bake in 2 greased and floured 9x1½-inch round pans at 350° till done, about 25 to 30 minutes.

Cool layers thoroughly. Split each layer in two, using a thread (wrap around center of layer, crossing ends; pull).

Put cake together, spreading sieved apricot preserves, then about 2 tablespoons Chocolate Torte Frosting between each layer. Frost top and sides of cake with remaining frosting. Serve with generous dollops of whipped cream.

SACK *(sak)* — Sherry and other strong, light-colored, sweet wines. Sack (also sherris sack) was the name for sherry in sixteenth-century England. There are references to sack in Shakespeare's *Henry IV.*

Sack was introduced to England from Spain and the Canary Islands. It was one of the first sipping wines to become popular in that country. Today, the name sack is carried over as a brand name of a sherry. (See also *Sherry.*)

SADDLE — A large cut of meat including the two, undivided loins of an animal. Mutton, venison, lamb, and veal are the types of meat cut into saddles. Roasting is the usual method of cooking this tender cut.

SAFFLOWER — A thistlelike herb with orange red flowers. Safflower seeds are used in making a vegetable oil. Spanish and Polish people sometimes substitute safflower for saffron in their cooking.

SAFFLOWER OIL — A vegetable oil extracted from safflower seeds. It is polyunsaturated and is used in making margarine, shortening, and salad oil. One tablespoon of safflower oil has 124 calories. (See also *Fat.*)

SAFFRON *(saf' ruhn)* — The orange stigma of purple crocus flowers that is used as a spice. Saffron is considered the world's most expensive spice because these orange filaments must be carefully gathered by hand. There are only three filaments per flower and it takes at least 75,000 blossoms to make 1 lb. of saffron.

Saffron has been prized since ancient times. It was used in Babylon, Rome, and Greece for a dye in both cloth and food, for a perfume, and for a seasoning. The Moors introduced it to Spain and the Roman legions introduced saffron to England. Many classic dishes from these countries include saffron. Bouillabaisse from France and paella and arroz con pollo from Spain contain saffron.

American cooks use saffron to add a bright yellow color and a pleasantly bitter flavor to foods. The spice is used in flavoring breads, cakes, puddings, rice dishes, fish, and chicken.

The saffron available in American markets is imported from Spain and Portugal. It comes in two forms: tiny strands and powder. Packages of saffron mixed with rice are also available in supermarkets.

Pork Chops with Saffron Rice

    6 pork chops, cut ½ to ¾ inch
        thick
    ½ teaspoon salt
        Dash pepper
    2 tablespoons shortening, melted
    1 6-ounce package saffron rice
        mix
    ½ cup chopped onion
            • • •
    1 beef bouillon cube
    1¾ cups hot water
    ½ cup dairy sour cream

Sprinkle chops with salt and pepper. In skillet slowly brown chops in melted shortening; drain off excess fat. Add rice mix and onion. Dissolve bouillon cube in hot water; pour over rice. Bring to boiling; reduce heat.

Cover and cook over low heat for 40 minutes, stirring occasionally, till chops are tender and water is absorbed. Remove chops to warm platter; stir sour cream into rice mixture. Cook over low heat till heated. Makes 6 servings.

Always use the amount of saffron specified—a little bit adds a lot of flavor and too much causes a bitter, medicinal taste. If the saffron threads are not cooked in boiling liquid during preparation of a dish, heat some of the liquid and add the saffron. Let it stand about five minutes to dissolve before returning the liquid to the dish, as illustrated in the following recipes. (See also *Spice*.)

Saffron Bread

    1 package active dry yeast
    2½ to 3 cups sifted all-purpose
        flour
    1 cup milk
    ¼ cup sugar
    2 tablespoons butter or margarine
    ½ teaspoon salt
    ⅛ teaspoon powdered saffron
            • • •
    ¼ cup raisins
    ¼ cup currants
    2 tablespoons chopped,
        toasted almonds

In large mixer bowl combine yeast and 1½ *cups* flour. Heat milk, sugar, butter, salt, and saffron just till warm, stirring occasionally to melt the butter. Add to dry mixture in mixing bowl. Beat at low speed with electric mixer for ½ minute, scraping sides of bowl often.

Beat 3 minutes at high speed. By hand, stir in raisins, currants, almonds, and enough of the remaining flour to make a soft dough. Knead till smooth and elastic, 8 to 10 minutes. Place in greased bowl; turn once to grease surface. Cover and let rise in warm place till double, about 1¾ hours. Punch down; turn out on lightly floured surface. Cover and let rest 10 minutes. Shape in loaf; place in greased 8½x 4½x2½-inch loaf dish. Let rise till double, about 1¼ hours. Bake at 375° till done, about 35 minutes. If necessary to prevent over-browning, cover with foil for last 15 minutes.

SAGE—An herb belonging to the mint family. The slender, grayish green leaves of sage give foods in which it is used a pungent, slightly bitter flavor.

Sage has been credited with many virtues through the centuries. It was once used as a medicine to lengthen one's life and also to improve the memory. This is noticeable in the traditional Christmas and Thanksgiving Day meat stuffings.

Sage has slender green leaves that turn a grayish color when dried. The plant has blue flowers and grows to a height of two feet.

Sage's value as a seasoning has made it one of the most popular herbs in America. It goes well with pork and stuffings.

Sausage Stuffing

½ pound bulk pork sausage
18 cups soft bread crumbs
2 cups diced apples
1 cup chopped onion
½ cup raisins
   Giblets, cooked, drained (reserve ½ cup broth), and chopped
4 teaspoons salt
2 teaspoons ground sage
¼ teaspoon pepper
3 beaten eggs

Cook sausage until it is lightly browned; drain. Add crumbs, apples, onion, raisins, giblets, and seasonings. Add eggs and reserved giblet broth; toss the stuffing to moisten. Enough stuffing for one 20-pound turkey.

Sage also accents poultry, cheese, meat loaves, breads, and vegetables such as brussels sprouts, carrots, and tomatoes. When adding sage, do not use too much or its flavor will dominate the food's flavor.

Several forms of sage, most of which are from Yugoslavia and southern Europe, are available in supermarkets. There are dried sage leaves, rubbed sage, and ground sage. The rubbed form is fluffy, while ground is finer in texture. You can grow sage plants in a home garden easily. (See also *Herb.*)

Herb Twists

1 13¾-ounce package hot roll mix
1 teaspoon rubbed sage
½ teaspoon dried basil leaves, crushed
2 tablespoons butter or margarine, melted

Prepare hot roll mix according to package directions, *adding* sage and basil to the dry mix. Turn out on lightly floured surface; knead till smooth, about 2 to 3 minutes.

Place dough in greased bowl, turning once to grease surface. Cover and let rise in warm place till double, about 45 minutes. Punch down. Cover; let rest 10 minutes. Turn out on lightly floured board. Roll to 18x8-inch rectangle. Brush *half* the dough, lengthwise, with melted butter. Gently fold unbuttered half over buttered to make 18x4-inch rectangle.

Slice dough crosswise into 1-inch wide strips. Holding strips by ends, twist several times; place on greased baking sheet. Let rise in warm place for 20 minutes. Bake at 425° till golden brown, about 8 to 10 minutes. Cool slightly on rack before serving. Makes 18 rolls.

SAGE CHEESE—A young Cheddar cheese flavored with sage. Sage cheese has a sharp flavor that connoisseurs appreciate.

This cheese is also called Vermont sage and, sometimes, green cheese because the cheese is mottled green. This coloring once was due to the leaves of sage. Now, a sage extract flavors the cheese and green corn or alfalfa contributes color.

SAGO *(sā′ gō)*—A dried, starchy substance made from the soft center of palms, and grown in the East Indies and Indonesia.

Sago is the basic food in the southwest Pacific. The people use it in making soups and cakes. In North America, sago is used occasionally in thickening puddings.

SAINT JOHN'S BREAD—A long fruit pod grown on a tree native to the Mediterranean. This fruit is also called carobs.

The dried pods consisting of hard seeds and a sweet pulp are eaten like raisins or are ground into flour.

SAKE *(sä′kē)*—A Japanese alcoholic beverage that is brewed from rice. Sake, the national beverage of Japan, is also called rice wine. However, it more closely resembles beer than wine.

Sake is colorless with a slightly sweet flavor and a faintly bitter aftertaste. It contains from 12 to 16 percent alcohol.

Custom is to serve sake before a meal in small porcelain cups. The drink is usually warmed to about 100°. Sake is popular as a flavoring in sauces and cocktails. (See also *Wines and Spirits.*)

SALAD

A wide variety of salad appetizers, side dishes, main dishes, and desserts.

A salad can be as simple as a bowl of greens dressed with oil and vinegar or lettuce or spinach leaves sprinkled with salt and eaten with the fingers, or as elaborate as a beautiful arrangement of vegetables, poultry, or seafood, a fancy gelatin mold, or a frozen delight. Although the traditional definition of a salad is a dish put together with a complementary dressing, today, the category salad also includes dishes that are not served with a dressing. In fact, there are an endless variety of salads, ranging from hot to frozen and from meat to fruit, which use an equally endless array of ingredients.

Salads of one kind or another have been enjoyed for centuries. Ancient Greeks and Romans ate salads made of greens. The Greeks, who regarded salad as food for the gods, often served it as the final course to clear the palate after sweets. A book of recipes written by a Roman during the first century mentions that salads, like many other foods at that time, were considered to have medicinal value. The Romans are also responsible for the name salad. Because these people sprinkled salt on greens as a salad dressing, the Latin word for salt, *sal*, was eventually expanded to salad as a name for this dish.

Although salads appeared during the ancient times, few salads were served during the Middle Ages. Even during the revival of interest in food that occurred in the Renaissance, it took quite awhile before salads were a fairly common menu item. By the late-seventeenth century, salads had become so popular that a book, *Acetaria, a Discourse on Sallets*, was written about them.

During the eighteenth century, salads gained popularity in Europe. This was a time of experimentation, and several different ingredients, seasonings, and dressings for salads were introduced. French and other European chefs sometimes concocted salads that had well over two dozen ingredients.

Salad-making remained primarily a European art until the late 1800s when wealthy Americans began importing French salad chefs. However, it still took several decades for salads to become a common menu item in America. Today, the people of the United States probably eat more salads than any other group of people. The traditional tossed salads, coleslaw, gelatin salads filled with fruits and vegetables, bean salads, pea salads, macaroni salads, potato salads, meat salads, seafood salads, egg salads, and numerous fruit combination salads are only a few of the salads that are enjoyed in this country today.

Salads are also a popular part of the menu in other countries. For example, Canadians relish sweet-savory salads such as tomatoes and oranges with a dressing of tomato sauce and orange juice. In France, the traditional salad of greens served with an oil and vinegar dressing remains the favorite. The Spanish enjoy vegetable combination salads such as tomatoes with beans. As can be seen from these examples, a compilation of the thousands of salad recipes used around the world would indeed be a diverse collection.

Crisp tossed salad

← Serve delectable Tossed Western Salad as an appetizer or side dish. Marinated artichokes and croutons make this salad special.

Tossing tips

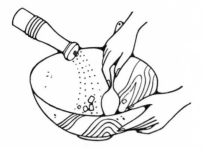

Add extra flavor to your salads with this trick. Sprinkle salt into a wooden salad bowl. Then, using the back of a spoon, mash a garlic clove into the salt. As the salad is tossed, it acquires a garlic flavor.

Place salad ingredients in a big bowl, add dressing, then mix using a roll-toss. To get the required down-and-over motion, use two salad tools and stroke down with one as the other comes up and over.

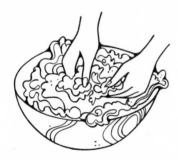

Enhance the appearance of tossed salads by tearing the salad greens into bite-sized pieces rather than by cutting them with a knife. Torn greens make a fresh-tasting salad that absorbs the dressing easily.

If the salad includes tomatoes, avoid diluting the dressing by reserving the juicy wedges or slices for a garnish. Give the salad crunch by adding crisp croutons or chopped walnuts lightly browned in butter.

Before adding oil-based dressings to the salad, shake them to emulsify the oil and vinegar and blend the other ingredients. Pour just enough dressing over the salad to lightly coat the greens; then toss gently.

If tossing the salad has to wait awhile, keep the torn salad greens fresh by covering them with damp paper toweling wrung out in ice water. For delays that are very long, refrigerate the bowl of covered greens.

Preparation

As was pointed out previously, salads are made from a wide variety of ingredients. Even so, they can be divided into five types – vegetable combinations; fruit combinations; meat, poultry, fish, and egg salads; gelatin salads; and frozen salads.

Vegetable combinations: In the United States, the most popular kind of salad is a crisp salad made of greens and other raw vegetables, and tossed with a salad dressing. By far the most common ingredient in tossed salad is iceberg lettuce. However, if you want to give variety to the salad, use a mixture of greens including Bibb lettuce, red lettuce, romaine, curly endive, escarole, watercress, or spinach. In addition to fresh greens, use other ingredients such as shredded carrot and red cabbage, sliced radish, sliced cucumber, crisp croutons, green pepper rings, ripe olives, crumbled bacon, and shredded cheese to add colors and flavors.

One of the most important parts of a tossed salad is the dressing. Even though choosing from the numerous types of salad dressings may be difficult, remember to choose a dressing that complements but does not overpower the other ingredients. (See also *Salad Dressing*.)

Preparing a fresh, crisp tossed salad is simple if you use the following tips. Several hours before the meal, carefully wash the salad greens in cool water, and then dry them by shaking them in a wire salad basket or by gently patting them with a kitchen towel. Next, store the greens in the refrigerator to crisp them. (Wilted greens don't have the appealing appearance that crisp greens do, so be sure to allow several hours of chilling.)

Shortly before serving time, tear the greens into bite-sized pieces. (Don't cut them with a knife as this hastens darkening of the edges.) Also, prepare the other vegetables for the salad. At serving time, gently toss the greens, other ingredients, and dressing together. Although you usually toss the salad in the kitchen, why not stage a small production by tossing the salad at the dinner table while your dinner guests watch?

Salad success tips

An appealing salad is an asset at any meal and it is so easy to make if you follow these preparation and serving suggestions.

Clean and chill all ingredients ahead of time. Also chill salad plates or bowl.

Leave salad ingredients in fairly large slices or chunks to give the salad a luscious look and a good texture.

Thoroughly drain fruits and vegetables before use, and dry the washed greens.

Toss salad ingredients together lightly; never stir vigorously.

Accent salads with simple trims such as tomato wedges, onion or green pepper rings, radish roses, pimiento strips or cutouts, egg slices or wedges, olives, small whole fruits, cherry tomatoes, nuts, or pickles.

Vegetable salads: Always tear salad greens into bite-sized pieces since cutting them with a knife hastens browning.

Give cooked vegetables an enticing flavor by marinating them for about an hour in French dressing; drain before using.

Peel tomatoes quickly by running the back of a knife over the skin to loosen it; then pull off the skin. Or loosen the skin by plunging the tomato into boiling water for a few seconds or by quickly twirling it on a fork over a flame.

Fruit salads: To make pretty orange or grapefruit sections, first peel the fruit closely, then cut down the side of one section membrane and slide the fruit off.

To seed grapes in a jiffy, cut them in half with kitchen scissors and remove the seeds with another snip or two.

Gelatin salads: When unmolding a gelatin salad, rinse the plate or platter with cold water. Loosen the salad with the tip of a knife, dip the mold just to the rim in warm water for a few seconds. Place wet plate or platter on top of mold, hold tightly together, and invert quickly. Lift off the mold, and center the salad by pushing it gently with the back of a spatula. As the finishing touch, tuck lettuce leaves around and under the salad.

Tossed Salad Combination Guide

Venture into the realm of leafy greens and vegetables with a flavorful salad creation that will give each menu spark and variety. To prepare the winning combinations given below, tear salad greens in bite-sized pieces unless otherwise indicated. Add remaining ingredients *except* garnish and toss lightly with your favorite dressing. Garnish the salad with the ingredient that is recommended in the last column; serve the tossed salad immediately.

To Go Along With	Add These	Garnish With
Bibb lettuce	Tomato, cut in wedges Unpared cucumber, sliced Avocado, peeled and sliced	Hard-cooked egg, sliced
Boston lettuce	Hard-cooked egg, chopped Fresh mushrooms, sliced Chives, snipped	Parsley sprigs
Boston lettuce	Watercress Anchovy fillets	Parmesan cheese, grated
Chinese cabbage	Leaf lettuce Celery, bias-cut Radishes, sliced Chives, snipped	Water chestnuts, sliced
Curly endive	Iceberg lettuce Bacon, crisp-cooked and crumbled Tomato, cut in wedges Celery, sliced Radishes, sliced Green onion, chopped	Hard-cooked egg, sliced
Iceberg lettuce	Carrot, shredded Celery, diced Mandarin oranges, well-drained	Raisins

Iceberg lettuce	Raw cauliflowerets,
	   thinly sliced
	Onion, sliced and separated
	   into rings
	Pimiento-stuffed green
	   olives, sliced
		Blue cheese, crumbled

Tossed Salad Combination Guide		
To Go Along With	Add These	Garnish With
Leaf lettuce	Chicory Watercress Tomato, cut in wedges Onion, thinly sliced Cucumber, sliced	Walnut halves
Leaf lettuce	Curly endive Tomato, finely diced Green onion, sliced	Cheddar cheese, cut in thin strips
Leaf lettuce	Watercress Raw spinach Carrot curls Pitted ripe olives, sliced	Almonds, toasted
Romaine	Tomato, diced Green pepper, chopped Romano cheese, grated	Artichoke hearts
Raw spinach	Bacon, crisp-cooked and crumbled Hard-cooked egg, chopped Carrot, thinly sliced	Canned French-fried onions
Raw spinach, shredded	Raw zucchini, sliced Radishes, sliced Green onion, sliced	Mushroom crowns
Raw spinach	Leaf lettuce Romaine Artichoke hearts Pimiento, chopped Celery, sliced	Pimiento-stuffed olives, sliced
Watercress	Iceberg lettuce Ripe olives, sliced Cucumber, sliced Tomatoes, cut in wedges Green pepper rings Green onion, sliced	Croutons

Tossed Western Salad

Cook one 9-ounce package frozen artichoke hearts according to package directions; drain. In screw-top jar combine ½ cup salad oil; ¼ cup lemon juice; 3 tablespoons tarragon vinegar; 2 tablespoons sugar; 2 tablespoons minced onion; 1 clove garlic, crushed; 1 teaspoon salt; ½ teaspoon dry mustard; and dash freshly ground pepper. Cover; shake. Pour over artichokes. Cover; chill well, stirring occasionally.

Several hours before serving, wash 3 heads Bibb or 2 heads Boston lettuce and 2 medium heads romaine. Drain well on paper toweling. Tear greens into bite-sized pieces and layer with paper toweling in large container. Cover with damp paper toweling; refrigerate. Slice ½ bunch radishes. Place in bowl; cover and chill. Slice 1 avocado and place in another small bowl. Sprinkle with a little of the artichoke dressing. Cover and chill. Brown 1 cup packaged croutons in 2 tablespoons butter, stirring till toasted on all sides.

To serve, fluff greens into bowl; add artichokes with dressing and radishes. Roll-toss. Season with salt and freshly ground pepper. Add avocado and croutons; toss. Serves 8.

Tossed green salads are by no means the only kind of vegetable salad. In fact, almost all vegetables are adaptable for use in salads. Everyone is familiar with the standard coleslaw, bean salad, and potato salad. However, perk up the standards by adding ingredients such as tomato, pineapple, or peanuts to coleslaw; pimiento or olives to bean salad; and cauliflower, cheese, or cucumber to potato salad.

Also try different combinations of other vegetables such as asparagus, corn, cauliflower, peas, tomatoes, radishes, cucumbers, celery, onion, green pepper, beet, carrot, and broccoli.

Italian Bean Toss

Cook two 9-ounce packages frozen Italian green beans according to package directions; drain and chill. Blend together ½ cup mayonnaise, 2 tablespoons grated Parmesan cheese, 1 tablespoon finely chopped canned pimiento, 1 teaspoon salt, and ¼ teaspoon curry powder. Add beans and toss; chill. Serves 6 to 8.

Potato Salad Special

Combine 3 cups diced cooked potatoes; 1½ cups sliced raw cauliflower; 1 cup diced celery; 2 hard-cooked eggs, chopped; ¼ cup chopped onion; and 6 slices bacon, crisp-cooked and crumbled. In small bowl mix 1 cup mayonnaise, 1 tablespoon bacon drippings, and 2 teaspoons caraway seed (optional); pour over salad. Toss lightly. Salt to taste. Chill. Serves 5 or 6.

Bean and Avocado Boats

Combine ¼ cup salad oil, 2 tablespoons vinegar, 2 tablespoons lemon juice, 1 tablespoon sugar, ½ teaspoon chili powder, ¼ teaspoon salt, dash garlic salt, and dash pepper. Pour over one 15-ounce can garbanzo beans, drained; one 8-ounce can kidney beans, drained; and 2 tablespoons sliced green onion. Chill well, stirring occasionally. Spoon beans into 2 avocados, halved lengthwise and seeded. Serves 4.

Fruit combinations: For a refreshing salad, select fruits from the wealth of fresh, canned, dried, and frozen fruits available and combine them with a tart-sweet dressing, dairy dressing, or cooked dressing. For a change from the salad-in-a-bowl, capitalize upon the appealing colors and shapes of various fruits by serving the salad in an attractive arrangement with a bowl of dressing.

Fresh fruits make particularly delicious salads. Although fruits such as bananas and some citrus fruits are widely available all year, many other fruits are seasonal. For example, watermelons, cantaloupes, peaches, strawberries, raspberries, and cherries are summer favorites, while apples, pears, cranberries, and pomegranates are more plentiful in the fall and winter. A salad that uses fresh fruits is a flavorful addition to any menu.

A make-ahead salad

As its name indicates, 24-Hour Salad should → be made a day before serving. Chilling the salad overnight allows the flavors to blend.

Fruit Combination Guide
Team the fruit with suggested counterparts at the right for a real taste treat. Then, arrange items on different varieties of greens each time. Top with a dressing.

To Go Along With	Choose These
Apple, diced	• Mandarin orange sections and diced celery
Unpeeled red apple slices	• Grapefruit sections, sliced avocado, and pomegranate seeds
Avocado, peeled and sliced	• Grapefruit sections and persimmon wedges • Sliced tomato
Apricots, halved and seeded	• Red grapes and sliced jellied cranberry sauce • Pineapple chunks and maraschino cherries
Banana, halved lengthwise	• Orange and grapefruit sections and pitted dates • Cottage cheese and salted peanuts
Banana, bias-cut	• Halved red plums, sliced pineapple, red raspberries, and coconut
Figs, halved and seeded	• Raspberries and cream cheese balls rolled in shredded coconut
Grapefruit sections	• Sweetened raw cranberries • Orange sections, pineapple spears, and ripe olives
Honeydew melon, peeled and crescent-cut	• Thinly sliced Prosciutto ham
Honeydew melon, peeled and sliced	• Raspberry, lemon, or lime sherbet
Melon, peeled and sliced	• Fresh sweet cherries, halved green grapes, and chopped pecans • Fruit cocktail and whipped cream
Melon, cubed	• Cottage cheese and fresh strawberries • Raspberries and bias-cut banana slices
Peach, halved	• Blueberries and raspberries • Cottage cheese and candied ginger
Peach, spiced	• Pineapple chunks and apple-mint jelly
Pear, halved	• Shredded American cheese • Sliced plums and blueberries • Halved green grapes and cream cheese
Pineapple, chunks	• Orange sections and fresh strawberries
Pineapple, sliced	• Watermelon chunks and sliced banana

24-Hour Salad

  1 20½-ounce can pineapple tidbits
  3 egg yolks
  2 tablespoons sugar
  2 tablespoons vinegar
  1 tablespoon butter or margarine
    Dash salt
  1 16-ounce can pitted light
    sweet cherries, drained
  2 peeled oranges, cut up and
    drained
  ¼ cup drained maraschino cherries
  2 cups miniature marshmallows
  1 cup whipping cream

Drain pineapple tidbits, reserving 2 tablespoons syrup. In top of double boiler beat egg yolks slightly; add reserved syrup, sugar, vinegar, butter or margarine, and salt. Place over *hot, not boiling* water; cook, stirring constantly, till mixture thickens *slightly* and *barely* coats a metal spoon (about 12 minutes). Cool to room temperature.

Combine *well-drained* fruits and marshmallows. Pour cooled custard over and mix gently. Whip cream; fold into fruit. Turn into serving bowl. Cover and chill 24 hours. Trim with fresh strawberry halves and seedless green grapes, if desired. Makes 6 to 8 servings.

Yogurt-Fruit Combo

Easy dressing is made of yogurt and mayonnaise—

  2 8-ounce cartons orange yogurt
  ⅓ cup mayonnaise or salad
    dressing
  1 11-ounce can mandarin orange
    sections, drained
  1 20-ounce can pineapple tidbits
    drained
  1 16-ounce can pitted light
    sweet cherries, drained
    and halved
  1 cup miniature marshmallows

Stir together orange yogurt and mayonnaise or salad dressing. Fold in mandarin oranges, pineapple tidbits, light sweet cherries, and miniature marshmallows. Chill at least one hour before serving. Makes 10 to 12 servings.

Date-Apple Waldorf

  1 orange
  2 cups diced, unpeeled apple
    (about 2 apples)
  ½ cup pitted dates, snipped
  ½ cup chopped celery
  ⅓ cup chopped walnuts
    • • •
  ¼ cup mayonnaise or salad
    dressing
  1 tablespoon sugar
  ¾ cup frozen whipped dessert
    topping, thawed

Peel orange; section over bowl to catch juices. Halve orange sections and reserve 1 tablespoon juice. In medium bowl combine apple, dates, celery, walnuts, and orange sections. Blend together mayonnaise, sugar, and the reserved orange juice. Fold in the thawed whipped dessert topping; combine with date mixture. Serve in lettuce cups. Makes 6 servings.

Meat, fish, poultry, and egg salads: When the menu calls for a hearty salad, turn to recipes that contain meat, fish, poultry, or egg. With choices such as chicken, turkey, or egg salad dressed with mayonnaise, a shrimp salad with an herb-vinegar dressing, a salad of meat, cheese, greens, and other vegetables dressed with French dressing, and a ham and cheese combination, you are sure to find just the right salad.

Leftover meats, such as roast beef and poultry, are adaptable to salads, too. Simply combine them with other ingredients such as salad greens, tomatoes, pickles, cheese, onion, or green pepper; then add a compatible dressing. These salads are more attractive if you cut the ingredients in bite-sized pieces.

Ham and Egg Salad

Combine 1½ cups cubed fully cooked ham; 6 hard-cooked eggs, coarsely diced; ½ cup chopped celery; and ½ cup chopped sweet pickle. Blend together ⅓ cup mayonnaise or salad dressing and 2 tablespoons prepared mustard. Toss with ham mixture. Chill. Serves 4.

San Marino Beef Salad

4 to 5 pounds beef short ribs
⅓ cup chopped carrot
⅓ cup chopped onion
• • •
¼ cup olive oil
¼ cup red wine vinegar
½ teaspoon dry mustard
½ teaspoon salt
Dash cayenne
1 medium red onion
½ sweet red pepper
3 medium carrots
3 branches celery
2 tablespoons cut celery leaves

In large saucepan cover beef short ribs, chopped carrot, and chopped onion with salted water. Bring to a boil. Cover and simmer till meat is tender, about 1½ to 2 hours. Strip meat from bone and trim off fat. Cut meat into julienne strips (3 cups); chill.

In a screw-top jar combine the ¼ cup olive oil, wine vinegar, dry mustard, salt, and cayenne. Shake well; chill. Shake again before using. Slice red onion and separate into rings. Cut red pepper, carrots, and celery branches into julienne strips.

To serve combine beef strips, onion rings, and the pepper, carrots, and celery strips. Toss with dressing. Sprinkle with cut celery leaves. Makes 4 servings.

Turkey-Mushroom Salad

2½ cups cubed cooked turkey
1½ cups sliced fresh mushrooms
1 cup chopped celery
2 tablespoons sliced pimiento-stuffed green olives
⅓ cup mayonnaise or salad dressing
1 tablespoon lemon juice
1 teaspoon finely chopped onion
½ teaspoon salt
Romaine leaves

Combine turkey, mushrooms, celery, and olives. Blend mayonnaise, lemon juice, onion, and salt. Add to turkey mixture; toss lightly. Chill. Line salad bowl with romaine. Spoon in turkey salad. Makes 6 servings.

Crab-Wild Rice Salad

1 6-ounce package long-grain, wild rice mix
1 7½-ounce can crab meat, drained, flaked, and cartilage removed
1 tablespoon lemon juice
¼ cup chopped green pepper
¼ cup chopped canned pimiento
2 tablespoons snipped parsley
½ cup mayonnaise or salad dressing
2 tablespoons Russian salad dressing
½ teaspoon salt
2 medium avocados, peeled and sliced*

Cook rice following package directions; cool. Mix together crab meat and lemon juice. Combine rice, crab, green pepper, pimiento, and parsley. Blend together mayonnaise, Russian salad dressing, and salt. Add mayonnaise mixture to vegetable-crab mixture and toss lightly. Chill. Serve with avocado slices. Serves 4 or 5.

*To keep avocado slices bright, dip in lemon juice mixed with a little water.

Gelatin salads: A mold of gelatin, with or without added ingredients, makes an enticing salad for any meal. When the meal is large, serve a simple salad of fruit-flavored gelatin. On the other hand, when the rest of the meal is light, serve a hearty salad of fruits, vegetables, meat, or cheese with a base of either unflavored or flavored gelatin.

Although gelatin is clear, ingredients such as whipped cream, ice cream, cream cheese, and mayonnaise give gelatin salads a creamy, opaque appearance as well as adding a delectable flavor to the gelatin. As a general rule, whipped cream and ice cream are particularly compatible with fruits, and mayonnaise is most commonly used with vegetables. However, whipped cream, ice cream, mayonnaise, and cream cheese can all be used with a wide variety of gelatin flavors and added ingredients.

Since gelatin requires several hours of refrigeration to set, this type of salad must be prepared quite awhile before it is served. However, if time is shorter than usual, you can hasten the setting of gelatin salads. Simply dissolve a 3-ounce package of flavored gelatin in 1 cup boiling water; then, add 8 to 12 ice cubes and stir constantly until the gelatin starts to thicken (this usually takes 2 to 3 minutes). Remove the unmelted ice and let stand at room temperature for about 5 minutes before folding in fruits and vegetables; then chill.

Harvest Fruit Mold

    1 11-ounce package mixed dried
        fruits
    1/3 cup sugar
    2 3-ounce packages orange-
        flavored gelatin
    2 cups boiling water

In saucepan combine fruit and enough water to cover; simmer gently, covered, 25 to 30 minutes, adding sugar for last 5 minutes of cooking. Drain fruit, reserving syrup. Add water to syrup to make 2 cups. Dissolve gelatin in the 2 cups boiling water; stir in syrup mixture. Chill till partially set.

Pit prunes; cut up all fruit. Fold fruit into gelatin. Pour into 6-cup ring mold; chill till firm. Makes 8 servings.

Confetti Relish Mold

    1 3-ounce package lemon-flavored
        gelatin
    2 beef bouillon cubes
    1 cup boiling water
    1 tablespoon tarragon vinegar
    1 cup dairy sour cream
    1/2 cup chopped, unpeeled cucumber
    1/4 cup sliced radishes
    1/4 cup finely chopped green pepper
    2 tablespoons sliced green onion

Dissolve gelatin and bouillon cubes in boiling water; stir in vinegar. Chill till partially set. Add sour cream to gelatin; beat with rotary beater till smooth. Fold in chopped cucumber, sliced radishes, chopped green pepper, and sliced green onion. Pour into a 3½-cup mold. Chill till firm. Makes 6 servings.

Shrimp in Avocado Ring

Dissolve one 3-ounce package lemon-flavored gelatin in 1 cup boiling water. Chill till partially set; whip till fluffy. Stir in 1 cup mayonnaise or salad dressing, 1 to 2 tablespoons lemon juice, and ½ teaspoon salt.

Whip 1 cup whipping cream. Fold whipped cream and 2 medium avocados, peeled and sieved (1 cup), into gelatin mixture. Pour into one 5½-cup ring mold or six to eight ½-cup ring molds. Chill till firm. Unmold on lettuce-lined plate; fill center with cleaned, cooked shrimp. Makes 6 to 8 servings.

Potato Salad Mold

Pimiento-stuffed olives add color and flavor—

In saucepan mix 1 envelope unflavored gelatin (1 tablespoon), 2 tablespoons sugar, and ¾ teaspoon salt. Add 1¼ cups water; stir over low heat till gelatin and sugar are dissolved. Add ¼ cup lemon juice. Cool to room temperature. Stir 4 cups diced, peeled, cooked potatoes; ¾ cup chopped celery; 3 hard-cooked eggs, chopped; ¼ cup sliced pimiento-stuffed green olives; ¼ cup chopped green pepper; and ¼ cup snipped parsley into gelatin mixture.

Whip ½ cup whipping cream. Fold whipped cream and 1 cup mayonnaise into gelatin. Spoon mixture into a 7½-cup mold or 9x9x2-inch pan. Chill till firm. Makes 8 or 9 servings.

Frozen salads: When the menu demands something refreshingly cold, serve a frozen salad. The smooth iciness of this type of salad depends on the inclusion of ingredients (interfering agents) that prevent the formation of large ice crystals. One of the ingredients most commonly used is whipped cream. A pudding-like base of mayonnaise or salad dressing is frequently used in frozen salads, too.

Frozen salads are usually made in refrigerator freezing trays or loaf pans. Since these salads are usually very firm when removed from the freezer, let the salad set at room temperature a few minutes before cutting it into slices or squares. A bed of greens makes an attractive background for frozen salad.

Frosty Salad Loaf

   1 **8-ounce package cream cheese**
   1 **cup dairy sour cream**
  ¼ **cup sugar**
  ¼ **teaspoon salt**
1½ **cups pitted, halved fresh dark sweet cherries**
   1 **16-ounce can apricot halves, drained and sliced**
   1 **8¾-ounce can crushed pineapple, drained**
   2 **cups miniature marshmallows**
     Few drops red food coloring
     Salad greens
     Pitted cherries
     Peach slices

Let cream cheese stand at room temperature to soften. Then, beat fluffy. Stir in sour cream, sugar, and salt, then fruits and marshmallows. Add few drops red food coloring to tint pale pink. Pour into an 8½x4½x2⅝-inch loaf pan. Freeze about 6 hours or overnight.

To serve let stand out a few minutes, then remove from container, slice, and place on crisp salad greens. Trim with pitted cherries and peach slices. Makes 8 servings.

Frozen Fruit Slices

In mixing bowl blend together two 3-ounce packages cream cheese, softened, and 1 cup mayonnaise or salad dressing. Stir in one 30-ounce can fruit cocktail, well drained; ½ cup maraschino cherries, well-drained and quartered; and 2½ cups miniature marshmallows. Whip 1 cup whipping cream; fold into fruit mixture. Tint with a few drops red food coloring or maraschino cherry juice, if desired.

Pour into two 1-quart round ice cream containers or refrigerator-freezer trays. Freeze firm, about 6 hours or overnight. To serve, let stand out a few minutes, then remove from containers; slice. Serves 10 to 12.

Meal in a bowl

← Succulent ham, pineapple, cheese, grapes, and lettuce are complemented by a sour cream dressing in Ham and Cheese Medley.

Uses in the menu

Not only are salads made from a wide variety of ingredients, they also are served in a variety of places in the menu—as an appetizer, a main dish accompaniment (side dish), the main dish itself, or as a dessert. Both personal preference and the ingredients in the salad help you to determine which course to serve the salad.

Appetizer: As with any appetizer, a salad served as the first course of a meal should be light. Its purpose is to stimulate the appetite. A simple tossed salad with a tangy dressing such as vinegar and oil or French dressing is the type of salad most frequently served as an appetizer. However, other salads, such as a fruit or relish assortment, are also suitable first courses.

❈MENU❈

SPECIAL COMPANY DINNER

Festive Lettuce Salad

Roast Pork with Applesauce

Hot Biscuits   Butter

Baked Potatoes   Sour Cream

Buttered Brussels Sprouts

Gingerbread with Lemon Sauce

Coffee   Tea

Festive Lettuce Salad

An easy first course—

    Lettuce
    Tomato slices
    Green pepper slices
    Onion rings
    Italian or French salad dressing

Cut lettuce in 1-inch slices. Place on salad plates. Top with tomato, green pepper, and onion. Serve with Italian or French dressing.

Accompaniment side dish: The most common way to serve a salad is as a side dish with the main course. A wide variety of salads including tossed salads, vegetable combination salads, fruit combination salads, fruit arrangements, molded fruit and vegetable salads, frozen salads, and deviled eggs all make delicious accompaniments. So many recipes for side dish salads are available that you will find many that appeal to you.

When trying to decide which side dish salad to serve, consider the salad's color, texture, and flavor. Remember that a good side dish salad complements the rest of the meal without overshadowing it.

❦MENU❦

FAMILY-STYLE SUPPER

Pan-fried Liver

Apricot-Fruit Salad

Green Beans with Bacon

Chocolate Pudding

Coffee   Milk

Apricot-Fruit Salad

1 22-ounce can apricot pie filling
1 11-ounce can mandarin orange
    sections, drained
1 30-ounce can pineapple chunks,
    drained
1 8½-ounce can grapefruit
    sections, drained
1 cup miniature marshmallows
2 bananas, sliced
    Lettuce
    Maraschino cherries

Have all fruits chilled, except bananas. In large bowl combine apricot pie filling, mandarin oranges, pineapple chunks, grapefruit sections, miniature marshmallows, and bananas. Garnish with lettuce and maraschino cherries. Serves 10 to 12.

Don't toss a salad—twirl it!

For a change of pace from the tried-and-true tossed salad, why not substitute a twirling relish tray? Here are a few creative ideas to make that salad course extra-special.

Let guests concoct their own salads from a variety of bite-sized vegetables. How about a tray of shredded red cabbage, crinkle-cut carrots, and bias-sliced celery with a bowl of assorted greens? Try fresh spinach, escarole, or Bibb.

How about a variety of "hot" nibbles: cauliflower buds, corn relish, tiny spiced sausages, and garlic-flavored olives?

Whet appetites with a tasty selection of out-of-the-ordinary cheeses: Roquefort, Brie, Feta, Gruyère, Monterey Jack, Muenster, Primost, Ricotta, Stilton, or Tilsit. To go along, serve tiny crackers or homemade bread sticks you've made from a biscuit mix.

Try a variety of relishes in pert containers such as cranberry relish made from canned sauce with a little orange peel, or corn relish, which starts with canned corn and peppers.

Dress up a cucumber-onion relish with a tangy sour cream sauce.

Here's a hostess' delight—a real make-ahead that doesn't even need dishing up at the last minute: tomato quarters, asparagus spears, broccoli buds, and artichoke hearts that have marinated in an oil and vinegar, herb-garlic, Italian, or French dressing. Marinate the vegetables in serving dishes.

Arrange fresh fruits of the season on a wooden or colorful china twirling platter: cantaloupe chunks, sugared grapes, slivers of watermelon, and orange and apple wedges. Garnish with fresh mint or lemon leaves.

Perk up appetites with an assortment of eye-appealing relishes such as baked chutney peaches, a curried fruit compote, mustard beans, and pickled beets.

Start the meal with a lazy Susan of condiments and relishes: spiced apple rings crowned with scoops of cottage cheese, kumquats topped with candied ginger, spiced cantaloupe and honeydew balls, a variety of crinkle-cut pickles—both dill and sweet, and some rosy, tangy crab apples.

MENU

STEAK NIGHT
Broiled T-bone Steaks
Wilted Spinach Toss
Spiced Apples
Scalloped Potatoes
Buttered Corn
Raspberry Shortcake
Iced Tea

Wilted Spinach Toss

- 3 slices bacon
- ¼ cup vinegar
- 1 tablespoon salad oil
- 1½ teaspoons sugar
- ⅛ teaspoon dried tarragon leaves, crushed
- Dash freshly ground black pepper
- ¼ cup chopped celery
- 1 tablespoon sliced green onion
- ½ pound fresh spinach, torn
- 2 medium oranges, peeled and cut in bite-sized pieces

In large skillet cook bacon till crisp; drain, reserving 2 tablespoons bacon drippings. Crumble bacon and set aside. Stir vinegar, oil, sugar, ¼ teaspoon salt, tarragon, and pepper into reserved drippings; bring to boiling. Add chopped celery and sliced green onion. Gradually add spinach, tossing just till leaves are coated and wilted slightly. Add oranges and crumbled bacon; toss lightly. Serves 6 to 8.

Harvest Toss

In screw-top jar combine 3 tablespoons salad oil, 2 tablespoons vinegar, 1½ teaspoons sugar, ½ teaspoon salt, and dash pepper; shake well. In bowl toss 6 cups torn leaf lettuce; 2 cups coarsely chopped, unpeeled red apple; 1 cup thinly sliced, unpeeled raw zucchini; and 1 small green pepper, cut in thin strips. Pour dressing over; toss. Makes 6 servings.

Asparagus Mold

- 2 envelopes unflavored gelatin
- ½ cup sugar
- 3½ cups cold water
- ⅓ cup white vinegar
- 3 tablespoons lemon juice
- 1 teaspoon grated onion
- 1 cup finely chopped celery
- ⅓ cup chopped canned pimiento
- 1 14½-ounce can asparagus cuts, drained
- Mayonnaise or salad dressing

In saucepan combine gelatin, sugar, and ¼ teaspoon salt. Add 1½ *cups* of the water and the vinegar; stir over low heat till gelatin and sugar are dissolved. Add lemon juice, onion, and remaining water. Chill till partially set. Fold in celery and pimiento. Arrange *one-third* of the asparagus in bottom of a 6½-cup mold. Carefully pour in *one-third* of the gelatin mixture. Repeat layers, ending with gelatin. Chill till firm. Serve with mayonnaise or salad dressing. Makes 10 to 12 servings.

Sea Lime Salad

Dissolve one 3-ounce package lime-flavored gelatin in 1 cup boiling water. Gradually stir hot gelatin into one 8-ounce package cream cheese, cubed and softened; beat till smooth. Chill till partially set. Fold in one 8¾-ounce can undrained crushed pineapple; 1 cup chopped peeled cucumber; and ¼ cup chopped walnuts. Whip ½ cup whipping cream; fold in. Pour into 5½-cup mold; chill. Serves 5 or 6.

MENU

CANDLELIGHT DINNER
Lamb Chops
Buttered Rice
Asparagus Mold
Hot Fruit Compote
Coffee   *Tea*

Main dish: For a delicious meal that is easy to prepare, serve a hot or cold salad as the main dish and complete the menu with bread, a dessert, and a beverage. Meat, fish, seafood, poultry, and eggs, frequently combined with salad greens, other vegetables, or gelatin, are the most popular ingredients for main dish salads.

One of the most noticeable differences between a main dish salad and a salad served as an appetizer, side dish, or dessert is the size of the serving—main dish salads are served in larger helpings.

❖MENU❖

BEFORE THE GAME
Baked Seafood Salad

Hot Rolls   Butter

Buttered Broccoli

Pickled Apples   Sweet Pickles

Angel Cake with Cherry Sauce

Baked Seafood Salad

      1 7-ounce can crab meat, drained, flaked, and cartilage removed
      1 4½-ounce can shrimp, drained
  1½ cups chopped celery
   ¼ cup chopped green pepper
   ¼ cup chopped onion
   ¼ cup chopped canned pimiento
   ¾ cup dairy sour cream
   ¼ cup mayonnaise
      1 tablespoon lemon juice
   ½ teaspoon salt
   ½ teaspoon Worcestershire sauce
      1 cup soft bread crumbs
      1 tablespoon butter, melted

Combine first 6 ingredients. Blend sour cream, mayonnaise, lemon juice, salt, Worcestershire sauce, and dash pepper; stir into seafood. Spoon into 10x6x1¾-inch baking dish. Mix crumbs and butter; sprinkle atop. Bake at 350° for 20 to 25 minutes. Makes 4 to 6 servings.

Ham and Cheese Medley

For an easy, delicious menu serve this tasty salad, bread sticks, a beverage, and a dessert—

Drain one 8¾-ounce can pineapple tidbits, reserving ¼ cup syrup. Toss together drained pineapple; 1 small head lettuce, torn in bite-sized pieces (4 cups); 1 cup cubed fully cooked ham; 1 cup halved seedless green grapes; and 2 ounces natural Swiss cheese, cut in strips. Line salad bowl with Bibb lettuce; spoon in salad mixture. Chill thoroughly.

For dressing, stir reserved ¼ cup pineapple syrup into 1 cup dairy sour cream till well blended; chill. To serve, spoon a little dressing atop salad. Garnish with additional green grapes and Bibb lettuce, if desired. Pass remaining dressing. Makes 6 servings.

Fruit-filled Frosty Salad Loaf contains pineapple in addition to the sweet cherries and canned apricots repeated as a garnish.

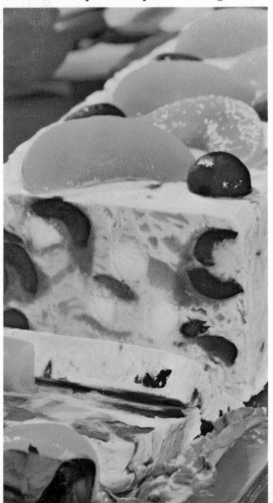

```
❧MENU❧

HOT WEATHER LUNCHEON
Chef's Salad Bowl
Hot Rolls      Butter
Watermelon
Iced Tea      Lemonade
```

Chef's Salad Bowl

Rub wooden salad bowl with cut clove of garlic. Separate leaves of 1 head romaine *or* 1 bunch leaf lettuce, Arrange romaine or lettuce in salad bowl, lining sides. Group atop lettuce: 2 cups fully cooked ham strips; 8 ounces sharp natural Cheddar cheese, cut in strips; and 3 hard-cooked eggs, sliced. Sprinkle with salt and freshly ground pepper. Pass Italian salad dressing. Makes 6 servings.

Dessert: As with other desserts, a salad served as the last course or refreshment is usually sweet. Many kinds of gelatin and frozen salads make delicious desserts, particularly those containing fruit. If the menu calls for a substantial dessert, serve a fruit-filled dessert salad rich with whipped cream. On the other hand, if you need a light dessert, try a simpler dessert salad such as a fresh fruit combination or whipped, fruit-flavored gelatin.

```
❧MENU❧

INSIDE BARBECUE
Oven-Barbecued Spareribs
Hashbrowns
Peas with Mushrooms
Emerald Salad Dessert
Coffee
```

Emerald Salad Dessert

An easy-to-fix salad dessert—

1 8¾-ounce can crushed pineapple
1 3-ounce package lime-flavored gelatin

• • •

2 cups miniature marshmallows
1 2-ounce package dessert topping mix

Drain pineapple, reserving syrup. Add water to syrup to make 2 cups; bring to boil. Add gelatin to boiling syrup and stir to dissolve. Add drained pineapple; pour into 10x6x1¾-inch dish. Cover immediately with a layer of marshmallows. Chill till gelatin is firm.

Just before serving, prepare topping mix according to package directions; spread over marshmallows. Makes 8 to 10 servings.

Lemon-Blueberry Salad

Canned pie filling furnishes the blueberries—

1 3-ounce package lemon-flavored gelatin
1 3-ounce package black raspberry-flavored gelatin
1 cup boiling water
½ cup cold water
1 tablespoon lemon juice
1 21-ounce can blueberry pie filling
½ cup whipping cream
Sifted confectioners' sugar
Lemon peel

Dissolve gelatins together in boiling water; add cold water and lemon juice. Gradually stir into blueberry pie filling. Pour into 8x8x2-inch baking dish; chill till firm. Whip cream; sweeten to taste by folding in confectioners' sugar. Spread over gelatin mixture. Chill till serving time. Cut in squares. If desired, garnish with lemon peel. Makes 8 servings.

SALAD BURNET—A perennial herb with a cucumberlike flavor and aroma. As its name suggests, this herb is used primarily in salads. (See also *Herb.*)

SALAD DRESSING

*Valuable hints on how to prepare and use
these essential partners for salad.*

Most people agree that a salad without dressing is lacking something—it's nice, perhaps, but not perfect. In saladmaking, the mixture of ingredients called the dressing serves two functions: it adds flavor to the salad and it binds the ingredients together, sometimes literally and sometimes by flavor accent only.

Quite naturally, the history of salad dressings is linked with the history of salad. In fact, like salad, salad dressings can be traced as far back as the ancient Greeks and Romans. Unlike most of the salad dressings of today, which contain several ingredients, the first definable salad dressing used by these people consisted of only one ingredient—salt.

The classic mixture of oil and vinegar is a dressing of long standing. In fact, a mixture of greens and sometimes other vegetables dressed with oil and vinegar was the only type of salad known in European countries several centuries ago.

By the 1700s, however, many chefs were becoming more experimental, and salad dressings were one of the things that received attention. Mayonnaise, a sauce that is considered as much of a classic dressing as oil and vinegar, was one of the developments of this time. Apparently, however, there were still rules on what constituted a good salad dressing because it is recorded that one of the French chefs of that time reprimanded Marie Antoinette for using an incorrect dressing.

Homemade dressings

← Easy Italian Dressing, Tomato Soup Dressing, and fluffy Lemonade Dressing are only a few of the salad dressings that you can make.

Another milestone in the history of salad dressing occurred in the 1920s when prepared salad dressings were first sold. Since then, the variety of prepared dressings available has increased continually. Today, homemakers have the choice of dressing salads with a homemade salad dressing or one of the dozens of dressing mixes and bottled dressings available.

How to complement salads

When adding a salad dressing to a salad, one of the most important things to remember is to use salad dressing with discretion. If you use too little dressing, the salad loses character. On the other hand, if you use too much dressing, you are likely to drown the basic salad flavor.

However, this reminder does not answer the question of what dressing goes with what salad. Although there are several standard combinations, such as French dressing on tossed salads and mayonnaise on meat salads, don't limit yourself to these. Start experimenting.

Your personal preferences and those of your family and guests are one of the most important guides to use when matching salads and dressings—if it has an appealing appearance and flavor, it is a good combination. As a starting place for finding out what combinations you like, use the following general hints.

One thing that helps you to determine which dressing to use is whether the salad is an appetizer, side dish, main dish, or dessert salad. Since the purpose of an appetizer salad is to whet the appetite, the dressing must help to accomplish this. Therefore, use a light dressing rather than a heavy dressing and a tart, spicy dressing rather than a sweet dressing on first-course salads. Dressings such as an oil-vinegar dressing and fruit juices fulfill these requirements.

The dressing for a side dish or main dish salad can range from light to heavy and from mild to highly seasoned, depending on the ingredients in the salad. Dressings for dessert salads are usually quite sweet, although they are sometimes flavored with a rather tart fruit juice.

The ingredients in the salad are another important guide when matching salads and salad dressings. Although flavor is probably the main consideration, also make sure that the texture and color of the salad dressing complement the salad.

The type of dressing you choose depends on what flavor you want to be dominant—the salad or the dressing. For example, a wedge of lettuce doesn't have much flavor by itself, so you can serve a dressing with a prominent flavor such as blue cheese dressing or a highly seasoned French dressing with it. However, if you are serving a deluxe tossed salad that includes several types of salad greens, red cabbage, shredded carrots, and other vegetables, put the emphasis on the salad flavor by using a simple dressing such as oil and vinegar or a basic French dressing. The following box gives some more guides on which dressing to use.

Dressing tips

French dressings cling readily to greens and are great for marinating vegetables. The tart-sweet ones add tang to fruit salads.

Cooked dressings add luscious appeal to potato salads. Sweet cooked dressings are especially good as fruit toppings.

Cheese-flavored dressings used with vegetables, make exciting companions.

Sour cream dressings add zip to fruit and vegetable salads. They're also delightful with main dish salad bowls.

Mayonnaise and salad dressing, with their varied combinations, heighten the flavor of meat, seafood, egg, and molded salads. When combined with whipped cream, mayonnaise is excellent on fruit salads.

How to prepare

Mixing a salad dressing can be as simple as shaking together several ingredients, or it can be a more complicated process that involves cooking or extended beating. But no matter what the preparation technique, the objective is to prepare a flavorful, enticing dressing. Numerous combinations of ingredients will fulfill this objective, but generally salad dressings are divided into four types—cooked, dairy, oil-based, and mayonnaise-based.

Cooked: This type of salad dressing is thickened with eggs (at least the yolks) and/or starch or a cooked syrup. Besides the thickening agent, cooked dressings usually include sugar, vinegar or another acid ingredient, and seasonings.

When making a cooked salad dressing, remember to follow directions. Specifically, pay careful attention to the length of cooking time and the adding of the eggs to the hot mixture (first, stir a little hot mixture into the eggs and then stir this into the remaining hot mixture).

The commercial product, salad dressing, fits into this category. Although this product is often substituted for mayonnaise, it doesn't have as much oil.

Fruit Dip Fluff

½ cup sugar
⅓ cup light corn syrup
¼ cup hot water
1 stiffly beaten egg white
   Dash salt
   Few drops vanilla
½ cup mayonnaise
1½ teaspoons shredded orange peel

In small saucepan combine sugar, light corn syrup, and hot water. Heat slowly, stirring till all sugar is dissolved. Then, boil without stirring till mixture reaches soft-ball stage (236°). Gradually beat hot syrup into stiffly beaten egg white. Add salt and vanilla. Cool mixture thoroughly.

Fold mayonnaise and shredded orange peel into cooled mixture; chill thoroughly. Serve as dressing on fruit salad. Makes 1⅔ cups.

Cooked Dressing

 2 tablespoons all-purpose flour
 2 tablespoons sugar
 1 teaspoon dry mustard
   Dash cayenne
 2 slightly beaten egg yolks
 ¾ cup milk
 ¼ cup vinegar
 1½ teaspoons butter

Mix together flour, sugar, mustard, ½ teaspoon salt, and cayenne in small saucepan. Add egg yolks and milk; cook, stirring constantly, over low heat till thick. Add vinegar and butter; mix. Cool thoroughly. Makes 1 cup.

Lemonade Dressing

 1 6-ounce can lemonade concentrate
 2 beaten eggs
 ⅓ cup sugar
 1 cup whipping cream

Thaw concentrate. In small saucepan combine eggs, lemonade concentrate, and sugar. Cook and stir over low heat till thickened. Cool. Whip cream; fold in. Chill thoroughly. Serve with fruit salads. Makes 3 cups dressing.

Dairy: Many salad dressings have dairy products as their main ingredient: Whipped cream, cream cheese, sour cream, yogurt, or cottage cheese combined with seasonings.

Dairy dressings are easy to prepare. Usually, it requires only a few minutes to stir the dressing ingredients together. However, as with most salad dressings, you should prepare dairy dressings several hours before serving to allow the flavors to blend while the dressing chills.

Berry-Sour Cream Dressing

 1 cup dairy sour cream
 ½ 10-ounce package frozen, sliced
   strawberries, thawed (½ cup)

Blend sour cream and fruit. Chill. Serve with fruit salads. Makes about 1¼ cups.

Mushroom Dressing

 1 3-ounce can chopped mushrooms, drained
 1 cup dairy sour cream
 ⅓ cup mayonnaise or salad
   dressing
 2 tablespoons well-drained
   pickle relish
 2 tablespoons milk
 ¾ teaspoon salt
 ½ teaspoon Worcestershire sauce

Chop any large pieces of mushrooms. Combine with sour cream, mayonnaise, pickle relish, milk, salt, and Worcestershire sauce; chill thoroughly. Serve with lettuce wedges or vegetable salads. Makes 2 cups dressing.

Western Blue Cheese Dressing

In pint-sized screw-top jar combine 2 ounces blue cheese, crumbled (½ cup), and ¾ cup dairy sour cream; stir in 2 tablespoons milk. Add 1 tablespoon salad oil, dash Worcestershire sauce, 2 teaspoons grated Parmesan cheese, dash onion salt, dash garlic salt, and dash pepper; mix well. Add 3 tablespoons white wine vinegar; cover jar and shake well. Chill. Serve over tossed green salads. Makes 1⅔ cups.

Sweet-Sour Dressing

 1 cup dairy sour cream
 2 tablespoons white vinegar
 2 tablespoons sugar
 ½ teaspoon salt

Combine sour cream and white vinegar. Stir in sugar and salt. Chill thoroughly. Toss with shredded cabbage. Makes 1 cup dressing.

Nippy Nectar Dressing

In small mixing bowl beat together one 3-ounce package cream cheese, softened; 2 tablespoons honey; 1 teaspoon grated lemon peel; 1 tablespoon lemon juice; and ⅛ teaspoon salt. Gradually add ½ cup salad oil, beating till mixture is thickened. Chill thoroughly. Serve with fruit salads. Makes about 1 cup dressing.

Horseradish Dressing

½ cup dairy sour cream
¼ cup mayonnaise or salad
    dressing
1 tablespoon prepared horseradish
1 teaspoon sugar
¼ teaspoon salt
2 drops bottled hot pepper sauce
2 drops Worcestershire sauce

Combine sour cream, mayonnaise, horseradish, sugar, salt, hot pepper sauce, and Worcestershire sauce; chill thoroughly. Serve with meat or seafood salads. Makes 2 cups.

Crunchy Cream Dressing

Tiny vegetable pieces add crunch—

½ cup finely chopped, unpeeled
    cucumber
2 tablespoons finely chopped
    green pepper
2 tablespoons finely chopped
    green onion
2 tablespoons thinly sliced
    radishes
• • •
1 cup dairy sour cream
½ teaspoon salt
  Dash pepper

Combine cucumber, green pepper, onion, and radishes. Stir in sour cream, salt, and pepper; mix well. Chill thoroughly. Serve over lettuce or cabbage salads. Makes 1½ cups.

Banana-Cheese Dressing

1 3-ounce package cream cheese,
    softened
2 tablespoons milk
1 fully ripe banana
1 tablespoon sugar
1 tablespoon lemon juice
  Dash salt

Blend softened cream cheese with milk. Mash banana; add sugar, lemon juice, and dash salt. Stir the banana mixture into cheese mixture. Serve with fruit salads. Makes 1 cup.

Dairy-Fruit Dressing

½ cup dairy sour cream
1 tablespoon honey
1 teaspoon lemon juice
¼ teaspoon salt

Combine sour cream, honey, lemon juice, and salt. Chill. Serve with sweetened or canned fruit. Makes about ½ cup dressing.

Tarragon Dressing

1 cup dairy sour cream
½ cup mayonnaise
1 teaspoon vinegar
½ teaspoon dried tarragon
    leaves, crushed
¼ teaspoon seasoned salt

Combine sour cream, mayonnaise, vinegar, tarragon, and seasoned salt. Chill. Serve with seafood or vegetable salads. Makes 1½ cups.

Rosy Salad Dressing

1 8-ounce package cream cheese,
    softened
1 cup dairy sour cream
¾ cup cranberry relish

Combine softened cream cheese and dairy sour cream; beat till smooth. Stir in cranberry relish. Chill at least 2 hours. Serve with fruit salads. Makes about 3 cups dressing.

Chef's Cheese Dressing

3 ounces blue cheese,
    crumbled (¾ cup)
½ cup olive *or* salad oil
2 tablespoons white vinegar
1 tablespoon lemon juice
1 teaspoon anchovy paste
½ clove garlic, minced
  Salt and pepper

Thoroughly combine blue cheese, olive *or* salad oil, white vinegar, lemon juice, anchovy paste, and garlic. Season with salt and pepper. Chill thoroughly. Stir before serving. Makes 1 cup.

Oil-based: The classic oil and vinegar dressing (usually three parts oil to one part vinegar), French dressing, and mayonnaise are all oil-based salad dressings (see *French Salad Dressing* and *Mayonnaise* for recipes). However, many variations of these classic recipes as well as numerous other dressings for fruit and vegetable salads also have oil as a base.

Most oil-based dressings are easy to prepare since mixing the ingredients is all that's required. The easiest way to mix a dressing of this type other than mayonnaise is in a screw-top jar. Simply measure the ingredients into the jar, screw the lid on tightly, and shake vigorously. However, as the dressing sets, the oil and other ingredients separate, so shake the dressing again just before using it.

Zippy Emerald Dressing

- 1 cup salad oil
- 1/3 cup vinegar
- 1/4 cup chopped onion
- 1/4 cup snipped parsley
- 2 tablespoons finely chopped green pepper
- 2 teaspoons sugar
- 1 1/2 teaspoons dry mustard
- 1/2 teaspoon salt
- 1/8 teaspoon cayenne

Combine salad oil, vinegar, onion, parsley, green pepper, sugar, dry mustard, salt, and cayenne in screw-top jar. Cover; let stand at room temperature for about 1 hour. Shake to blend thoroughly. Serve with seafood or tossed green salads. Makes about 1 1/2 cups.

As the perfect finishing touch for a fruit-filled, molded gelatin salad as well as for other fresh or canned fruit salads generously spoon on rich, creamy Banana-Cheese Dressing.

Glossy Fruit Dressing

½ cup sugar
¼ cup vinegar
1 teaspoon celery salt
1 teaspoon paprika
1 teaspoon dry mustard
½ teaspoon salt
½ teaspoon grated onion
1 cup salad oil

In small saucepan combine sugar and vinegar; heat and stir just till sugar is dissolved. Cool. Add celery salt, paprika, mustard, salt, and onion. Add oil in slow stream, beating with an electric mixer or a rotary beater till dressing is thick. Makes 1½ cups.

Fruit French Dressing

1 cup salad oil
¼ cup orange juice
3 tablespoons lemon juice
1 tablespoon vinegar
⅓ cup sugar
1 teaspoon salt
1 teaspoon paprika
1 teaspoon grated onion

Mix salad oil, orange juice, lemon juice, vinegar, sugar, salt, paprika, and onion in screw-top jar; cover and shake vigorously. Chill. Shake before serving. Makes about 1⅔ cups.

Shawano Dressing

½ cup salad oil
⅓ cup sugar
⅓ cup catsup
¼ cup vinegar
1 teaspoon salt
1 teaspoon paprika
½ teaspoon dry mustard
2 teaspoons grated onion
1½ teaspoons bottled steak sauce
1 clove garlic, minced

In bowl combine salad oil, sugar, catsup, vinegar, salt, paprika, dry mustard, grated onion, bottled steak sauce, and minced garlic. Blend mixture thoroughly with a beater. Serve with fruit. Makes about 1⅓ cups dressing.

Tomato Soup Dressing

1 10¾-ounce can condensed
   tomato soup
1 cup vinegar
½ cup salad oil
1½ teaspoons Worcestershire sauce
2 tablespoons sugar
1 tablespoon grated onion
2 teaspoons dry mustard
½ teaspoon paprika
¼ teaspoon garlic powder
Dash cayenne

In screw-top jar combine tomato soup, vinegar, salad oil, and Worcestershire sauce. Add sugar, grated onion, dry mustard, 1½ teaspoons salt, paprika, garlic powder, and cayenne. Cover; shake. Chill thoroughly. Makes 2¼ cups.

Celery Seed Dressing

½ cup sugar
⅓ cup lemon juice
1 teaspoon celery seed
1 teaspoon dry mustard
1 teaspoon paprika
¾ cup salad oil

Combine sugar, lemon juice, celery seed, dry mustard, paprika, and ½ teaspoon salt. Slowly add oil, beating with electric or rotary beater till thick. Makes 1⅓ cups dressing.

Italian Dressing

1 cup salad oil
¼ cup vinegar
1 clove garlic, minced
1 teaspoon salt
½ teaspoon white pepper
½ teaspoon celery salt
¼ teaspoon cayenne
¼ teaspoon dry mustard
Dash bottled hot pepper sauce

Combine salad oil, vinegar, garlic, salt, white pepper, celery salt, cayenne, dry mustard, and hot pepper sauce in screw-top jar. Cover and shake well. Chill mixture thoroughly. Shake again just before serving. Serve with vegetable salads. Makes 1¼ cups dressing.

Dressing dictionary

French Dressing: Both clear and creamy French dressings are a mixture of oil, vinegar or lemon juice, and seasonings. Clear dressings separate and must be shaken well before using. Creamy dressings are homogenized; thus, they do not separate.

Mayonnaise: This creamy dressing is made by beating oil very slowly into egg, vinegar or lemon juice, and seasonings. The egg emulsifies and prevents separation.

Salad Dressing: Oil and egg are used in lower proportions than in mayonnaise. Starch pastes may be used as thickening agents, as also emulsifiers. The flavor is more tangy than mayonnaise.

Cooked Dressing: Also called boiled dressing, this type is high in egg and low in fat. It is made by cooking a white sauce-egg base to which vinegar, butter or margarine, and seasonings are added.

Sesame Dressing

Toasted sesame seeds give crunch—

Combine ⅔ cup sugar, and ⅓ cup vinegar; blend in 2 tablespoons finely chopped onion, ½ teaspoon salt, ½ teaspoon Worcestershire sauce, ¼ teaspoon dry mustard, ¼ teaspoon paprika, and 4 to 5 drops bottled hot pepper sauce. Gradually add 1 cup salad oil, beating constantly with rotary beater or electric mixer till thick; chill. Stir in 2 to 3 tablespoons toasted sesame seed just before serving. Serve with fruit salads. Makes 1¾ cups.

Snappy Garlic Dressing

In screw-top jar combine ⅔ cup salad oil; ¼ cup vinegar; 1 small clove garlic, minced, 1 teaspoon sugar; ¾ teaspoon salt; ¾ teaspoon dry mustard; and dash freshly ground pepper. Cover and chill several hours. Shake well before serving with salad greens or shredded cabbage. Makes 1 cup dressing.

Mayonnaise-based: As expected, the main ingredient in this type of salad dressing is mayonnaise. Although mayonnaise alone is used as a dressing for some kinds of salads, the addition of other ingredients not only varies the flavor but also increases the versatility.

Preparing mayonnaise-based dressings simply requires blending the ingredients together. Sometimes, however, the blending of ingredients is done in two steps. First, the mayonnaise and seasonings are mixed and then a fluffy ingredient such as whipped cream is folded in. The dressing is chilled before serving.

Apricot Dressing

⅓ cup mayonnaise or salad dressing
⅓ cup apricot preserves
½ cup whipping cream

Blend together mayonnaise or salad dressing and apricot preserves. Whip cream till soft peaks form; gently fold into apricot mixture. Serve with fruit salads. Makes 1⅓ cups.

Parmesan Dressing

1 cup mayonnaise
1 tablespoon anchovy paste
½ envelope Parmesan salad dressing mix (1 tablespoon)
¼ cup water
2 tablespoons vinegar

In small mixing bowl combine mayonnaise and anchovy paste. Stir in Parmesan salad dressing mix, water, and vinegar. Serve with vegetable salads. Makes 1½ cups dressing.

Red Currant Dressing

½ cup currant jelly
¼ cup mayonnaise
¼ cup whipping cream

With rotary beater, beat currant jelly till soft and smooth. Blend in mayonnaise. Whip cream; fold into mixture. Makes about 1 cup.

Using herbs and spices

A sprinkling of various herbs and spices gives salads distinction. Add them in small amounts, about ¼ teaspoon for four servings. Taste before adding more. For best flavor results, blend the seasonings with a little oil, then stir into the chosen dressing.

Crush dried herbs or snip fresh ones before using. If substituting fresh for dried, use 3 times more fresh herbs. Below are basic types of salads with the herbs and spices that accent them best.

Bean: oregano, savory, tarragon.

Beet: chervil, dill, thyme.

Coleslaw: caraway seed, celery seed, dill, poppy seed, tarragon, thyme.

Cucumber: basil, chervil, dill, tarragon.

Egg: caraway seed, chili powder, curry powder, dill, tarragon.

Fish and seafood: basil, celery seed, curry powder, dill, oregano, tarragon.

Fruit: allspice, cinnamon, clove, ginger, mint, nutmeg, rosemary, tarragon.

Meat: basil, celery seed, chervil, dill, parsley, rosemary, tarragon, thyme.

Potato: caraway seed, chervil, curry powder, dill, oregano, savory.

Poultry: basil, curry powder, marjoram, parsley, poultry seasoning, tarragon, thyme.

Tomato: basil, celery seed, chervil, dill, oregano, savory, thyme.

Tossed green: basil, chervil, dill, marjoram, sesame seed, tarragon.

Vegetable: basil, chervil, dill, mustard seed, oregano, savory, tarragon.

Peanut-Mallow Dressing

½ 7-ounce jar marshmallow creme
¼ cup orange juice
• • •
½ cup peanut butter
¼ cup mayonnaise or salad dressing
1 tablespoon lemon juice

Combine marshmallow creme and orange juice; whip till very fluffy with electric beater. Blend peanut butter, mayonnaise, and lemon juice; fold into marshmallow mixture. Serve over fresh or canned fruit. Makes 2 cups.

Honey Mayonnaise

Blend ½ cup mayonnaise, 2 tablespoons honey, 1 tablespoon lemon juice, ½ teaspoon celery seed, and ¼ teaspoon paprika. Serve with fruit salads. Makes about ¾ cup dressing.

Cream Goddess Dressing

Combine 1 cup mayonnaise, ½ cup dairy sour cream, ⅓ cup snipped parsley, 3 tablespoons snipped chives, 3 tablespoons anchovy paste, 3 tablespoons tarragon vinegar, 1 tablespoon lemon juice, and dash freshly ground pepper. Chill. Serve with salad greens. Makes 2 cups.

Blue Cheese Mayonnaise

In mixing bowl combine 2 tablespoons crumbled blue cheese, softened, and ½ cup mayonnaise. Beat till smooth. Stir in 4 teaspoons milk and few drops bottled hot pepper sauce. Serve with salad greens. If desired, crumble extra blue cheese over top. Makes ½ cup.

Uses

While the most common use for salad dressings is on salads, these flavorful mixtures have several other uses. It is easy to make one kind of salad dressing or another an ingredient in the menu.

Dressings such as mayonnaise, French dressing, and the thick, creamy mixture sold as salad dressing are especially tasty spread on sandwiches, used as a binder for sandwich fillings, or used in appetizer dips or spreads. Steaks and roasts as well as fish and seafood are particularly flavorful when marinated in a highly herbed salad dressing before cooking. And broiled or barbecued meat is tasty when brushed during cooking with a tangy salad dressing.

In addition to homemade salad dressings, you can choose from the wide selection of prepared dressings and dressing mixes (mixed at home with oil or mayonnaise) that are available in the supermarket. Using prepared dressings cuts down the preparation time of salads and other dishes that use salad dressing.

Liver with Mushrooms

A low-calorie main dish—

>   1 4-ounce can sliced mush-
>   rooms, drained
>   ⅓ cup low-calorie French-style
>   salad dressing
>   1 pound calves liver, cut ½
>   inch thick

Marinate mushrooms in salad dressing for 30 minutes. Meanwhile, remove membrane from calves liver; cut in serving-sized pieces.

Drain mushrooms, reserving marinade. Brush both sides of liver with reserved marinade. Broil 3 inches from heat for 4 minutes. Turn; top with mushrooms. Broil till liver is tender, about 4 minutes longer. Serves 4.

Pickled Shrimp

A tasty appetizer—

Cover 1 pound fresh or frozen shrimp in shells with boiling water; add ¼ cup celery leaves, 2 tablespoons mixed pickling spices, 1½ teaspoons salt. Cover; simmer for 5 minutes. Drain; peel and devein shrimp under cold water.

Mix shrimp, ½ cup sliced onion, and 4 bay leaves; arrange in shallow dish. Combine ¾ cup low-calorie Italian salad dressing, ⅓ cup white vinegar, 1 tablespoon capers with liquid, 1 teaspoon celery seed, ½ teaspoon salt, and few drops bottled hot pepper sauce; mix well. Pour over shrimp mixture. Cover; marinate in refrigerator at least 24 hours, spooning marinade over shrimp occasionally. Makes about 2½ cups pickled shrimp and onions.

Accent the flavor of fresh or canned fruits with sweet-sour Celery Seed Dressing. Substitute poppy seed for celery seed, and use this delicious dressing on vegetable salads, too.

Herbed Steak Broil

Sure to become an over-the-coals favorite—

½ cup clear French salad dressing
with herbs and spices
½ cup dry sherry
2 tablespoons sliced green onion
1 tablespoon Worcestershire sauce
Dash pepper
1 2½- to 3 pound chuck steak, cut
1½ inches thick

Combine salad dressing, dry sherry, sliced green onion, Worcestershire sauce, and pepper. Pour over steak in shallow dish. Cover and marinate several hours at room temperature or overnight in refrigerator, turning at least once and spooning sauce over occasionally. Drain, reserving marinade. Broil steak over hot coals for 40 to 50 minutes, turning every 10 to 15 minutes, and brush with marinade. Steak will be rare; cook longer for desired doneness. Makes 6 to 8 servings.

Tuna-Berry Sandwiches

A tasty tuna and cranberry combination—

1 6½- or 7-ounce can tuna,
drained and flaked
¼ cup finely chopped celery
2 tablespoons chopped walnuts
¼ cup mayonnaise or salad
dressing
8 slices white bread
1 8-ounce can jellied cranberry
sauce, sliced ¼ inch thick
• • •
2 slightly beaten eggs
3 tablespoons milk
Dash salt

In mixing bowl combine flaked tuna, finely chopped celery, chopped walnuts, and mayonnaise or salad dressing. Spread filling on 4 slices bread. Arrange cranberry slices atop filling; top with remaining bread.

In shallow bowl combine slightly beaten eggs, milk, and the dash salt. Dip sandwiches in egg mixture. Grill on medium-hot, lightly greased griddle till browned, about 6 to 8 minutes, turning once. Makes 4 servings.

SALAD OIL—Any one of several vegetable oils commonly used in making salad dressings. This type of oil is usually extracted from corn, olives, cottonseed, safflower seeds, soybeans, or peanuts.

After extraction, the oil is refined, bleached, and deodorized. Another process frequently used for salad oil is called winterizing. This consists of chilling the oil and then filtering out any crystals. If salad oil does not undergo winterizing, it will become cloudy if stored at refrigerator temperatures.

Besides its use in salad dressings, salad oil is used also in baked goods and for frying foods. In fact, salad oil can be used wherever vegetable oil or cooking oil is called for. (See also *Fat.*)

Rare Roast Beef Salad

1 1-pound T-bone steak, cut
1 inch thick
⅔ cup salad oil
1 teaspoon grated lemon peel
⅓ cup lemon juice
1 teaspoon Worcestershire sauce
1 teaspoon prepared mustard
½ teaspoon salt
• • •
4 ounces natural Swiss cheese,
cut in strips (1 cup)
¼ cup diced green pepper
2 tablespoons sliced green onion
6 cups torn romaine
Dash salt
Dash freshly ground pepper

Trim fat from steak. In screw-top jar combine oil, lemon peel and juice, Worcestershire sauce, mustard, and salt. Cover and shake vigorously to blend. Pour over steak in shallow baking dish. Cover; marinate 4 hours at room temperature or overnight in refrigerator. Drain off marinade; reserve for dressing. Broil steak 3 inches from heat to rare doneness, about 5 minutes per side; cool. Slice steak into thin strips; chill.

In salad bowl arrange steak strips, cheese strips, diced green pepper, and sliced onion over the 6 cups torn romaine. Toss with some of the reserved marinade, dash salt, and freshly ground pepper. Makes 4 servings.

Spiced Applesauce Bread

- 1¼ cups applesauce
- 1 cup granulated sugar
- ½ cup salad oil
- 2 eggs
- 3 tablespoons milk
- 2 cups sifted all-purpose flour
- 1 teaspoon baking soda
- ½ teaspoon baking powder
- 1 teaspoon ground cinnamon
- ¼ teaspoon *each* salt, ground nutmeg, and ground allspice
- ¾ cup chopped pecans
- ¼ cup brown sugar

Thoroughly combine first 5 ingredients. Sift together flour, baking soda, baking powder, ½ *teaspoon* cinnamon, salt, nutmeg, and allspice. Stir into applesauce mixture; beat well. Fold in ½ *cup* pecans; turn into well-greased 9x5x3-inch loaf pan. For topping, combine remaining pecans, brown sugar, and remaining cinnamon; sprinkle over batter. Bake at 350° for 1 hour. Remove from pan; cool on rack.

SALAMI (*suh lä′ mē*)—A highly seasoned sausage made of pork and usually beef. Two types of salami are commonly available—hard and soft. Hard salami is an air-dried sausage that will keep without refrigeration until it is cut. Fresh (soft) salami has not been dried and must be kept refrigerated. Differences in seasonings and the proportion of pork to beef account for the various kinds of salami such as Italian, Genoa, and cotto salami.

Use salami on appetizer trays, plates of cold cuts, and in hot dishes, especially Italian dishes. (See also *Sausage*.)

Salami–Cheese Salad

- 6 cups torn lettuce
- 1 cup sliced salami, cut in quarters
- 4 ounces natural Swiss cheese, cut in strips
- ½ cup sliced pitted ripe olives
- 3 tablespoons chopped canned pimiento
- 1 2-ounce can anchovy fillets, drained and chopped
- ⅓ cup salad oil
- 3 tablespoons wine vinegar
- ½ clove garlic, crushed

Combine lettuce, salami, cheese, olives, pimiento, and anchovies. In screw-top jar combine oil, vinegar, and garlic for dressing. Cover; shake well. Makes 8 servings.

Aladdin's Salad Bowl

- 4 cups torn lettuce
- 2 cups torn endive
- 1 4-ounce package sliced, jellied beef loaf, cut in strips
- 1 4-ounce package sliced salami, cut in strips
- 6 ounces sliced natural Muenster cheese, cut in strips
- 2 hard-cooked eggs, sliced
- ½ cup mayonnaise
- ¼ cup Russian salad dressing

Combine lettuce and endive in salad bowl. Arrange beef, salami, cheese, and egg slices atop greens. Season to taste with salt and pepper. Combine mayonnaise and Russian dressing. Serve with salad. Serves 4 to 6.

At left: Highly seasoned dry salami is great for snacking. Garlic is one of the predominant flavors in this chewy sausage, which is air-dried but not smoked.

At right: Scattered whole peppercorns and a mild garlic flavor distinguish cotto salami. This pork and beef sausage is both cooked and smoked during processing.

SALISBURY STEAK *(sôlz′ber′ē, -buh rē)* —
A mixture of ground beef formed into a
patty. This mixture often contains bread
or cracker crumbs, egg, onion, green pepper, and seasonings, and it may be served
with a sauce. The patty can be broiled,
panbroiled, or panfried. Salisbury steak
closely resembles a hamburger patty.

Salisbury Steak

>   1 beaten egg
>   ½ cup soft bread crumbs
>   ¼ cup finely chopped onion
>   2 tablespoons finely chopped
>   green pepper
>   1½ teaspoons salt
>   ¼ teaspoon pepper
>   2 pounds ground beef

Combine egg, crumbs, onion, green pepper,
salt, and pepper. Add the ground beef and mix
well. Shape into 6 patties, ¾ inch thick. Broil
3 inches from heat for 6 minutes. Turn and
broil 4 minutes longer. Makes 6 servings.

SALLY LUNN —A coffee cake-type bread
most often leavened with yeast; however,
baking powder is sometimes used in place
of the yeast. This bread may be baked in
a loaf pan, square pan, muffin pan, Turk's
head pan, or 10-inch tube pan. It is
especially delicious when served hot.

This coffee bread is said to have been
named after an eighteenth-century English woman by the name of Sally Lunn.
She baked and sold the bread in her tea-
shop, which was located in Bath, England.

Sally Lunn

Good for brunch or breakfast—

>   1 package active dry yeast
>   ¼ cup warm water
>   ¾ cup milk, scalded
>   3 tablespoons butter or margarine
>   3 tablespoons sugar
>   2 eggs
>   3½ cups sifted all-purpose flour
>   1¼ teaspoons salt

Soften yeast in warm water (110°). Cool milk
to lukewarm. Add to yeast mixture and set
aside. Cream butter and sugar. Add eggs, one
at a time, beating after each addition. Add
flour and salt to creamed mixture *alternately*
with yeast mixture, beating well after each addition. Beat till smooth. Cover; let rise in
warm place till double, about 1 hour.

Beat down and pour into a well-greased
Turk's head mold or a 10-inch tube pan. Let
the dough rise till double, about 30 minutes.
Bake at 350° till golden brown and crusty,
about 40 to 45 minutes. Serve hot.

SALMAGUNDI *(sal′muh gun′dē)* — 1. A medley or mixture of foods usually containing
chopped meat (often leftover) or fish,
vegetables, and eggs. 2. A salad made of
cooked meat served with mayonnaise or
salad dressing. The origin of the word
salmagundi is not known, although some
say it was named after a recipe prepared
by an eighteenth-century French chef,
Salmis De Gonde. Today, it is associated
with a number of mixed casserole dishes.

Salmagundi Bake

>   1 8-ounce can tomato sauce
>   ¾ cup uncooked long-grain rice
>   1 cup chopped onion
>   ½ cup chopped green pepper
>   1 teaspoon salt
>   Dash pepper
>   1 pound ground beef
>   1 teaspoon salt
>   1 12-ounce can whole kernel corn,
>   drained
>   1 to 2 teaspoons chili powder
>   1 8-ounce can tomato sauce

Combine 1 can tomato sauce, uncooked rice,
1 cup water, onion, green pepper, 1 teaspoon
salt, and pepper. Turn into a 2-quart casserole.
Layer uncooked beef on top. Sprinkle with 1
teaspoon salt. Evenly spread the drained corn
over beef. Add chili powder to 1 can tomato
sauce; pour mixture over corn.

Cover and bake at 375° for 1 hour. Uncover
and bake till rice is tender, about 10 minutes
longer. Garnish with crisp bacon curls, if
desired. Makes 6 to 8 servings.

SALMI *(sal′ mē)*—An elaborate dish of French origin made traditionally with wild game birds such as pheasant. After the bird is partially roasted, the meat is removed from the bones and cooked with truffles and mushrooms in a white wine sauce. The sauce can be prepared in a chafing dish at the table. The mixture is then served on bread spread with pate.

SALMON—A finfish that lives in the Pacific and Atlantic oceans and also in some freshwater lakes. It has an elongated body with a pointed snout. The word salmon comes from the Latin word *saline*, meaning to leap, which is exactly what salmon do as they make their way back to native streams for the spawning season.

From early times, salmon was important as a food to the American Indian, especially the Indians of the Pacific Northwest. Salmon is mentioned often in Indian legend as being symbolic of the whale in the biblical story of Jonah.

Early colonists and pioneers ate fresh salmon, too. In fact, many of these people settled in the New England area because of the abundance of salmon. Both the Indians and the colonists smoked the fish as a method of preserving it for use when the fish were not "in season." Since those early times, the waters along the East Coast have been overfished and polluted; consequently, salmon have become scarce along the Eastern seaboard.

Types of salmon: Because of the scarcity of Atlantic salmon, the majority of these food fish are found in the Pacific Ocean. The largest percent come from the Pacific Northwest—Alaska, Washington, and Oregon.

The following life cycle is true for all types of Pacific salmon. Prior to the spawning season, salmon courageously swim back to their native freshwater streams, often leaping up waterfalls and traveling several hundred miles. As they reach the mouth of the river where they spawn, the salmons' stomachs shrink and their throats narrow, which lessens their appetites. This makes the salmon flesh watery, soft, and light in color. Shortly after spawning, most of the adult Pacific salmon die, and only a small number of the newly hatched fish ever reach maturity. These salmon stay in the fresh water until they are old enough to migrate to the ocean, and then they repeat this cycle.

There are five major types of salmon—chinook, coho, sockeye, pink, and chum. The largest of these types, the chinook, is named after an Indian word meaning spring. It is also called the king salmon, probably because it averages between 20 and 25 pounds. The flesh of this fish is usually very red, but it can be almost white, especially at spawning time. The flesh of chinook salmon is firm.

Another type of salmon, the coho, is also called the silver salmon because of its silvery skin. The flesh of this type fades as it is cooked. Coho salmon average about nine pounds, but they can weigh up to 30 pounds.

One of the most familiar types of salmon to homemakers is the sockeye, also named the blueback or red salmon. The flesh is deep red, firm, sweet, and contains much oil. The sockeye averages between three and five pounds.

The pale-fleshed, pink or humpback salmon is the smallest salmon and weighs three to six pounds. It has a moderate amount of oil and breaks into small flakes.

The last type of Pacific salmon is the chum, keta, or dog salmon. It has the palest flesh with the least amount of oil of all the types. Chum salmon is used for canning and seafood dishes where color and texture are not important.

The salmon in the Atlantic Ocean average in weight from 10 to 20 pounds. Their life cycle is different from the Pacific salmon in that they survive several spawnings. The few salmon that are still taken from the Atlantic come mostly from the east coast of Canada and Maine. Nova Scotia salmon is considered a delicacy. The eastern salmon has a paler flesh.

The color of the different types varies from deep red to pale pink. These types, ranging from the deepest red to the lightest pink, are sockeye, chinook, coho, pink, and chum. The deeper red the color, the higher the oil content, and most often, the higher the price the fish will command.

Nutritional value: Salmon contains some sodium, calcium, phosphorus, iodine, vitamin A, and the B vitamins thiamine and riboflavin. The calcium content is higher if the skin, bones, and liquid are included when preparing canned salmon.

Salmon is a fat fish, and the fat is poly-unsaturated, the type recommended for low cholesterol diets. Salmon is also a good source of protein, which is greatly needed for body building.

As far as calories are concerned, one-half cup of canned chinook salmon equals 262 calories; one-half cup canned pink salmon equals 176 calories; and one-half cup canned sockeye equals 213 calories. A 3½-ounce uncooked portion of Atlantic salmon equals 217 calories; of chinook salmon equals 222 calories; and of pink salmon equals 119 calories. A 3½-ounce portion of smoked salmon has 176 calories.

How to select: Salmon comes in a variety of forms—smoked, salted, canned, fresh, and frozen. Whole fresh salmon should have the same general characteristics as any other fresh fish—firm flesh, fresh odor, bright and clear eyes, and shiny skin. Fresh fillets, steaks, and rounds should have a fresh-cut appearance and a fresh odor. Frozen fish have no odor.

Poached Salmon with Cucumber Sauce is a make-ahead main dish. Both salmon and sauce are chilled thoroughly before serving. Remember this tasty sauce to dress up canned salmon.

Canned salmon is identified by the name of the species. The grades from high to low are sockeye, chinook, coho, pink, and chum. Choose chinook and sockeye for salads, as they are deep in color and break into large flakes. Coho is also good for salads and creamed dishes. Pink and chum salmon break into small flakes and are tasty in salmon loaves, sandwiches, soups, and casseroles.

How to store: Keep frozen salmon solidly frozen and tightly wrapped in freezer until ready to use. It should be used within six months. Store fresh salmon in the refrigerator and use within a day or two after purchase. Store canned salmon on the shelf in a cool, dry place.

How to use: Since salmon is a fat fish, it can be prepared by any of the basic fish cooking methods—baking, broiling, frying, poaching, and steaming.

Fresh or frozen salmon lends itself to many elegant dishes. Poached salmon, for example, is excellent with a sauce.

Salmon with Cucumber Sauce

```
  1 quart water
1½ tablespoons salt
  2 tablespoons lemon juice
  6 fresh or frozen salmon steaks*
  1 unpeeled cucumber
½ cup dairy sour cream
¼ cup mayonnaise
  1 tablespoon minced parsley
  2 teaspoons grated onion
  2 teaspoons vinegar
¼ teaspoon salt
    Dash pepper
    Shredded lettuce
```

In large skillet bring water, 1½ tablespoons salt, and lemon juice to boiling. Add 3 salmon steaks. Simmer till fish flakes, 5 to 10 minutes. Remove steaks with slotted spatula. Repeat with remaining salmon in same cooking water. Chill salmon thoroughly.

Meanwhile, prepare cucumber sauce by shredding enough cucumber to make 1 cup (do not drain). Add remaining ingredients, except salmon and lettuce. Blend well. Chill.

Arrange salmon on a bed of shredded lettuce. Serve with lemon wedges, if desired, and cucumber sauce. Makes 6 servings.

*If using frozen salmon, thaw before cooking.

Salmon with Crab Sauce

```
  2 cups water
  2 lemon slices
½ teaspoon salt
½ teaspoon dillseed
  1 bay leaf
  2 12-ounce packages frozen salmon
    steaks (6 steaks), partially
    thawed
  1 cup chicken broth
  4 teaspoons cornstarch
¼ cup dairy sour cream
  2 tablespoons butter or margarine
    Dash ground nutmeg
  1 7½-ounce can crab meat, drained,
    flaked, and cartilage removed
```

In a large skillet combine water, lemon slices, salt, dillseed, and bay leaf; heat to boiling. Add salmon steaks and return to boiling. Reduce heat; simmer till salmon flakes easily when tested with a fork, 5 to 10 minutes.

Meanwhile, prepare crab sauce by gradually stirring cold broth into cornstarch in saucepan. Cook quickly, stirring constantly, till mixture is thick and bubbly. Cook 1 minute more. Then, remove from heat. Stir in sour cream, butter or margarine, and nutmeg; add crab meat. Heat through *but do not boil.*

Place salmon on warm serving platter. Serve with crab sauce. Makes 6 servings.

Dilled Salmon Steaks

Place 4 fresh or frozen salmon steaks in lightly greased baking dish (thaw steaks if they are frozen). Combine 2 tablespoons lemon juice and 2 teaspoons instant minced onion; sprinkle over salmon. Season with ½ teaspoon salt and dash pepper. Bake, uncovered, at 400° till fish flakes easily, about 15 to 20 minutes. Remove the fish from the oven.

Spread ¼ cup dairy sour cream over salmon. Sprinkle with 1 teaspoon grated lemon peel and ½ teaspoon dried dillweed. Return to oven; bake 3 minutes longer. Makes 4 servings.

Salmon Steaks

     4 fresh or frozen salmon steaks,
        1 inch thick
    1/3 cup butter, melted
     1 teaspoon Worcestershire sauce
     1 teaspoon grated onion
    1/4 teaspoon paprika

Place steaks in shallow baking pan (thaw frozen steaks). Blend remaining ingredients; brush some lightly on salmon. Sprinkle with salt. Bake at 350° till fish flakes easily, about 25 minutes. Pass remaining sauce. Serves 4.

Grilled Salmon Steaks

    1/2 cup salad oil
    1/4 cup snipped parsley
    1/4 cup lemon juice
     2 tablespoons grated onion
    1/2 teaspoon dry mustard
    1/4 teaspoon salt
        Dash pepper
     6 fresh or frozen salmon steaks

Combine oil, parsley, lemon juice, onion, mustard, salt, and pepper. Mix well. Place salmon steaks in shallow dish (thaw steaks if frozen). Pour on marinade mixture. Let stand at room temperature for 2 hours, turning occasionally. (Or marinate in refrigerator for 4 to 6 hours.) Drain, reserving marinade.

Place fish in greased, wire broiler basket. Broil over *medium-hot* coals till slightly brown, about 8 to 10 minutes. Baste with marinade and turn carefully. Brush again with marinade. Broil till fish flakes easily with a fork, about 8 to 10 minutes longer. Makes 6 servings.

Canned salmon adds variety to the menu because it can be used for many different types of dishes, from salads that are cold to piping-hot casserole dishes.

Fancy enough for a bridge luncheon

← A perky lemon twist and curly endive trim Salmon-Avocado Mold, which is frosted with an avocado-sour cream mixture.

Salmon-Avocado Mold

     1 envelope unflavored gelatin
        (1 tablespoon)
     2 tablespoons sugar
     1 tablespoon lemon juice
     1 tablespoon vinegar
     2 teaspoons grated onion
    1/2 teaspoon prepared horseradish
     1 16-ounce can salmon, drained
        and flaked
    1/2 cup mayonnaise
    1/3 cup sliced pitted ripe olives
    1/4 cup finely chopped celery
     1 large avocado
    1/2 cup dairy sour cream

In saucepan soften gelatin in 1 cup cold water. Stir over low heat till gelatin is completely dissolved. Stir in sugar, lemon juice, vinegar, onion, 1/2 teaspoon salt, and horseradish. Chill till the mixture is partially set.

Fold in flaked salmon, mayonnaise, olives, and celery. Spoon into a 3½-cup mold; chill till the gelatin mixture is firm.

To prepare avocado dressing, peel and mash avocado. Blend the mashed avocado (about 2/3 cup), sour cream, and 1/2 teaspoon salt. Chill. Unmold salmon salad onto serving platter. Spread avocado dressing mixture evenly over outside of salad. If desired, garnish with curly endive and lemon twist. Serves 4.

Salmon-Filled Tomatoes

     6 medium tomatoes
     1 16-ounce can salmon, drained and
        broken into small chunks
    1½ cups diced, peeled cucumber
    1/2 cup mayonnaise
     1 tablespoon chopped onion
     1 tablespoon chopped, canned
        pimiento
        Lettuce

Scoop out centers of tomatoes. Invert; chill. Combine salmon, cucumber, mayonnaise, onion, pimiento, 1/4 teaspoon salt, and dash pepper. Chill the salad mixture thoroughly.

Just before serving, sprinkle insides of tomatoes with salt. Spoon chilled salmon mixture into tomato cavities. Serve on lettuce-lined plates. Makes 6 servings.

For something special, serve smoked salmon on black bread or pumpernickel and accompany with cucumber slices and lemon wedges.

Salmon and Potato Chip Casserole

An easy main dish to fix when there are a large number of people to serve—

- ½ cup butter or margarine
- 1 large onion, chopped (1 cup)
- ¼ cup all-purpose flour
- 5 10½-ounce cans condensed cream of mushroom soup
- 4 cups milk

• • •

- 1¼ pounds potato chips, coarsely crushed (12 cups)
- 5 16-ounce cans salmon, drained and flaked
- 2 10-ounce packages frozen peas, cooked and drained

In a 3-quart saucepan melt butter; add onion and cook till tender but not brown. Blend in flour, stirring till bubbly. Stir in soup. Gradually add milk, stirring till smooth. Set aside about *2 cups* crushed potato chips. In two 13x 9x2-inch metal baking pans, layer the remaining potato chips, salmon, peas, and the soup mixture alternately. Sprinkle reserved chips over top. Bake at 350° till heated through, about 40 to 45 minutes. Makes 25 servings.

Salmon Loaf

- 1 beaten egg
- ½ cup milk
- 2 cups soft bread crumbs (about 3 slices)
- 1 tablespoon butter, melted
- 1 tablespoon chopped onion
- ½ teaspoon salt
- 1 16-ounce can salmon, drained and flaked

• • •

- Piquant Sauce

In a bowl combine egg, milk, soft bread crumbs, melted butter, chopped onion, and salt; add salmon; mix thoroughly. Shape into a loaf on a greased shallow baking pan or in a 7½x3¾x 2¼-inch loaf pan. Bake at 350° for 35 to 40 minutes. Serve with Piquant Sauce or creamed peas. Makes 3 or 4 servings.

Piquant Sauce: Cook 2 tablespoons chopped green onion in 3 tablespoons butter or margarine till onion is tender but not brown. Blend in 2 tablespoons all-purpose flour, ½ teaspoon dry mustard, ½ teaspoon salt, and dash pepper. Add 1¼ cups milk and 1 teaspoon Worcestershire sauce. Cook, stirring constantly, till the sauce thickens and bubbles.

Salmon Balls in Caper Sauce

Drain one 16-ounce can salmon, reserving liquid; flake salmon. In a bowl combine 2 beaten eggs, 1 cup soft bread crumbs (about 1½ slices), 2 tablespoons snipped parsley, 1 tablespoon grated onion, ½ teaspoon salt, ½ teaspoon grated lemon peel, 2 teaspoons lemon juice, and dash pepper. Mix ingredients. Shape into 8 balls; place in a medium skillet.

Combine ½ cup dry white wine and reserved salmon liquid. Add water to make 2 cups liquid. Pour over salmon balls. Heat to boiling. Reduce heat; cover and simmer 10 minutes. Remove the salmon balls to serving dish.

Combine 2 tablespoons softened butter or margarine and 2 tablespoons all-purpose flour. Stir into hot liquid. Cook and stir over high heat till the mixture thickens and bubbles. Stir in ½ cup light cream, 1 tablespoon snipped parsley, and 1 tablespoon capers, drained. Heat the mixture to boiling. Serve the sauce over cooked salmon balls. Makes 4 servings.

Salmon Roll-Ups

> 1 7¾-ounce can salmon, drained and flaked
> 1 beaten egg
> 1 teaspoon dried parsley flakes
> 1 teaspoon instant minced onion
> ½ teaspoon dried dillweed
> 1 8-ounce package refrigerated crescent rolls (8 rolls)
>
> •   •   •
>
> 2 tablespoons butter or margarine
> 2 tablespoons all-purpose flour
> ½ teaspoon salt
> Dash pepper
> 1 cup milk
> 2 ounces sharp process American cheese, shredded (½ cup)
> 2 beaten egg yolks
> 1 tablespoon lemon juice

Combine salmon, egg, parsley, onion, and dillweed. Separate crescent rolls and spread each with about 1 tablespoon of the salmon mixture. Roll up from wide end. Bake on baking sheet at 375° for 12 to 15 minutes.

Serve with Cheese Sauce. In saucepan melt butter; blend in flour, salt, and pepper. Add milk; cook and stir until thickened and bubbly. Stir in cheese, egg yolks, and lemon juice; heat till cheese melts. Makes 4 servings.

Salmon Tetrazzini

Cook 4 ounces spaghetti according to package directions; drain. Meanwhile, drain one 16-ounce can salmon, reserving liquid. Add milk to salmon liquid to make 2 cups. Break salmon into large pieces; set aside.

Melt 2 tablespoons butter or margarine in a saucepan. Blend in 2 tablespoons all-purpose flour, ¼ teaspoon salt, dash pepper, and dash ground nutmeg. Add salmon liquid and milk all at once. Cook over medium heat, stirring constantly, till mixture is thickened and bubbly. Add 2 tablespoons dry red wine.

Stir in cooked spaghetti; one 3-ounce can sliced mushrooms, drained; and salmon pieces. Turn into 1-quart casserole. Combine 2 tablespoons fine dry bread crumbs and 2 tablespoons grated Parmesan cheese. Sprinkle cheese-crumb mixture over top. Bake at 350° for 35 to 40 minutes. Makes 6 servings.

Salmon Casserole

Cook ¼ cup chopped onion and ¼ cup chopped celery in 1 tablespoon butter till tender. Blend cooked vegetables with one 7¾-ounce can salmon, flaked (with liquid); one 10½-ounce can condensed cream of mushroom soup; ½ cup shredded sharp process American cheese; and 2 cups cooked rice. Turn the mixture into a 1-quart casserole. Sprinkle ½ cup buttered soft bread crumbs atop. Bake at 350° for about 30 minutes. Makes 4 servings.

Smoked salmon is available in slices that make delicious main dishes, appetizers, and sandwiches. Cured and smoked red salmon is sometimes referred to as lox, a Jewish favorite served with bagels and cream cheese. (See also *Fish.*)

SALMONBERRY—A type of wild raspberry, also called cloudberry, that grows in the Pacific Northwest. (See also *Raspberry.*)

SALMONELLA—A family of bacteria that causes food poisoning, especially in eggs, poultry, milk, fish, and other animal products. The organisms can be destroyed if heated above 165°. (See also *Food Poisoning.*)

SALMON TROUT—Another name for a steelhead salmon. Although it looks like a salmon, this fish is a large trout. It lives in fresh water. (See also *Trout.*)

SALSA *(säl′suh)*—The Italian and Spanish word for sauce or condiment.

SALSIFY—A root vegetable sometimes called oyster plant or vegetable oyster. The root, the part usually eaten, has a mild, oysterlike flavor and the shape of a carrot. It grows up to 10 inches long and is about 2 inches across at the top. Native to Europe, salsify is more popular there than it is in the United States.

When salisfy is prepared, it discolors readily, so keep it in water with some type of acid, such as lemon juice. Serve salsify boiled, mashed, riced, or sauced. It can also be cooked, then marinated and served cold. (See also *Vegetable.*)

SALT—1. The household name for sodium chloride (white, granular substance). **2.** To season a food or to preserve meat and fish with salt.

Undoubtedly one of the most important chemical substances known to man, salt is used in cooking primarily as a seasoning and as a preservative for meat and fish. It is also necessary to the diet.

Salt was especially important for preserving foods prior to the advent of refrigeration. It was used to preserve meats for long periods, such as on sailing voyages. Rich and poor alike kept a salt larder—or ate spoiled meat.

Until modern-day mining techniques were developed, the tiny crystals that you sprinkle liberally on your food were an expensive commodity. In fact, the word salary stems from the Latin *salarium*, the monetary allowance that was given to Roman soldiers to buy salt. Salt's importance can be seen, too, in its use in food terms: salad comes from the Latin *salada*, a dish of salted vegetables; and sauce comes from the Latin *salsus*, a salty seasoning, which, by common usage, became sausage.

It's not too difficult to see that when someone was "not worth his salt," he wasn't regarded too highly by others.

How salt is produced: Originally, salt was an impure product, often mixed with other materials. Now, it is available in various qualities and grades for both table and commercial uses. Salt is made by evaporating a concentrated brine (water with a high concentration of salt), or by mining underground rock salt. It is then cleaned, purified, ground, sieved, and graded before it is put on the market.

Types of salt: There are various forms of cooking salt: regular or iodized table salt, or salt flavored with garlic, celery, onion, hickory, or a mixture of seasonings. You can also buy coarse salt, or Kosher salt, which has large crystals, absorbs moisture slowly, and will not cake easily when introduced to moisture; and the familiar rock salt used for freezing homemade ice cream or for cooking some types of shellfish on the half shell.

Nutritional value: Salt is important to the body, for it regulates the water and nutrients that pass in and out of the body tissues. Salt also helps in the digestion of food. In the stomach, chloride from the salt changes into hydrochloric acid, which is a vital part of the digestive juices. In addition, iodized salt is a major source of iodide in areas where the soil and water content of this nutrient are low. This mineral prevents goiter.

Normally, the food consumed each day provides an adequate supply of salt. Occasionally, however, in cases where there is excessive perspiration due to extreme heat, it may be necessary to take salt tablets to replace the salt lost by the body. However, this is more the exception than a common occurrence.

How to use: The principal uses for table salt or flavored salts in cookery are to add flavor to many foods and to bring out the basic flavor in others. Unless special diet restrictions prohibit the use of salt, add it with discretion. Salting with a heavy hand makes food taste of salt. On the other hand, salting too lightly can cause the food to taste insipid.

Flavored salts add a delightful flavor to a variety of foods. In this recipe, onion salt is added to a jiffy bread.

Crescent Roll-Ups

Unroll one package refrigerated crescent rolls (8 rolls) and separate; spread with ½ cup dairy sour cream and sprinkle with ½ teaspoon onion salt. Cook ½ pound bacon till crisp; drain and crumble. Sprinkle over sour cream. Cut each roll lengthwise into 3 equal wedges. Roll up each wedge, starting at point of wedge. Place on greased baking sheet. Bake at 375° till golden brown, about 12 to 15 minutes. Serve warm as appetizers. Makes 24.

Follow recipe directions carefully when adding salt to foods. For example, salt sprinkled on meat that is broiled or panfried causes juices to flow, making the cooked meat a bit dry. Therefore, season the meat after it is browned.

Not only does salt add flavor, but it has additional functions. In yeast breads it restrains a too-rapid growth of the yeast. Salt is also used to pickle and preserve foods such as hams and cucumbers.

Several other types of salt have cooking functions, too. Coarse salt is often sprinkled on bread sticks. Because the crystals absorb moisture so slowly, they will remain in crystals on the top of the bread stick. Rock salt, a coarser type, is used in the preparation of oysters and clams on the half shell. It helps balance the shells during baking. Rock salt is also necessary in the freezing process for homemade ice cream.

Homemade Strawberry Ice Cream

    2 3¾- or 3⅝-ounce packages
        instant vanilla pudding mix
    4 eggs
    ½ cup sugar
    2 cups whipping cream
    4 10-ounce packages frozen
        strawberries, thawed
    1 teaspoon vanilla
    ½ teaspoon red food coloring
        • • •
    Crushed ice
    Rock salt

Prepare pudding following package directions; chill till set. Beat eggs till light and fluffy. Beat in sugar, cream, and pudding. Stir in strawberries, vanilla, and food coloring.

Pour mixture into freezer can, filling only ⅔ full. Adjust dasher and cover. Fit can into freezer. (If using electric ice cream freezer, follow manufacturer's directions.) Pack ice and salt around can, using 6 parts ice to 1 part rock salt. Turn dasher slowly till ice partially melts and forms a brine. Add more ice and salt, as needed. Turn handle constantly till crank turns hard. Remove ice to below lid of can; remove lid and dasher.

To ripen ice cream, plug opening in lid. Cover can with several thicknesses of waxed paper or foil for tight fit; replace lid. Pack more ice and salt (use 4 parts ice to 1 part salt) around can to fill freezer. Cover freezer with heavy cloth or newspapers. Let ice cream ripen about 4 hours. Makes about 2 quarts.

SALT COD—A cod fish that has been split, salted, and dried. (See also *Cod.*)

SALT FISH—Fish that has been preserved by dry-salting or by being put into a salted brine. Salting fish is a technique that has been used since ancient times to prevent fish from spoiling.

Varieties of fish that are commonly salted include cod, bloaters, and herring. The salt must be removed from the fish before it is cooked. The most common procedure for removing the salt is soaking the fish in water for several hours. The water should be changed several times. Then, the fish can be used in entrees and casseroles. (See also *Fish.*)

SALTIMBOCCA *(säl′ tim bôk′ uh)*—An Italian dish consisting of thin slices of ham and veal rolled up around cheese, then cooked in butter in a skillet.

SALT PORK—A thick, fat portion of pork from the belly of the pig that is cured with dry salt. Salt pork is almost all fat, occasionally streaked with lean.

It is used to flavor baked beans and vegetables. Crisp, fried salt pork is frequently an ingredient in chowders. Occasionally, you will find salt pork baked or panfried for a main dish. (See also *Pork.*)

SALT-RISING BREAD—An old-fashioned raised bread that is made without yeast. A mixture of salt, sugar, milk, and sometimes cornmeal is allowed to stand in a warm place until fermentation begins. This leavens the bread.

SALT STICK—A white or rye roll that is shaped like a thick pencil, generously covered with coarse salt crystals.

SAND DAB—A saltwater flatfish related to the flounder. Sand dabs are usually associated with the Pacific Coast; however, small ones are found on the East Coast.

Sand dabs are commonly available fresh near the source of supply. These lean, delicately flavored fish are cooked by boiling, steaming, or frying. They can be baked or broiled if extra butter or a sauce is added. (See also *Flounder.*)

SANDWICH

How to combine breads and fillings to create
unique sandwiches for everyday or party fare.

There's hardly a person alive who is not familiar with a variety of sandwich combinations. To some people the word sandwich brings fond memories of peanut butter and jelly spread on bread, while to others it conjures up the thought of mustard-slathered ham and cheese on rye or a flavorful tuna salad sandwich with a crisp piece of lettuce. But no matter how you stack it, a sandwich always has certain basic ingredients—one, two, or more slices of bread (sometimes buttered, sometimes unbuttered) or rolls or buns, plus a filling or well-seasoned spread. As a matter of fact, a sandwich can be almost any food served on or between slices of bread or on or in rolls.

A sandwich can be a meal-in-one such as the heroes, poor boys, or grinders, or a dainty tea sandwich. It can be hot or cold. It can be a finger food or one that necessitates the use of a knife and fork.

Regardless of the combination, sandwiches are internationally popular. In fact, they have become a part of everyday cooking because of their convenience, the food value they contribute to the diet, and because they are an outlet for the creativity of the modern-day homemaker.

Because of the countless variations of sandwiches that are made, it is rather difficult to trace the history of sandwiches. It is said that people of ancient times used their unleavened bread as a wrapper or liner for other foods, similar to today's open-faced sandwich.

He-man sandwich

← Start with a loaf of unsliced bread to make Dilly Beef Cartwheel (see *Beef* for recipe). Then, slice sandwich into separate wedges.

Some authorities say that during pre-Christian times an unleavened wafer spread with honey was eaten by the high priests, and that Rabbi Hillel, the Jewish teacher, invented the custom of eating a sandwich of matzoh spread with bitter herbs. However, the most familiar story credits an Englishman, John Montague, the Fourth Earl of Sandwich, with the invention of the sandwich. It is said that he liked to gamble, and that one day he decided that he would eat while at the gaming tables. He needed a food that could be held in one hand while he continued playing with the other hand. His "sandwich" consisted of a piece of meat between two pieces of bread.

Fellow gamblers began following his example, and the sandwich was popularized and named after the Earl. This was in the eighteenth century. Since then, sandwiches have become common fare.

Basic ingredients: The essential ingredients of a sandwich are bread, sometimes butter, margarine, or salad dressing, and a filling. Other ingredients, such as lettuce and tomato, can also be added for flavor and texture.

Don't discount the importance of bread in a sandwich because it makes up about two-thirds of most sandwiches. Use fresh bread for sandwiches and don't forget to vary the bread you use. Granted, the most popular is the old standby, white bread; however, there are countless other types of breads and rolls that make the perfect base for the sandwiches you prepare. Choose from whole wheat, cracked wheat, light or dark rye, pumpernickel, sourdough, poppy seed, oatmeal, cheese, onion, nut breads, and fruit loaves. For variety, use hamburger or frankfurter buns, English muffins, French or Italian rolls or bread, and the other types of buns, rolls, and biscuits on the bakery shelf.

If possible, leave the crusts on sliced bread to prevent the sandwich from drying out. Exceptions to this are some of the fancy tea and party sandwiches from which crusts are trimmed off for appearance purposes. When using toasted bread for sandwiches, make sure it's fresh and warm. Toast seems to toughen as it cools.

The next ingredient is butter or margarine. Have the butter softened before you begin making sandwiches. Use a flexible spatula or blunt knife for spreading to avoid tearing the bread. Spread the butter to the edges of the slices. Hit a happy medium between too thin and too heavy a spreading. The butter will keep soft fillings from soaking in, yet avoid any dry bites. For a variation, add flavoring to the butter, such as mustard, garlic, or horseradish. In place of the butter, some people prefer to use mayonnaise or salad dressing. The choice is yours.

Now, you're ready for the filling. You'll find that the combinations for sandwich fillings are almost limitless. This is where the homemaker can let her imagination run loose to create a masterpiece.

There are a few points about fillings to keep in mind, however. Keep juicy fillings, jellies, and the like for sandwiches that are going to be eaten before the bread has a chance to become soggy. Also, when choosing meat for the filling, slice the meat paper-thin and stack four or five slices deep. The sandwich will be easier to bite through than if one thick slice is used. Season salad-type mixtures to taste and add salad dressing or mayonnaise to achieve desired consistency. Fillings should be moist, but should not squeeze out between the bread slices.

In addition to homemade fillings, there are many prepared fillings and spreads on the market. Meat spreads and cream cheese spreads are examples of these.

There are also a variety of additional ingredients available to make sandwiches more appealing. A leaf or two of lettuce adds a bit of crispness to a sandwich, while a slice of tomato adds both a flavor note and a touch of color. A slice of pickle also can be added to a sandwich both for its flavor and for its crisp texture. Add these types of ingredients just before eating the sandwich to keep them crisp and fresh and to prevent the bread from becoming soggy. For lunch boxes or picnics, carry these ingredients separately and add at the last minute.

Nutritional value: Because of its component parts, a sandwich is a very nutritious food. Enriched breads contribute B vitamins and iron to the diet. Bread also contains small amounts of calcium and protein. One slice of enriched white bread contains about 62 calories.

Butter, in addition to contributing calories, adds needed fat to the diet. One tablespoon furnishes 100 calories.

Fillings can also add important nutrients to the diet. Meat, poultry, egg, cheese, and peanut butter fillings contribute protein, vitamins, and minerals.

Preparation: To make batches of sandwiches in a hurry, set up an assembly line for easy preparation. Have the fillings ready before you begin and have the butter softened, ready to spread. Line up slices of bread in pairs, side by side, on a cutting surface. Spread all the bread slices with butter out to the edges. Then top alternate slices of bread with the filling. Make all of one type of sandwich at one time, cut (see suggestions in box on page 1972), and wrap individually, sealing well to keep sandwiches fresh.

Storing and freezing: If circumstances prevent you from preparing sandwiches just before they are eaten, you can make them up ahead of time, wrap them well, and refrigerate or freeze till they are needed. When refrigerating sandwiches, wrap in waxed paper, then cover with a dampened towel to keep them moist.

A meal in a sandwich

Deviled ham, cheese, and tomato go into the →
makings for easy Triple-Layered Sandwiches. Add an apple or orange for dessert.

When time permits, make a batch of sandwiches at one time and store them in the freezer. This way you can make good use of leftover meat and poultry that you may have on hand. Spread fresh bread with butter or margarine rather than mayonnaise or salad dressings, since these products tend to separate when frozen. Wrap and tightly seal each sandwich in a moisture-vaporproof material such as clear plastic wrap, foil, or small plastic bags suited for sandwiches. Label with contents and date, then freeze. You can freeze sandwiches up to two weeks.

Take wrapped sandwiches from the freezer in the morning when it's time to tote them, and they'll be thawed and right for eating at lunchtime. Eat them immediately after they are unwrapped because the bread dries out quickly after it has been frozen and thawed.

Sandwiches that freeze best include hard-cooked egg yolk, sliced or ground meat and poultry, tuna or salmon, and peanut butter. Those fillings not recommended for freezing include cheeses (except blue cheese), lettuce, celery, tomatoes, cucumbers, parsley, watercress, white of hard-cooked eggs, and jelly. Avoid very moist fillings that are made with mayonnaise or salad dressing.

Ways to cut a sandwich

- Since smaller sandwich pieces are easier to handle, cut sandwiches into halves, quarters, or thirds. Use a sharp or serrated, long-bladed knife for quick and easy cutting. Stack two or three and cut all at once.

- Cut sandwich crosswise and lengthwise, making four quarters. Or make four triangles by cutting diagonally.

- Cut diagonally forming two triangles.

- Cut sandwich in thirds, either crosswise, diagonally, or into pie-shaped pieces. Or slice the sandwich in half, either lengthwise or diagonally, and cut one of the halves in half, making three smaller sandwiches.

Types of sandwiches

Sandwiches come in cold or hot versions. Some, such as the open-faced sandwiches of Denmark, a three-decker club sandwich, or a hero sandwich by any of its names, are large enough to be the entire main course. Main dish hot sandwiches include hot, sliced meat in gravy, a scrambled egg sandwich called a Denver or Western, and poultry in cream sauce spooned over a slice of toast. Then, there are the dainty, chilled sandwiches for a tea party or an appetizer buffet.

Cold sandwiches: The open-faced sandwich is good to fix when counting calories. By eliminating the extra slice of bread, you trim some calories. But, when piled high with ingredients, it can satisfy the heartiest appetites.

Fruit Wheels

2 bagels, split and toasted
1 tablespoon cream cheese
Ground cinnamon
Thin peach slices
Thin honeydew melon slices
Thin banana slices

Spread bagel halves thinly with cream cheese; sprinkle with ground cinnamon. Arrange fruit slices atop each. Makes 4 sandwiches.

Garden Cottage Cheese Sandwiches

1½ cups small curd cream-style
cottage cheese
½ cup diced celery
¼ cup shredded carrot
¼ cup chopped radish
½ teaspoon caraway seed
6 slices thinly sliced white
bread
Butter or margarine, softened
Lettuce

Mash cottage cheese with fork; stir in vegetables and caraway. Chill. Butter bread; top with lettuce. Spread about ⅓ cup cottage cheese mixture atop lettuce. Serves 6.

Tuna Open-Facer

A sandwich especially suited for dieters—

- 1 6½-ounce can dietetic-pack tuna, drained
- ½ cup coarsely grated cabbage
- ¼ cup coarsely grated carrot
- 1 tablespoon sliced green onion
- ⅓ cup low-calorie mayonnaise-type dressing
- 1 tablespoon catsup
- 1 tablespoon lemon juice
- ½ teaspoon seasoned salt
  Dash pepper
- 4 lettuce leaves
- 2 hamburger buns, split and toasted

Break tuna in chunks; combine with cabbage, carrot, and onion. Blend together low-calorie mayonnaise, catsup, lemon juice, seasoned salt, and pepper; add to tuna mixture and toss lightly. Place 1 lettuce leaf on each toasted bun half; spoon tuna salad mixture on top of the lettuce leaves. Makes 4 servings.

Open-Face Sandwich Supreme

Hearty sandwich for a big appetite—

- ½ cup mayonnaise or salad dressing
- ½ cup catsup
- ¼ cup pickle relish
- 2 tablespoons prepared mustard
- 1 tablespoon milk
- 4 slices rye bread
  Butter or margarine, softened
  Leaf lettuce
- 4 ounces brick or provolone cheese (4 slices)
- 8 thin slices cooked roast beef
  Tomato slices
- 2 hard-cooked eggs, sliced
  Bacon curls

Combine mayonnaise, catsup, pickle relish, mustard, and milk. Spread bread with butter. Top with lettuce, cheese, roast beef, and tomato slices. Spoon ¼ cup of the mayonnaise mixture over each; garnish with egg slices and bacon curls. Pass additional dressing. Serves 4.

┌─────────────────────────────┐

❊MENU❊

LOW-CALORIE LUNCHEON
Fresh Fruit Cup
Tuna Open-Facer
Baked Custard
Coffee   Skim Milk

└─────────────────────────────┘

Cold sandwiches with two or more slices of bread make filling lunchtime entrées. And unsliced loaves of French bread an impressive luncheon main dish.

Triple-Layered Sandwiches

- 1 4½-ounce can deviled ham
- 2 tablespoons pickle relish
- 2 tablespoons finely chopped green pepper
- 12 slices whole wheat bread
  Mayonnaise or salad dressing
- 8 tomato slices
- 4 slices mozzarella cheese

Combine first 3 ingredients. Lightly spread 4 slices bread with mayonnaise; spread each with ham. Top each with another slice bread; spread lightly with mayonnaise. Add tomato and cheese. Dot with mayonnaise; top with remaining bread. Halve; secure with wooden picks. Makes 4.

Fish Salad Club Sandwich

Cook one 16-ounce package frozen perch; flake cooked fish (2 cups). Combine perch with ½ cup chopped celery, ½ cup bottled tartar sauce, and ¼ teaspoon salt. Chill. Spread 18 slices toasted bread with softened butter.

Spread about ⅓ cup perch mixture on each of 6 slices toast. Top each with second slice of toast; place lettuce and tomato slices atop. Cover with third slice of toast. Secure with wooden picks and cut sandwich diagonally into quarters. Makes 6 sandwiches.

Quick Cold Sandwich Ideas

Add avocado slices to bacon, lettuce, and tomato sandwiches. Serve open-face with Thousand Island dressing; homemade or bottled.

Add coleslaw with a little prepared mustard to corned beef on rye sandwiches.

Blend softened cream cheese with orange marmalade, cranberry jelly, or crushed pineapple. Spread the mixture on nut bread.

Combine 1 cup chopped cooked chicken or turkey, 1/3 cup well-drained crushed pineapple, 1/3 cup mayonnaise or salad dressing, 2 tablespoons chopped walnuts, and dash salt.

Blend softened cream cheese with chopped pimiento-stuffed green olives or finely chopped candied ginger. Also a good celery stuffer.

Spread some peanut butter on buttered bread slices. Add crumbled cooked bacon, jelly, pickle slices, or thin slices of banana.

Arrange thinly sliced onion or pickle on buttered bread. Spoon a mixture of baked beans and chili sauce atop the onion or pickle.

Arrange thinly sliced radishes on buttered whole wheat or rye bread.

Mix flaked tuna, crab, or lobster with finely chopped celery and blend with mayonnaise.

Moisten sardines and chopped hard-cooked egg with a little lemon juice.

Layer liverwurst, lettuce, and sliced tomato on buttered whole wheat or white bread.

Chop hard-cooked eggs and pimiento-stuffed green olives. Add mayonnaise to moisten. Spread on rye bread and add a leaf of lettuce.

Mix diced cooked chicken, chopped celery, and chopped sweet pickle with mayonnaise.

Mix cottage cheese, finely chopped onion and green pepper, salt, and paprika.

Spread Russian rye bread with mustard sauce. Top with liver sausage and Swiss cheese.

Golden Gate Salad Loaf

 1 unsliced loaf French bread
   Butter or margarine, softened
 1 1/2-pound piece bologna, cut in
   1/2-inch cubes (2 cups)
1/2 cup sliced radishes
1/3 cup mayonnaise
1/4 cup pickle relish
   Dash pepper
 2 cups shredded lettuce

Cut French bread in half lengthwise; wrap top half and store for later use. Cut thin slice off bottom of remaining half to make it sit flat. Scoop out center to make slight hollow; spread inside with softened butter.

Combine bologna and radishes. Blend together mayonnaise, relish, and pepper. Add to bologna mixture; toss lightly. Place shredded lettuce in bottom of hollow; spoon bologna mixture over. Garnish with radishes and sweet pickle slices, if desired. Makes 6 servings.

Shrimp Boat

 3 cups cooked, cleaned shrimp
 1 cup diced celery
 4 hard-cooked eggs, chopped
1/3 cup sliced green onion
1/4 cup chopped dill pickle
 2 tablespoons drained capers
   (optional)
 1 cup mayonnaise
 2 tablespoons chili sauce
 2 teaspoons prepared horseradish
 1 teaspoon salt
 1 loaf Vienna bread (11x5 inches)
   Butter or margarine, melted
   Lettuce

Reserve a few large shrimp for garnish; cut up remainder. Combine first 6 ingredients. Blend mayonnaise and next 3 ingredients. Add to shrimp mixture and toss lightly. Chill.

Meanwhile, cut a large, deep wedge out of Vienna loaf to make "boat." Brush the cut surfaces with melted butter. Place loaf on *ungreased* baking sheet. Toast at 350° till lightly browned, 15 minutes. Cool before filling.

Line bread with lettuce; mound with shrimp salad. Trim with whole shrimp. If desired, pass lemon wedges. Cut in 6 to 8 slices.

Hot sandwiches: Perhaps the hamburger or frankfurter (coney) sandwich is at the top of your favorite hot sandwich list. With the addition of a few ingredients, a hamburger is turned into gourmet fare. Grilled sandwiches and the king-sized sandwiches served on a loaf of French bread are also treats for large appetites.

Tangy Kraut Burger

1½ pounds ground beef
  1 8-ounce can sauerkraut, drained and snipped
  ¼ cup Italian salad dressing
  1 tablespoon instant minced onion
  ½ teaspoon caraway seed
  ¼ teaspoon salt
  6 hamburger buns, split and toasted

Combine ground beef, sauerkraut, dressing, onion, caraway, and salt. Shape into 6 patties, ¾ inch thick. Broil 3 inches from heat for 6 minutes. Turn; broil 6 to 8 minutes longer. Serve in buns. (Top burgers with hot sauerkraut, if desired.) Makes 6 sandwiches.

Quick Hot Sandwich Ideas

Spread French bread slices with butter or margarine and prepared mustard. Spoon on baked beans and top with shredded sharp process American cheese. Broil till cheese melts.

Spread 2 tablespoons seasoned ground beef on sliced bread. Broil about 3 minutes.

Scramble eggs with finely chopped onion, chopped green pepper, and diced ham. Serve the scrambled eggs on toast.

Before forming hamburger patties, spark ground beef with one or more of the following ingredients: Worcestershire sauce, chopped onion, chopped green pepper, soy sauce and ginger, mustard, catsup, pickle relish, barbecue sauce, or prepared horseradish.

Toast bread on one side. Top untoasted side with cheese and tomato slices. Broil to melt cheese. Top with a cooked bacon slice or two.

Hot Dog Burgers

  1 pound ground beef
  ⅓ cup evaporated milk
  3 frankfurters, halved lengthwise
  3 frankfurter buns, split, toasted, and buttered

Combine beef, 1 teaspoon salt, dash pepper, and milk. Shape into 6 flat rectangles the size of buns. Press half of a frank into each burger. Broil 3 inches from heat, 8 to 10 minutes; turn once. Serve in buns. Serves 6.

Besides ground beef, there are other ingredients that make great hot sandwiches. Grilled cheese and oven or broiled seafood sandwiches are always popular. Or how about a breakfast main dish made with corn bread and sausage links?

Breakfast Corn Bread Stacks

Prepare one 10-ounce package corn bread mix following package directions. Cut into 6 servings; keep warm. Cook one 8-ounce package brown-and-serve sausage links following package directions. Split lengthwise; keep warm.

In saucepan combine ¼ cup sugar, 2 tablespoons cornstarch, and ⅛ teaspoon salt; stir in 1½ cups orange juice. Cook and stir till thickened and bubbly. Remove from heat; stir in 2 tablespoons butter and 1 orange, peeled and sectioned. Split corn bread in half lengthwise. Layer bottom halves with sausage and a little orange sauce. Replace tops. Spoon sauce over each serving. Serve warm. Serves 6.

❧MENU❧

LAZY SATURDAY BREAKFAST
Pineapple-Grapefruit Drink
Breakfast Corn Bread Stacks
Cinnamon-Apple Rings
Coffee   Tea

Stroganoff Sandwich

1 unsliced loaf French bread
1 pound ground beef
¼ cup chopped green onion
1 cup dairy sour cream
1 tablespoon milk
1 teaspoon Worcestershire sauce
¾ teaspoon salt
⅛ teaspoon garlic powder
  Butter or margarine, softened
• • •
2 tomatoes, sliced
1 green pepper, cut in rings
4 ounces sharp process American
  cheese, shredded (1 cup)

Cut loaf in half lengthwise; wrap in foil. Heat at 375° for 10 to 15 minutes. In skillet cook beef with onion till meat is browned; drain off fat. Stir in sour cream, milk, Worcestershire sauce, salt, and garlic powder; heat, *but do not boil.* Butter cut surfaces of bread.

Spread half of *hot* meat mixture on each loaf half. Arrange tomato slices alternately with green pepper rings atop meat. Sprinkle with cheese. Place on baking sheet; bake at 375° for 5 minutes. Cut each half in 4 slices.

Pizza by the Yard

1 unsliced loaf French bread
1 6-ounce can tomato paste
⅓ cup grated Parmesan cheese
¼ cup finely chopped onion
¼ cup chopped, pitted ripe olives
¾ teaspoon salt
½ teaspoon dried oregano leaves,
  crushed
⅛ teaspoon pepper
1 pound ground beef
4 tomatoes, sliced (16 slices)
1 8-ounce package sliced sharp
  process American cheese

Cut loaf in half lengthwise. Combine tomato paste, Parmesan cheese, onion, olives, salt, oregano, and pepper. Add meat; mix well. Spread atop loaf halves. Place on baking sheet. Bake at 400° for 20 minutes. Remove from oven; top with tomato slices. Cut cheese in 1-inch strips. Crisscross strips atop tomatoes. Bake 5 minutes. Makes 4 or 5 servings.

Meat Loaf Splits

For easier eating, split sandwich in center—

1 unsliced loaf Italian or French
  bread
¼ cup butter, softened
⅛ teaspoon garlic powder
8 slices process American cheese
4 slices leftover meat loaf, sliced
  ⅜ inch thick
  Grated Parmesan cheese

Cut ends from loaf; store for later use. Slice loaf crosswise into 8 pieces. In each piece make 3 slashes, *almost to bottom.*

Blend butter with garlic powder; spread on all cut surfaces of bread. Quarter cheese and meat slices. Place meat slice between 2 cheese slices; repeat to make 16 meat-cheese stacks.

Insert stacks in the *two* end slashes in each bread piece. Sprinkle sides of sandwiches with grated Parmesan cheese. Place on baking sheet. Bake at 400° till lightly browned, 8 to 10 minutes. Makes 8 servings.

Corned Beef Hash Burgers

1 15-ounce can corned beef hash
⅓ cup dairy sour cream
1 tablespoon pickle relish
1 teaspoon prepared horseradish
• • •
8 onion rolls, split and toasted
8 slices tomato
8 ounces process American
  cheese (8 slices)

Combine corned beef hash, sour cream, pickle relish, and horseradish; spread about ¼ cup mixture on bottom halves of rolls. Broil 3 to 4 inches from heat till hot, about 5 minutes. Top each with a tomato slice, then a cheese slice; broil just till cheese melts. Cover with tops of rolls. Makes 8 sandwiches.

Teen-age party favorites

Vary sandwiches with French bread loaves → by preparing Stroganoff Sandwich and Meat Loaf Splits, both hot from the oven.

❋MENU❋

AFTER THE GAME
Mexi-Taco Sandwiches
Pickles   Olives
Raisin-Sugar Cookies
Hot Chocolate

Mexi-Taco Sandwiches

  1 pound ground beef
  ½ cup chopped onion
     • • •
  1 8-ounce can tomato sauce
  1 teaspoon Worcestershire sauce
  ¼ teaspoon chili powder
  ⅛ teaspoon garlic powder
1½ cups corn chips, crushed (½ cup)
12 hamburger buns, split and
    toasted
  3 cups shredded lettuce
  2 tomatoes, diced
  3 ounces natural Cheddar cheese,
    shredded (¾ cup)
    Taco sauce

Cook beef and onion till meat is browned and onion is tender. Add tomato sauce, next 3 ingredients, add ¼ teaspoon salt. Mix well; simmer 10 minutes. Fold in corn chips. Immediately spoon mixture onto toasted bun halves. Top with lettuce, tomato, cheese, and tops of buns. Pass taco sauce. Makes 12 servings.

Paul Revere Cheesewiches

Using 1 package refrigerated biscuits (10 biscuits), roll each to a 4-inch circle on a lightly floured surface. Combine 3 ounces natural Cheddar cheese, shredded (¾ cup); 4 slices bacon, crisp-cooked, drained, and crumbled; and 2 tablespoons pickle relish.

    Place a rounded tablespoon of mixture in center of each circle. Fold up 3 sides; pinch edges to seal. Place biscuits on lightly greased baking sheet. Bake at 425° till golden brown, 8 to 10 minutes. Serve warm. Serves 10.

Creole Sandwiches

  2 tablespoons chopped onion
  2 tablespoons chopped green
    pepper
  1 tablespoon butter or margarine
  1 8-ounce can whole tomatoes,
    cut up
  3 tablespoons sliced, pimiento-
    stuffed green olives
  1 teaspoon sugar
  ¼ teaspoon salt
    Dash garlic salt
    Dash pepper
  4 frozen fish portions
  4 hamburger buns, split and
    toasted

In small saucepan cook onion and green pepper in butter or margarine till tender but not brown. Stir in tomatoes, olives, sugar, salt, garlic salt, and pepper. Simmer till thickened, about 15 to 20 minutes. Panfry fish portions according to package directions. Butter buns, if desired. Place fish portions on bottom halves of buns. Spoon some sauce over fish. Then, put tops of buns in place. Makes 4.

Salmon-Blue Cheese Broilers

  1 16-ounce can salmon, drained
    and flaked
  ⅓ cup mayonnaise
  1 3-ounce can chopped mushrooms,
    drained
  2 tablespoons crumbled blue
    cheese
  8 slices white bread, toasted
    and buttered
    Grated Parmesan cheese

Combine salmon with next 3 ingredients. Spread toasted bread with mixture. Sprinkle Parmesan over sandwiches. Broil 5 inches from heat till hot, about 6 to 7 minutes. Serves 8.

Simple-to-fix fishwiches

Tomato mixture adds a colorful and flavorful → touch to Creole Sandwiches. Make plenty of these sandwiches for second helpings.

Party sandwiches: Small, fancy sandwiches arranged on a silver tray or a cheese-frosted sandwich loaf make an impressive showing at an afternoon tea, bridal or baby shower, or cocktail party. The small sandwiches include checkerboards, cornucopias, ribbons, and various-shaped pieces of bread spread with an enticing filling. Many of these tidbits are easy to make, and preparation speeds along once you've mastered the techniques. (See box below for some clues that will be helpful.)

Sandwich loaves are a good choice when you've got a group to feed. The sandwich loaf is more filling than the tiny sandwiches, and it can be used for a luncheon main dish. Choose complementary, yet contrasting flavors for the filling—anything that is easy to cut with a fork, since this sandwich is usually eaten with a fork.

Party sandwich tips

● Freeze bread for meat sandwiches. Then, cut and spread while bread is frozen.

● Trim off crusts for fancy sandwiches.

● Use thinly sliced bread or buy an unsliced loaf of bread and thinly cut it lengthwise. There will be less waste when cutting the bread into shapes.

● Use cookie cutters for fancy shapes.

● Vary the type of bread used for an assortment of colors and flavors.

Teatime Sandwiches

Soften two 3-ounce packages cream cheese. Blend in $\frac{1}{3}$ cup mayonnaise and 2 tablespoons crumbled blue cheese. Add $\frac{1}{2}$ cup finely chopped nuts, $\frac{1}{2}$ teaspoon Worcestershire sauce, $\frac{1}{4}$ teaspoon salt, and $\frac{1}{4}$ teaspoon grated onion; mix well. Chill. Using a cookie or biscuit cutter, cut out bread rounds and spread with butter, then cheese mixture. Makes $1\frac{1}{3}$ cups.

Seafood Diamonds

Combine flaked canned tuna, crab meat, or lobster with an equal part of finely chopped celery. Moisten with mayonnaise or salad dressing, adding lemon juice to taste. Spread mixture on diamonds cut out of whole wheat bread slices. Trim tops with pimiento cutouts.

Orange-Date Fold-Ups

$\frac{1}{2}$ cup finely snipped dates
$\frac{1}{4}$ cup finely chopped walnuts
$\frac{1}{3}$ cup orange juice
8 slices white bread
Butter or margarine, softened

Combine dates, nuts, and orange juice; let stand about 20 minutes. Trim crusts from bread; spread slices with butter, then date mixture. Bring two opposite corners of each square together at center. Secure with wooden pick; garnish with sprig of watercress, if desired.

Cornucopias

Trim off the crusts from slices of bread. Spread bread with softened pineapple-cheese spread. Roll bread into a cone shape (cornucopias). Secure, if necessary, with wooden picks. Trim with ripe olive pieces cut in the shape of petals. Chill sandwiches, seam side down.

Party sandwiches include Checkerboards, Orange-Date Fold-Ups, Seafood Diamonds, Cornucopias, and Date-Roll Sandwiches.

For making Ribbon Sandwiches and Checkerboards, cut two loaves bread (white and whole wheat) in six ½-inch thick slices.

For Ribbon Sandwiches, stack two long slices whole wheat and two white bread slices, alternating bread. Slice crosswise.

For Checkerboards, make loaves for Ribbon Sandwiches. Cut in six lengthwise slices. Put four slices together, alternating colors.

Date-Roll Sandwiches

  1 3-ounce package cream cheese,
      softened
  1 tablespoon milk
  1 tablespoon very finely chopped
      candied ginger
    Canned date-nut roll

Combine cream cheese, milk, and candied ginger. Slice date-nut roll ⅜ inch thick. Spread half the slices with cheese mixture. Top with remaining slices. Cut a crescent from one side of each sandwich using a round cutter. Remaining piece makes a petal-shaped sandwich.

Ribbon Sandwiches

  1 unsliced loaf white sandwich
      bread
  1 unsliced loaf whole wheat
      sandwich bread
  1 5-ounce jar sharp process
      cheese spread
  ½ cup butter, softened

Remove crusts from bread loaves. Cut each loaf into 6 lengthwise slices ½ inch thick. Beat together cheese and butter. Spread on one side of all but 3 of the white bread slices. Make 3 ribbon loaves by stacking 4 long slices together for each, starting with whole wheat, then alternating types of bread, ending with a slice of white bread not spread with the cheese mixture. Wrap; chill. Thinly slice crosswise.

Checkerboards: Prepare 2 ribbon loaves as for Ribbon Sandwiches. Cut each ribbon loaf into 6 lengthwise slices. Put 4 slices together with cheese mixture, alternating colors of bread, making 3 checkerboard loaves. Wrap and chill. Thinly slice the loaves crosswise.

Diploma Sandwiches

Trim crusts from unsliced sandwich loaf. Slice crosswise in very thin slices. Place slices between dampened towels to keep soft. Add a little pickle relish to canned deviled ham. Spread mixture on bread, rolling up immediately. Place seam side down; cover and chill. Before serving, tie in center with ribbon.

Uses in menus

Appetizer or snack-type sandwiches are a simple answer to the question of what to serve at an afternoon or evening gathering when you don't want to present an entire meal. Accompany the sandwiches with a beverage and perhaps a few relishes or delectable tidbits.

Fruit Tea Sandwiches

    1 3-ounce package cream cheese,
        softened
    2 tablespoons drained, crushed
        pineapple
    ½ teaspoon grated lemon peel
    ½ cup halved seedless green grapes
    ¼ cup miniature marshmallows
        Raisin or nut bread, buttered

Beat first 3 ingredients and dash salt together till fluffy. Add grapes and marshmallows. Spread between slices of bread. Makes 1 cup.

Party Sandwiches

Soften one 3-ounce package cream cheese; blend in 1 tablespoon milk, 1 teaspoon Worcestershire sauce, and 4 or 5 slices crisp-cooked bacon, crumbled. Cut 2-inch rounds with cookie cutters from white, whole wheat, and rye sliced sandwich loaves. Spread *half* of the rounds (use a variety of breads) with mixture. Top with remaining rounds. If desired, use small hors d'oeuvre cutters to cut shapes from centers of rounds.

> # ❦MENU❦
>
> ## FOR THE NEW NEIGHBOR
> *Fruit Tea Sandwiches*
> *Party Sandwiches*
> *Nuts*   *Mints*
> *Tea*   *Punch*

> # ❦MENU❦
>
> ## STAG PARTY
> *Big Western Bean Burgers*
> *Corn Chips*
> *Radishes*   *Dill Pickles*
> *Spice Cake*
> *Coffee*

Often, sandwiches are featured as the main dish for a luncheon, stag supper, picnic, or lunch box. For the ladies, serve a cheese-frosted sandwich loaf. Serve the men a he-man sandwich stacked with meat and cheese or a hearty, hot sandwich on a hamburger bun.

Big Western Bean Burgers

    2 tablespoons onion soup mix
    1 18-ounce jar baked beans
        in molasses sauce
    1 4-ounce package smoked
        sliced beef, snipped
    3 tablespoons frankfurter relish
    8 sesame seed hamburger buns,
        split and toasted

In saucepan combine ½ cup water and soup mix; let stand till softened, about 5 minutes. Stir in beans, beef, and relish. Cook over medium heat till heated, stirring occasionally. Spoon onto toasted buns. Makes 8 servings.

Salad Sandwich Tower

For each serving, butter a large, round slice of rye bread. Place, buttered side up, on plate. Add lettuce, then slices of Swiss cheese and slices of chicken or turkey.

Stir ½ cup chili sauce into 1 cup mayonnaise or salad dressing. Pour desired amount of mixture over the sandwich. Top with tomato slice, hard-cooked egg slice, hot cooked bacon, ripe olive slices, and a sprig or two of parsley.

Frosted Ribbon Loaf

     1 **unsliced sandwich loaf**
       Butter or margarine, softened
     1 **cup Ham Salad Filling**
     1 **cup Egg Salad Filling**
     4 **3-ounce packages cream cheese,**
       softened
    ⅓ **cup milk**
       Snipped parsley

Slice bread lengthwise in 3 layers; trim crusts. Butter layers with the softened butter. Spread first layer with Ham Salad Filling and spread Egg Salad Filling on second layer. Assemble loaf using 2 spatulas to support layers, placing third bread layer on top. Wrap loaf tightly in foil; chill the loaf thoroughly.

Before serving, beat cream cheese with milk till fluffy. Frost top and sides of loaf. Sprinkle with snipped parsley. (Or frost early, cover loosely, and chill.) Makes 10 slices.

Ham Salad Filling: In mixing bowl combine 1 cup ground fully cooked ham, ⅓ cup finely chopped celery, 2 tablespoons drained pickle relish, ½ teaspoon prepared horseradish, and ¼ cup mayonnaise. Makes 1½ cups.

Egg Salad Filling: In mixing bowl combine 4 hard-cooked eggs, chopped; ⅓ cup chopped pimiento-stuffed green olives; 2 tablespoons finely chopped green onion; 2 teaspoons mustard; and ¼ cup mayonnaise. Makes 1½ cups.

The next time you hostess a shower, prepare a Frosted Ribbon Loaf. Most of the work is done ahead of time. Then, at serving time, all you need to do is add a few simple garnishes.

SANGRIA *(sang grē' uh)* — A refreshing, sweet beverage usually made with wine, fruit, and nutmeg. Ale, beer, and other liquors are sometimes used in place of the wine. The punchlike mixture is poured into tall glasses of crushed ice.

Sangria, which in Spanish means "the act of bleeding," gets its name from the traditional blood red color of the drink, which is obtained by using red wine.

Summer Sangria

      ¾ cup light corn syrup
      ⅓ cup lemon juice
      8 drops yellow food coloring
           • • •
      2 cups sparkling water, chilled
        Ice
      2 cups port

Blend light corn syrup, lemon juice, and yellow food coloring; stir in sparkling water. Divide mixture among 4 tall glasses. Add ice cubes or crushed ice. Then, carefully pour ½ cup of the wine down side of each glass. Serve with straws, if desired. Makes 4 servings.

SANTA CLAUS MELON — A name for the large, oblong, green and gold Christmas melon. (See also *Christmas Melon*.)

SAPODILLA *(sap' uh dil' uh)* — A tropical evergreen tree that bears fruit called sapodilla plums. The fruit looks like a russet apple and has large black seeds, orange pulp, soft flesh, and a thin skin. The flavor of this fruit resembles that of a pear, being sweet when ripe.

Sapsago cheese; for appetizers or main dishes.

This tree grows wild in Central America and in northern parts of South America. It is also found in parts of Florida. The sapodilla tree attains a height of about 20 feet. In addition to the fruit that it produces, the tree also yields chicle, which is combined with sugar, caramel, and flavorings in chewing gum.

SAPSAGO CHEESE *(sap' suh gō')* — A hard, light green-colored cheese that originated in Glarus, Switzerland. The cheese gets its color and pungent flavor from the four-leaf clovers that are added to the cheese, a tradition that was started by Irish monks who lived in Switzerland.

Sapsago is made with sour skim milk, buttermilk, and sour whey. The curd that forms is cured under light pressure. The mixture then is formed into the shape of a cone about four inches tall and weighing between 1 and 2¼ pounds.

Sapsago is used mostly for grating. The grated cheese is sprinkled over scrambled eggs or salads, or is used in sauces. Purchase the whole or grated cheese at specialty food stores. (See also *Cheese*.)

SARATOGA CHIP — A name for potato chips that originated in Saratoga, New York.

SARDINE *(sär dēn')* — Various types of fish caught while they are small or immature. The sardine can be a herring, alewife, or pilchard. Herring sardines are taken along the northern Atlantic coast, primarily from Maine. Those from Norway are called brisling or sprat. Pilchards are caught in the Mediterranean Sea, English Channel, and along the Pacific coast.

Sardines, named for the island of Sardinia, have green or blue coloring with a silvery cast. Their habit of rising to the surface at night to feed stirs up organisms that give off a phosphorescent glow. This alerts the fisherman of their position so that nets can be set to capture them. This, however, is only one of the methods that is used to catch the fish. Sardines usually measure three to eight inches and weigh about two ounces.

Processing begins as quickly as the sardines are caught. While they are being pumped aboard, the scales are removed and then the fish are salted. At the cannery, the sardines are washed and precooked, and their heads and tails are removed. Then, they are packed into cans with an oil or sauce, sealed, cooked, and sterilized under inspection.

Not all sardines are canned in this manner. Some are sold fresh, salted and preserved in brine, or smoked. However, the majority on the market are canned with an oil or sauce, such as tomato or mustard.

Fresh sardines are available in April and May. They can be cooked like other fat fish. Frying is one of the most popular methods. All forms of sardines are used as appetizers, in hot or cold sandwiches, snacks, and as an ingredient in preparing main-dish casseroles.

The nutritional value of sardines is found in the high-quality protein, minerals, and B vitamins. One and one half large sardines have 160 calories when raw or 197 when canned in tomato sauce. A 3½-ounce serving canned in brine or mustard sauce has 196 calories. (See *Fish, Herring* for additional information.)

Sardine Appetizer Spread

Trim this unusual spread with a small sprig of parsley or watercress—

>   1 3¾-ounce can sardines in oil,
>   drained
>   ¼ cup butter or margarine, softened
>   2 tablespoons finely chopped
>   green onion
>   2 tablespoons chili sauce
>   1 tablespoon lemon juice
>   ¼ teaspoon dry mustard
>   Few drops bottled hot pepper sauce
>
>   •   •   •
>
>   Rye wafers

Mash the sardines with a fork. Combine with the ¼ cup butter or margarine, onion, chili sauce, lemon juice, the ¼ teaspoon mustard, and hot pepper sauce. Blend the mixture thoroughly. Chill. Let stand at room temperature a few minutes before serving. Serve the spread with crisp rye wafers. Makes ¼ cup spread.

Sardine Sandwiches

>   2 3¾-ounce cans sardines in oil
>   2 hard-cooked eggs, chopped
>   2 tablespoons snipped chives
>   2 tablespoons mayonnaise
>   1 tablespoon lemon juice
>   12 slices whole wheat bread
>   Mayonnaise

Drain sardines and mash. Combine sardines, eggs, chives, 2 tablespoons mayonnaise, and lemon juice. Spread whole wheat bread with additional mayonnaise. Spread sardine filling on 6 slices of bread. Top with lettuce, if desired, and remaining 6 slices of bread. Serves 6.

Sardine and Cheese Sandwich

>   4 slices rye bread, toasted
>   Butter
>   2 3¾-ounce cans sardines in oil,
>   drained
>   ⅓ cup chili sauce
>   2 tablespoons chopped onion
>   2 ounces process American cheese,
>   shredded (½ cup)

Spread toasted bread with butter. Arrange sardines on toast. Combine chili sauce and onion; spoon over sardines. Place on baking sheet and bake at 450° for 10 minutes. Top with shredded cheese. Return to oven and heat just till cheese melts. Makes 4 sandwiches.

SARSAPARILLA (*sär suh puh ril' uh, sär spuh-, sas' puh-*)—A soft drink flavored with the dried roots of a tropical American climbing plant related to the lily.

SASSAFRAS—A tree of the laurel family, native to America. The powdered leaves are used to make filé powder. This powder typically is used to thicken and season gumbos and stews in Creole cookery. Because of their bitey and spicy flavor, the bark and roots are used in flavoring sassafras tea and other beverages, and as one of the ingredients in root beer.

SATSUMA—A mandarin orange variety. (See also *Mandarin Orange.*)

SAUCE

*Master the art of saucemaking, and turn
any dish into a glamorous treat.*

A sauce is the crowning glory of any dish with which it is served. This liquid or semiliquid blend of ingredients not only adds flavor but it enhances the appearance of foods. The sauce should complement, contrast, and cling to the food on which or beside which it is served.

Tracing the origins of sauce is a difficult task, as is the case with many other foods. The word sauce evolved from the Latin word *salsus* (salted), and it is known that the early Greeks and Romans used sauces on their foods. Whether or not sauces were used earlier than this is, at best, only conjecture.

During medieval times in England, people did not think highly of simple dishes. To overcome this stigma, they added a sauce. These early sauces consisted of either a heavy gravy made by boiling down meat stock or a sweet mixture of honey or sugar, vinegar, and spices.

Sauces remained relatively simple creations until the seventeenth and eighteenth centuries when French chefs added a new dimension to the art of saucemaking. These inventive men transformed simple sauces into classic ones by adding other ingredients, such as herbs, eggs, vegetables, and cheeses. Many of the now-famous sauces were developed in the kitchens of French nobility. Kings generously rewarded chefs who created new sauces. Then, as now, being the sauce chef in a kitchen was an important duty.

Tantalizing seafood sauces

← Choose Jiffy Hollandaise (see *Hollandaise* for recipe)—top; Easy Seafood Sauce—middle; Tartar Sauce Deluxe—bottom; or Clarified Butter to top off seafood dishes.

The names given to the sauces created during this period often indicated the origin of the particular sauce. For example, Béarnaise was named for a region in southwestern France called Béarn. Béchamel was named for Louis de Béchamel, head steward of the kitchen in which the meals of Louis XIV were prepared. Another sauce, mayonnaise, named for the town of Mahon on the Spanish island of Minorca, was first made for the Duc de Richelieu; and the famous sauce, Bordelaise, was named after the Bordeaux region of France.

Basic ingredients: A sauce is only as good as the ingredients you put into it *and* the care you take when preparing it. Basic ingredients for sauces include cream, milk, stock, or wine for the liquid; butter for richness; eggs, flour, bread or starch for thickening; and herbs, spices, vegetables, and fruits for flavor.

While it's important to use the kinds of ingredients called for to duplicate a sauce, you can add your own creative touch by experimenting with flavor ingredients such as herbs rather than changing the basic ingredients.

To simplify saucemaking, make full use of the many high-quality, ready-to-use ingredients, mixes, and bottled and canned products that are available in the supermarket. Some of the bottled products, such as hot pepper sauce, Worcestershire sauce, and chili sauce, can be used as the base for many other sauces.

A few of the traditional bottled meat sauces have been on the market for generations. Today, they are joined by Hollandaise and Bordelaise, as well as various dessert or sundae sauces and sauces for use on pasta and meats. With

Know Your Classic Sauces		
Names of Sauces	Basic Ingredients	Characteristic Ingredients
White Sauces		
Béchamel Sauce* (classic White Sauce)	white roux, milk	
Caper Sauce Egg Sauce* Mornay Sauce (Cheese Sauce) Nantua Sauce Raifort Sauce Soubise Sauce Véronique	” ” ” ” ” ” ”	capers hard-cooked egg cheese, cream crayfish butter, cream horseradish puréed onion cream, white grapes
Velouté Sauce*	white roux; chicken, fish, or veal stock	
Allemande* or Parisienne Sauce Bercy Sauce (Shallot Sauce)	” ”	cream, egg yolks shallots, white wine, veal or fish stock to thin
Brown Sauces		
Espagnole Sauce	browned roux, white wine, meat stock	carrot, onion, celery, bouquet garni, tomato sauce or purée
Demi-Glaze Sauce Bordelaise Sauce* Chasseur Sauce (Hunter's Sauce) Diable* (Deviled Sauce) Duxelles Sauce	” ” ” ” ”	cooked down to concentrate red wine (Bordeaux), garlic, shallots mushrooms, shallots, white wine, tomato Worcestershire sauce, vinegar, white wine mushrooms, white wine, tomato
Emulsified Sauces		
Hollandaise Sauce* (cooked)	egg yolks, butter, lemon juice or vinegar	
Béarnaise Sauce* Mousseline Sauce*	” ”	shallots, tarragon, vinegar, white wine whipped cream folded in
Mayonnaise* (uncooked)	egg yolks, oil, lemon juice or vinegar	
Aïoli Sauce Rémoulade Sauce Tartar Sauce*	” ” ”	garlic mustard, gherkins, capers, parsley, herbs herbs, pickles, onions
Vinaigrette Sauces		
Basic Vinaigrette* (Clear French Dressing)	vinegar, oil	herbs and seasonings
*See also individual listings.		

all of the convenience products that are available on the market, there is little excuse for doing without a sauced food.

Remember that the sauce on a food is usually the first thing to touch your tongue. Always put a good sauce on good food, as this will enhance the food's taste appeal. However, a good sauce does little to make a poor food taste better.

Types of sauces

The art of saucemaking that has developed over the years stems from the classic sauce types, often referred to as the "mother sauces." These sauces include the white sauces—Béchamel and Velouté; Espagnole or Brown Sauce; two basic emulsified sauces—Hollandaise and Mayonnaise; and Vinaigrette or oil and vinegar sauces. When you prepare sauces, you use endless variations of these basic sauce types. In addition, these classic sauces have been joined by modern-day dessert sauces, sundae sauces, barbecue and brush-on sauces, and a wide variety of gravies.

The method of preparing the various types of sauces incorporates some of the same techniques. For example, a roux is basic to many of the white and brown sauces. This cooked mixture of flour and butter is an important contribution to the saucemaking art. (See also *Roux*.)

The classic white sauce is often known as cream sauce because of its appearance. It is the king of all sauces in the United States and is probably used most frequently in all types of dishes. As can be seen on the Know Your Classic Sauces chart, many different sauces start out as basic white sauce. (See also *White Sauce*.)

Brown sauces are also starch-thickened. However, the fat-flour roux is browned before the other ingredients are added. There are also variations of this classic type as seen on the chart.

Hollandaise and Mayonnaise are two sauces that are made with an emulsion of egg yolks and fat. These emulsified sauces have several variations, too.

Vinaigrette sauces are a simple blend of oil, vinegar, salt, and pepper, and actually are a clear French salad dressing.

Creamy Mustard Sauce (see *Egg* for recipe) adds both flavor and color contrast to broccoli, other green vegetables, or ham loaf.

A simplified version of white sauce makes use of an electric blender and eliminates the step of making the roux. The blender can also be used for bread sauce, a bread-thickened white sauce.

Blender White Sauce

Thin:
    1 cup milk
    1 tablespoon all-purpose flour
    1 tablespoon butter or margarine
Medium:
    1 cup milk
    2 tablespoons all-purpose flour
    2 tablespoons butter or margarine
Thick:
    1 cup milk
    ¼ cup all-purpose flour
    3 tablespoons butter or margarine

Put milk, flour, butter, and ¼ teaspoon salt in blender container; blend smooth. In saucepan cook and stir till bubbly. Makes 1 cup.

Bread Sauce

   1 cup hot milk
   2 tablespoons butter or margarine
   ¼ teaspoon salt
   White bread, crusts removed*

Warm blender container by filling with hot water and letting stand a minute or two; empty water. Put hot milk, butter or margarine, and salt in blender container; blend till ingredients are mixed. With blender running, break bread into pieces and add to blender container. Stop blender occasionally to check sauce consistency. Serve at once. Makes 1¼ cups.

   *Use 3 to 4 slices of bread for thin sauce, 6 to 7 slices of bread for medium sauce, and 9 to 10 slices of bread for thick sauce. Unless a white-colored sauce is desired, leave the bread crusts on and use less bread.

Sauce success tips

● Stir constantly while starch-thickened sauces cook to prevent lumping. If you must leave the sauce for a few seconds, set the pan off the heat during that time.
● If the starch-thickened sauce develops a few lumps, beat them out with a rotary beater or a wire whisk. As a last resort, strain sauce with sieve to remove lumps.
● Cook egg-thickened sauces over low heat, preferably using a controlled-heat burner or element. Or cook these sauces in the top of a double boiler over hot, not boiling, water. First, warm the egg yolks by stirring in a little of the hot sauce mixture. Then add to the remainder of the sauce mixture. Never let a sauce boil after the egg yolks are added. Sauce may curdle.
● Don't let water boil in the bottom of the double boiler if you use it to make a custard sauce. Also, make sure the water doesn't touch bottom of pan holding custard.
● Mayonnaise or mayonnaise-based sauces, such as Tartar Sauce, may separate if put on very hot foods. Pass the sauce after the food reaches the table and has cooled a bit.
● To make sauces with a rich color, add Kitchen Bouquet to gravies or yellow food coloring to cream sauces made with egg.

Mayonnaise is the basic for a gamut of cold sauces. One of the most famous of these is Tartar Sauce, a seafood favorite.

Blender Tartar Sauce

   1 cup mayonnaise or salad dressing
   1 tablespoon lemon juice
   1 large dill pickle, cut in pieces
   ¼ small onion
   1 hard-cooked egg, quartered
   1 tablespoon capers, drained
   1 teaspoon snipped chives

Put all ingredients in blender container; blend till ingredients are chopped. Chill thoroughly. Serve with fish. Makes 2 cups.

Tartar Sauce Deluxe

   ½ cup dairy sour cream
   ¼ cup mayonnaise or salad dressing
   1 hard-cooked egg, chopped
   2 tablespoons pickle relish
   2 tablespoons chopped green onion
   2 tablespoons sauterne
         ● ● ●
   Sieved egg yolk
   Sliced green onion

Blend together the sour cream, mayonnaise or salad dressing, chopped hard-cooked egg, pickle relish, chopped green onion, and sauterne. Chill the mixture thoroughly. Garnish top of sauce with sieved egg yolk and sliced green onion. Makes 1½ cups sauce.

Some of the other sauces that, strictly speaking, don't fit under the previous categories include marinades, basting sauces, sauces that coat the food as an integral part of the mixture, some types of fruit sauces, and pan gravies.

An elegant candlelight dinner

The sauce for Creamy Ham Rolls, a conve- →
nient main dish, starts with a mix to which frozen onions in cream sauce are added.

Instead of serving plain fried chicken, try Chicken with Orange Rice, which features pieces of chicken with a currant-orange sauce. You'll also find sunny orange flavor in the rice.

Burgundy Sauce

½ cup salad oil
½ cup Burgundy *or* claret
2 tablespoons finely snipped candied ginger
2 tablespoons catsup
2 tablespoons molasses
1 large clove garlic, minced
½ teaspoon curry powder
½ teaspoon salt
½ teaspoon pepper

Combine all ingredients. Use as a marinade or basting sauce for barbecued meat. Makes 1 cup.

Tangy Cranberry Sauce

Mix one 16-ounce can jellied cranberry sauce, ⅓ cup bottled steak sauce, 1 tablespoon *each* brown sugar and salad oil, and 2 teaspoons prepared mustard. Beat with rotary beater. Serve warm or as is with ham or pork. Makes 2 cups.

Think of sauces as both complementing and contrasting the food on which or beside which they are served. Hollandaise, for example, contrasts in color and texture, and complements in flavor a vegetable such as broccoli. The sharp seasoning of barbecue sauce cuts the richness of spareribs, while the colors of the meat and the sauce blend together attractively.

Light sauce can be used on light foods, but there should be a subtle difference of shading. Pale golden cheese sauce, for instance, is more appealing on macaroni than the best flavored white sauce ever could be. Milk chocolate sauce looks better on vanilla or coffee ice cream than on chocolate ice cream which has the same brown shade, but deep-colored fudge sauce on chocolate ice cream is perfect.

When you sauce a food, use a light hand. Don't use so much that the food is masked, but let some of the food show through. Or, for a change, put the sauce beside rather than on top of the food. Serve the sauce attractively, then pass around the remaining for seconds.

Sauces can be used on any type of food, no matter whether it's a main dish, a vegetable, or a dessert.

Main-dish sauces: Add a spark of additional flavor to main dishes. Flavorwise, some sauces go better with one type of meat than with another. For example, mint and dill are naturals with lamb, while mustard, cheese, or cherries are partners with ham. Poultry and fruit go together like steak and mushrooms or seafood and mayonnaise or butter sauces.

Chicken with Orange Rice

     ½ cup currant jelly
     ¼ cup frozen orange juice
          concentrate
     2 teaspoons cornstarch
     1 teaspoon dry mustard
          Dash bottled hot pepper sauce

          •   •   •

     ½ cup all-purpose flour
     1 teaspoon salt
     1 2½- to 3-pound ready-to-cook
          broiler-fryer chicken, cut up
          Shortening
          Orange Rice

Combine jelly, orange juice concentrate, and ⅓ cup water; cook and stir till smooth. Blend cornstarch, mustard, hot pepper sauce, and 1 tablespoon cold water; stir into jelly mixture. Cook and stir till thickened; set aside. Combine flour and salt in paper bag. Add 2 or 3 pieces of chicken at a time; shake to coat. Brown chicken in hot shortening, turning occasionally. Drain excess fat; add the currant-orange sauce. Cover; simmer over low heat till tender, 45 minutes. Baste occasionally with sauce. Serve with Orange Rice. Serves 4.

Orange Rice: Cook 1 cup chopped celery and ¼ cup chopped onion in ¼ cup butter till tender. Add 2 tablespoons frozen orange juice concentrate, 1¼ cups water, and ½ teaspoon salt. Bring the mixture to boiling. Add 1⅓ cups uncooked packaged precooked rice. Continue cooking as directed on the package.

Bacon-wrapped Lamb Patties with Dill Sauce will delight lamb lovers. The creamy sauce combines dill and Parmesan flavors.

Lamb Patties with Dill Sauce

     1 beaten egg
     ½ cup quick-cooking rolled oats
     ¼ cup finely chopped onion
     1 teaspoon salt
     ¼ teaspoon dried thyme leaves,
          crushed
          Dash pepper
     1½ pounds ground lamb
     6 slices bacon
          Dill Sauce

Combine egg, oats, onion, salt, thyme, and pepper. Add lamb and mix well. Shape mixture into 6 patties. Wrap each patty with 1 slice bacon; secure with wooden pick. Broil 5 inches from heat for 10 minutes. Turn; broil 5 minutes longer. Serve with Dill Sauce. Serves 6.

Dill Sauce: Cook 1 tablespoon finely chopped onion in 1 tablespoon butter or margarine till tender. Blend in 2 tablespoons all-purpose flour, 2 tablespoons grated Parmesan cheese, ½ teaspoon dried dillweed, ½ teaspoon paprika, and dash salt. Add 1 cup milk all at once. Cook and stir till thickened and bubbly.

Fresh Mint Sauce

Combine ¼ cup snipped, fresh mint leaves, ¼ cup light corn syrup, and 1 tablespoon lemon juice. Blend together ¼ cup water and 1½ teaspoons cornstarch; add to mint mixture. Cook and stir over medium heat till thickened and bubbly; strain. Stir in 1 drop green food coloring. Serve with lamb. Makes ½ cup sauce.

In-a-Hurry Mint Sauce

Combine ½ cup mint jelly and 2 teaspoons lemon juice. Heat slowly, stirring occasionally, till jelly melts. Serve with lamb. Makes ½ cup.

Creamy Ham Rolls

    1 12-ounce package frozen rice with
         peas and mushrooms
    2 ounces sharp process American
         cheese, shredded (½ cup)
    8 slices boiled ham
    1 10-ounce package frozen onions
         in cream sauce
    1 envelope white sauce mix

Prepare frozen rice according to package directions. (Omit Parmesan cheese if called for.) Stir in American cheese; spoon about ¼ *cup* mixture on each ham slice. Roll up jelly-roll fashion. Prepare frozen onions in cream sauce according to package directions.

In blazer pan of large chafing dish, prepare white sauce mix over direct heat following package directions. Add cooked onions with cream sauce. Arrange ham rolls in sauce. Cover and heat through. Makes 4 servings.

Hot Mustard Sauce

In saucepan melt 3 tablespoons butter or margarine; blend in 1 teaspoon all-purpose flour. Add ¼ cup vinegar, ¼ cup beef broth, ¼ cup prepared horseradish mustard, and 3 tablespoons brown sugar. Cook slowly, stirring constantly, till thickened. Gradually add a little hot mixture to 1 slightly beaten egg yolk; return to hot mixture. Bring sauce just to boiling point, stirring constantly; serve hot with corned beef or ham. Makes 1 cup.

Spicy Cherry Sauce

    ¾ cup sugar
       Dash salt
    2 tablespoons cornstarch
    ¾ cup orange juice
    1 tablespoon lemon juice
    1 16-ounce can pitted, tart
         red cherries (water pack)
    1 1-inch stick cinnamon
    ½ teaspoon whole cloves
    ¼ teaspoon red food coloring

Combine sugar, salt, and cornstarch. Stir in orange and lemon juices. Add undrained cherries, spices, and food coloring. Cook, stirring constantly, over medium heat till mixture thickens and comes to a boil. Boil 2 minutes. Before serving, remove the cinnamon and cloves. Serve warm with ham. Makes 3 cups.

1-2-3 Sauce

Combine one 12-ounce bottle extra-hot catsup, 2 teaspoons celery seed, 3 tablespoons vinegar, and 1 clove garlic, halved. Chill several hours; remove garlic before serving. Grill hamburgers a few minutes on each side, then baste with sauce. Makes 1¼ cups sauce.

Wine-Mushroom Sauce

Cook 1 cup sliced fresh mushrooms and ¼ cup finely chopped green onion in ¼ cup butter till tender. Blend in 4 teaspoons cornstarch. Add ¾ cup Burgundy, ¾ cup water, 2 tablespoons snipped parsley, ¾ teaspoon salt, and dash pepper. Cook and stir till thickened and bubbly. Serve with steak. Makes 1½ cups.

Easy Seafood Sauce

    ½ cup mayonnaise or salad dressing
    3 tablespoons catsup
    1 teaspoon prepared horseradish
    ¼ teaspoon garlic salt
       Snipped parsley

Combine mayonnaise, catsup, horseradish, and garlic salt; blend together. Chill thoroughly. Sprinkle with snipped parsley. Makes ¾ cup.

Clarified Butter

Melt butter over low heat without stirring; cool. Pour off oily top layer; discard bottom layer. Keep butter warm over candle warmer. Serve with steamed or poached fish or shellfish.

Vegetable sauces: Spoon a creamy or buttery sauce over garden-fresh vegetables. The smooth sauce contrasts in texture and at the same time gives an added flavor that's hard to beat. Cheese sauces are good accompaniments for vegetables, as are herbed butter sauces or creamy sauces delicately flavored with mustard.

Blue Cheese Sauce

    2 tablespoons butter or margarine
    2 tablespoons all-purpose flour
    1 chicken bouillon cube
    1 cup milk
    ¼ cup dairy sour cream
    ¼ cup crumbled blue cheese

In saucepan melt butter; stir in flour. Add crushed bouillon cube and milk all at once. Cook, stirring constantly, till mixture thickens and bubbles. Remove from heat; stir in sour cream and blue cheese. Heat through, *but do not boil*. Serve with baked potatoes or green vegetables. Makes 1¼ cups sauce.

Fix a quick sundae sauce by simply combining butter-toasted nuts and a milk chocolate bar. Complete the sundae by spooning warm Chocolate-Walnut Sauce over chocolate ripple ice cream.

Parmesan Cheese Sauce

  1 tablespoon butter or margarine
  1 tablespoon all-purpose flour
  ¼ teaspoon salt
     Dash pepper
     Dash paprika
     Dash dry mustard
  1 cup milk
  2 tablespoons grated Parmesan
     cheese
  2 tablespoons toasted, slivered
     almonds

In saucepan melt butter; stir in flour, salt, pepper, paprika, and dry mustard. Add milk all at once. Cook and stir till sauce thickens and bubbles. Add cheese and almonds; stir the mixture till cheese melts. Serve over drained, cooked vegetables. Makes 1 cup sauce.

Sour Cream Sauce

Combine ½ cup dairy sour cream, 2 tablespoons salad dressing, 2 teaspoons chopped green onion, 1½ teaspoons lemon juice, ½ teaspoon sugar, ¼ teaspoon dry mustard, and dash salt. Heat mixture, stirring constantly, till warm, *but do not boil.* Makes ½ cup sauce.

Dessert sauces: Top off dessert foods, such as puddings, cakes, ice cream, or fruits, with a luscious sauce. Classic examples of dessert sauces include brandy, foamy, or hard sauces spooned over warm plum puddings and spice cakes. Ice cream sauces can be as simple as fudge or mint sauce purchased at the store, or as elegant as Cherries Jubilee or other fruit sauces served over various flavors of ice cream or sherbet. A favorite sauce for fruit desserts is a creamy custard sauce.

Cherry Sundae Sauce

Combine ½ cup sugar and 2 teaspoons cornstarch. Add to 2 cups quartered, fresh dark sweet cherries in a saucepan. Heat and stir till sugar dissolves and mixture thickens slightly. Stir in 1 tablespoon lemon juice. Chill. Serve over ice cream. Makes 1⅔ cups sauce.

Fruit Sparkle Sauce

  1 30-ounce can fruit cocktail
  ¼ cup sugar
  1 tablespoon cornstarch
  ¼ teaspoon salt
  ¼ cup water
  ½ 6-ounce can frozen orange juice
     concentrate, thawed
     (⅓ cup)
  ¼ cup coarsely chopped pecans

Drain fruit cocktail, reserving syrup. In a saucepan combine sugar, cornstarch, and salt; blend in water. Add syrup and orange juice concentrate. Cook and stir till mixture thickens and boils. Add drained fruit cocktail; chill. Stir in pecans. Serve the sauce over vanilla ice cream. Makes 3½ cups sauce.

Tropical Sundae Sauce

  1 8¾-ounce can pineapple tidbits
  1½ cups sugar
  1½ tablespoons lemon juice
  3 drops peppermint extract
  2 medium oranges, peeled,
     sectioned, and seeded
  ½ cup green maraschino cherries,
     halved

Drain pineapple, reserving syrup; add enough water to syrup to make ½ cup. In a saucepan cook sugar and syrup over low heat till thickened, about 12 minutes. Add lemon juice and peppermint extract; chill. Before serving the sauce, add oranges and cherries. Serve over vanilla ice cream. Makes 2 cups sauce.

Hot Fudge-Peanut Butter Sauce

  1 6-ounce package semisweet
     chocolate pieces
  1 cup milk
  ½ cup sugar
  ½ cup peanut butter

In small saucepan combine chocolate, milk, and sugar. Bring to boiling, stirring constantly. Gradually stir chocolate mixture into peanut butter. Ladle warm sauce atop ice cream or over pound cake a la mode. Makes 2 cups.

Fruit sauce over fruit is the main theme for this fancy dessert called Bananas aux Fruits. Crumb-coated bananas are baked with an apricot mixture, then topped with cherry-wine sauce.

Bananas aux Fruits

   1 **slightly beaten egg**
   1 **tablespoon lemon juice**
   6 **firm, medium-sized bananas**
   9 **soft macaroon cookies**
   2 **tablespoons all-purpose flour**
¼ **cup apricot preserves**
   2 **tablespoons butter, melted**
   2 **teaspoons lemon juice**
     Cherry Sauce

Combine egg and 1 tablespoon lemon juice. Peel bananas and coat with egg mixture; place on greased baking sheet. Break cookies into coarse crumbs (1½ cups); stir in flour and pile mixture on bananas. Bake at 375° for 8 to 10 minutes. Combine preserves, butter, and 2 teaspoons lemon juice. Spoon over bananas. Bake till hot, 3 to 5 minutes more. Serve with hot Cherry Sauce. Makes 6 servings.

Cherry Sauce: Drain one 8¾-ounce can pitted dark sweet cherries, reserving syrup. Halve cherries. Add enough port wine to syrup to make ¾ cup. In saucepan combine 2 tablespoons sugar, 1 tablespoon cornstarch, and dash salt. Stir in reserved syrup mixture. Cook, stirring constantly, till mixture thickens and bubbles. Add cherries and heat just to boiling.

Chocolate-Walnut Sauce

¼ **cup butter or margarine**
½ **cup coarsely chopped walnuts**
   1 **4½-ounce milk chocolate bar, broken in pieces**

In heavy skillet melt butter. Add nuts; cook and stir over medium heat till nuts are toasted. Add chocolate; stir till melted and smooth. Serve warm over ice cream. Makes 1 cup.

SAUCE BOAT—A serving dish shaped like a low, oval pitcher with a pouring lip. A plate or tray is often attached at the bottom to catch drips. Larger sizes with attached trays are called gravy boats.

SAUCEPAN—A cooking pot that ranges in capacity from one cup to four quarts and has a handle. Most types are deep in proportion to width and have a flat bottom, straight or slightly sloping sides, and a tight-fitting cover. Saucepans are made of plain metal, porcelain-coated metal, glass ceramic, or heatproof glass. These utensils are used for boiling, simmering, and stewing foods as well as for making sauces. (See also *Pots and Pans.*)

SAUCISSON (*sō sē sôn*)—The French word for a large, smoked, pork sausage.

SAUERBRATEN (*sour'brät'uhn*)—German-style beef pot roast that is marinated and cooked in a vinegar mixture. The cooking liquid is often thickened, usually with gingersnaps, and served with the meat.

Sauerbraten

            2 medium onions, sliced
           ½ lemon, sliced
          1½ cups red wine vinegar
           12 whole cloves
            6 bay leaves
            6 whole peppercorns
            1 tablespoon sugar
           ¼ teaspoon ground ginger
            1 4-pound beef rump roast
            2 tablespoons shortening
              Gravy

In large bowl or crock combine first 8 ingredients, 2½ cups water, and 1 tablespoon salt. Add roast, turning to coat. Cover and refrigerate about 36 hours; turn meat several times. Remove meat; wipe dry. Strain; reserve marinade. In Dutch oven, brown meat in hot shortening; add strained marinade. Cover and cook slowly till tender, about 2 hours. Remove meat. Serve with Gravy. Makes 10 servings.

Gravy: For each cup of gravy combine ¾ cup meat juices and ¼ cup water; add ⅓ cup broken gingersnaps. Cook and stir till thick.

SAUERKRAUT, KRAUT (*sour' krout', sou' uhr-*)—Shredded cabbage that is fermented in a brine of salt and cabbage juice. The brine serves the double purpose of preserving the cabbage and giving it the sour flavor that accounts for the name, literally "sour cabbage."

The people of the Orient first made sauerkraut several thousand years ago. Much later, during the thirteenth century, invading Tartars introduced this dish to eastern Europe. The people of this area, particularly the Germans, soon became so fond of sauerkraut that even today it is associated with this area.

In Germany, you'll not only find the world-famous sauerkraut but also sauerkraut and sausage, sauerkraut cooked with fruit such as pineapple, sauerkraut cooked in beer or wine, and sauerkraut seasoned with spices. However, sauerkraut is not limited to Germany; it is enjoyed in all parts of the world.

Some homemakers still make their own sauerkraut, but today, most sauerkraut is packed commercially. Even though the commercial operations involve tremendous quantities of raw materials, the technique for making sauerkraut has changed very little in the past several centuries. Basically, cabbage and salt are layered in a deep container, and this mixture is pounded to start release of the juice. Then, the mixture is allowed to ferment. After several weeks, the sauerkraut has developed a full flavor and is ready to be eaten fresh or packed.

Although the flavor of fresh sauerkraut is quite mild, older sauerkraut is apt to have a strong flavor that is objectionable to some people. To tame this flavor, rinse the sauerkraut several times with cold water before cooking it.

The flavor alone is enough to make many people enjoy sauerkraut, but when you also consider that 1 cup of drained sauerkraut has only about 30 calories, this vegetable becomes enticing to weight watchers. Sauerkraut also has vitamin C and other vitamins and minerals.

The flavor of heated sauerkraut blends well with pork products and sausages. Corned beef and sauerkraut are a popular combination in a Reuben sandwich. Cold sauerkraut is delicious in salads or as a relish. Also try sauerkraut in combination with other meats, poultry, and vegetables, and remember that sauerkraut juice adds flavor to vegetable juice cocktails.

Frankrauts

Using 1 pound frankfurters, slit frankfurters lengthwise *not quite through*. Lightly brush cut surfaces with liquid smoke. Combine 1 cup drained sauerkraut, ¼ cup chili sauce, and 1 teaspoon caraway seed; stuff franks. Wrap *each* stuffed frank with a strip of partially cooked bacon; use wooden picks to hold bacon in place. Grill over *hot* coals, turning occasionally, 10 to 15 minutes. Serves 4 or 5.

Quick Frank-Kraut Dinner

    ¼ cup milk
    1 10¾-ounce can condensed
        Cheddar cheese soup
    ½ teaspoon caraway seed
    ½ teaspoon prepared mustard
    1 27-ounce can sauerkraut,
        drained and snipped
    1 pound frankfurters (8 to 10)

Gradually stir milk into cheese soup till well blended; add caraway seed and mustard. Fold in sauerkraut; heat through, stirring frequently. Turn into a 10x6x1½-inch baking dish. Slash each frankfurter diagonally at 1-inch intervals; arrange frankfurters atop sauerkraut mixture. Bake at 375° till frankfurters are heated through, 15 to 20 minutes. Serves 4.

Sausage-Potato Skillet

Using 1 package dry scalloped potatoes, combine dry potatoes and the packaged seasoned sauce mix. Add water to potatoes to equal *total liquid* called for on package. Heat to boiling; stir occasionally. Reduce heat; simmer, covered, till potatoes are tender, 30 minutes. Stir in one 16-ounce can sauerkraut, drained; sprinkle with ½ teaspoon caraway seed. Arrange 1 pound smoked pork sausage links, spoke-fashion, on top of mixture. Cover, cook about 10 minutes more. Serves 4 to 6.

Cut Sauerbraten into thick slices and serve it with Potato Pancakes (see *Kartoffel Pfannkuchen* for recipe) for a delectable meal.

Frank and Kraut Stew

A hearty stew—

    1 large onion, sliced (1 cup)
    ½ cup chopped green pepper
    2 tablespoons shortening
    1 16-ounce can sauerkraut
    1 16-ounce can tomatoes
    3 potatoes, peeled and cubed
    2 medium carrots, thinly sliced
        (about ½ cup)
    ½ cup water
    2 tablespoons brown sugar
    1 teaspoon salt
    ¼ teaspoon pepper
    1 pound frankfurters, quartered

In Dutch oven or large skillet cook sliced onion and chopped green pepper in shortening till tender. Add sauerkraut, tomatoes, potatoes, carrots, water, brown sugar, salt, and pepper. Simmer, covered, till vegetables are tender, about 35 minutes. Add frankfurters; simmer 10 minutes longer. Makes 5 or 6 servings.

Spareribs with Kraut

    3 pounds pork spareribs
    2 teaspoons salt
 ¼ teaspoon pepper
    1 27-ounce can sauerkraut
    1 cup finely chopped, unpeeled,
        tart apple
    1 cup shredded carrot
 1½ cups tomato juice
    2 tablespoons brown sugar
    2 teaspoons caraway seed

Cut ribs in pieces; season with salt and pepper; place in Dutch oven and brown well. Combine sauerkraut (including liquid) with chopped apple, shredded carrot, tomato juice, brown sugar, and the 2 teaspoons caraway seed; spoon over ribs. Simmer, covered, till the ribs are done, about 1¾ hours; baste with juices several times during the last hour of cooking. Skim off excess fat. Makes 6 servings.

Place prebrowned meatballs atop the sauerkraut-rice mixture for Meatball-Sauerkraut Skillet. Then, add tomatoes and cook.

Sauerkraut Provençale

An unusual vegetable dish—

 ⅓ cup chopped onion
    2 tablespoons butter or margarine,
        melted
 ⅓ cup canned condensed beef broth
    1 14-ounce can sauerkraut,
        drained
    2 tablespoons chopped, canned
        pimiento
            • • •
 ½ cup dairy sour cream
    Poppy seed

Cook chopped onion in melted butter or margarine till tender but not brown. Add condensed beef broth, drained sauerkraut, and chopped pimiento; mix lightly. Simmer, covered, for 10 minutes. Serve topped with dairy sour cream and dashed with poppy seed. Makes 4 servings.

Meatball–Sauerkraut Skillet

A tasty combination—

    1 pound ground beef
    3 cups soft bread crumbs
        (3 to 4 slices bread)
 ¼ cup milk
    1 egg
 ¾ teaspoon salt
    Dash pepper
    2 tablespoons shortening
            • • •
    1 27-ounce can sauerkraut,
        drained
 ½ cup chopped onion
 ½ teaspoon salt
 ¾ cup uncooked long-grain rice
 1½ cups water
    1 16-ounce can tomatoes, cut up

In bowl combine ground beef, bread crumbs, milk, egg, ¾ teaspoon salt, and pepper. Mix well. Shape into 12 meatballs. Brown in shortening in large skillet; remove meatballs.

In same skillet combine drained sauerkraut, chopped onion, and ½ teaspoon salt. Stir in uncooked rice and water. Add meatballs and tomatoes. Bring to boiling; reduce heat and simmer, covered, for 30 to 35 minutes. Serves 6.

SAUSAGE—A general name for over 200 meat products made of chopped or ground, seasoned meat and frequently stuffed into casings. Sausages are prepared from beef, veal, pork, lamb, liver, poultry, or a mixture of meats that are flavored with spices and herbs, and can be processed by salting, pickling, or smoking. The variety of sausages available includes mild, hot, moist, and dry sausages as well as thick or thin tubes, small or large links, and even loose sausage meat.

Federal regulations specify the ingredients, including the amount of fat and the additives that are used in each kind of sausage. For example, pork sausage can contain up to 50 percent fat, while frankfurters are limited to 30 percent.

Sausage has been used for such a long time that it is thought that a caveman was probably responsible for discovering how to preserve meat by hanging it over the smoke and heat of a fire or by letting it dry in the sun. As man became more sophisticated in his food habits, it was found that curing and then smoking meats improved keeping quality. It is known that sausagelike meats were prepared and eaten by the ancient Babylonians and the Chinese more than a thousand years before the Christian Era.

In 900 B.C., Homer wrote of a sort of sausage in the Odyssey. Other ancient Greeks also referred to sausage in their plays, and one writer about 500 B.C. spoke of salami, a sausage named for the ancient city of Salamis on Cyprus.

The Romans called sausage meats *salsus*, meaning salted. One of their specialties was made of fresh pork, pine nuts, cumin, bay leaves, and pepper.

By the Middle Ages, sausagemaking was a flourishing business. Sausagemakers wisely used the meats and seasonings that were plentiful in their regions. This practice resulted in distinctive sausages that were famous throughout Europe. Many of these local sausages carried with them the name of the city of their origin—Bologna sausage and Genoa salami. In some countries, sausages contained other foods of the area mixed with the meat, such as oatmeal in Scotland and cabbage in Luxembourg.

The popular pair, frankfurters and sauerkraut, combine in a delicious way in this easy-to-make Frank and Kraut Stew.

When early settlers arrived in America, they found the Indians making a sausage of chopped dried beef and berries. As people came from different countries to live in the New World, they brought their knowledge of making European-type sausages. Soon, some local, community sausage kitchens began to duplicate the homemakers' recipes commercially.

As the years passed new types of sausages were invented, too. One of these, scrapple, a mixture of pork, cornmeal, and spices cooked together and then shaped into a loaf, was created by the thrifty Pennsylvania Dutch to use up every bit of meat after butchering a hog.

Nutritional value: Like all meats, sausage is a source of high-quality protein, vitamins, and minerals. However, since the ingredients in different sausages vary greatly, the amount of these nutrients in sausage depends on the kind of sausage. The caloric value of sausage also depends on the kind of sausage. For example, three cooked, brown-and-serve sausages yield about 280 calories. The same portion of bologna provides 130 calories.

How sausage is manufactured: Although the recipes and some of the processing steps for sausage vary depending on the type of sausage being made and who's making it, there are several processes that are used in making any sausage.

The very important first step in making sausage is chopping or grinding and mixing the sausage ingredients. This is accomplished quickly by large, high-speed machines. Interestingly, in the making of some sausages, ice or cold water (the amount is regulated by law) is added to the mixture during the chopping process. This not only lowers the mixture to the proper temperature, but it also facilitates the mixing of seasonings and helps to control the texture of the sausage.

The next step in making most sausages is the stuffing process. Again, large machines are used. First, the sausage mixture is packed into the machine as tightly as possible to eliminate air pockets from forming. Then, the machine stuffs the meat mixture into either natural or cellulose casings of various diameters.

Since the sausage is in a very long tube when it leaves the stuffing machine, it is next sent to the linking machine, which twists or ties off the sausage into shorter lengths. The length of each sausage link depends on the type of sausage. Although most sausages are eventually cut into individual links, usually the links are left hooked together until later.

The smokehouse is the next stop in sausage processing. Originally, sausage was smoked to preserve it, but today refrigeration takes care of preservation. The smoking now is done for flavoring. The hardwood sawdust used, the amount of smoke, and the length of time the sausage is smoked differ, depending on the type of sausage, but all are carefully controlled to produce the desired flavor.

Sausages that are ready to eat when purchased have either been cooked or dried during processing. If the cooked sausages are also to be smoked, the two processes are often combined by cooking the sausage in the smokehouse. However, sausages may also be cooked with separate hot water or steam equipment. Dry sausages undergo two special processes—fermentation and drying. Fermentation is responsible for the tangy flavor of dry sausages, and the controlled air-drying of these sausages makes them ready to eat without cooking.

Types of sausages: Depending on their processing, sausages are grouped into one of five types—fresh; uncooked; smoked; cooked, smoked; and dry.

Fresh sausage is made by seasoning uncured, fresh meat, usually pork or beef. All fresh sausages, such as fresh pork sausage, bratwurst, weisswurst, and bockwurst, must be cooked.

The second type of sausage—uncooked, smoked sausage made from cured meat—also requires cooking by the homemaker. This type includes country-style pork sausage, linguisa, and mettwurst.

Sausages classed as cooked sausages are usually made from uncured meat, but cured meat is sometimes used. After stuffing, these sausages are thoroughly cooked in special hot water or steam cooking equipment. Blood sausage, liver sausage, and blood and tongue sausage are examples of this type of sausage. Often, these fully cooked sausages are served cold, but they may be heated.

The two most popular kinds of sausages, frankfurters and bologna, are both cooked, smoked sausages as are Berliner sausage, Polish sausage, knackwurst, and smokie links. Cured meat is usually used for this type of sausage. After they have been stuffed into casings, these sausages are smoked and cooked. These smoked sausages are fully cooked.

The last type of sausage is dry sausage. Besides chopped meat and spices, a curing agent such as salt or saltpeter is added to the initial sausage mixture. This meat mixture is then allowed to cure (or ferment) for several days, either before or after it is stuffed into casings. If

A variety of sausage links

Complementary sausage accompaniments → include cheese, potato salad, sauerkraut, pickled beets, cucumber pickles, and mustard.

	Sausage Chart	
Name	**Description**	**Serving Suggestions**
Berliner	A cooked, smoked sausage made of cured pork and usually some beef. Keep refrigerated.	Serve cold with beer and rye bread.
Blood sausage	Cooked sausage of pork, seasonings, and beef blood. Refrigerate.	Serve in sandwiches or on cold plates.
Bockwurst	Fresh sausage made of ground pork, veal, eggs, and spices. Keep refrigerated; use promptly.	Simmer, then fry. Serve with sauerkraut, cabbage, or beans.
Bologna	Mild, smoked and cooked, beef and pork sausage. Sold in rings, sticks, and slices. Refrigerate.	Serve cold with cheese or in sandwiches.
Bratwurst	Made of pork and beef or pork and veal, and spices. Keep refrigerated; use promptly.	Grill or simmer and fry.
Cappicola	A lightly smoked, dried pork sausage seasoned with paprika and red pepper. Keep refrigerated.	Serve in sandwiches or on cold plates.
Cervelat	Smoked, dried sausage made of beef and pork. Keep refrigerated.	Serve on cold plates, in sandwiches, or creamed on toast.
Chorizos	Lightly smoked, dried pork sausage containing pimiento. Refrigerate.	Use in soups and in vegetable combinations.
Cotto salami	Pork and beef sausage seasoned with garlic and whole peppercorns. Keep refrigerated.	Use on pizza, in other Italian dishes, or serve cold in salads.
Frankfurters	Ground pork and beef. Fully cooked and smoked during manufacture. Keep refrigerated.	Use in buns, with sauerkraut, or in casseroles.
Fresh pork sausage	Ground pork seasoned with spices. Sold in bulk, patties, or links. Keep refrigerated; use promptly.	As an accompaniment for eggs or pancakes and in casseroles.
Frizzes	All-pork sausage sold in two types—with sweet spices and with hot spices. Refrigerate.	Good sandwich meat. Also serve in Italian dishes.
Genoa salami	All-pork dry sausage seasoned with garlic and sometimes wine. Keep refrigerated.	Use in sandwiches or in Italian dishes.

Sausage Chart		
Name	Description	Serving Suggestions
Italian pork sausage	Made of pork, and highly seasoned with garlic and other spices. Keep refrigerated; use promptly.	Use on pizza or in spaghetti sauce.
Italian salami	A pork and beef, dry sausage that is highly seasoned. Refrigerate.	Serve with dark bread or crackers as a snack.
Knackwurst	Similar to frankfurters in ingredients but seasoned with garlic. Keep refrigerated.	Serve with sauerkraut, with potato salad, and in casseroles.
Lebanon bologna	All-beef, cooked and smoked sausage. Keep refrigerated.	Serve on cold plates, in salads, or with sharp cheese.
Liver sausage	Made of pork and pork livers. Smooth texture; slices or spreads easily. Keep refrigerated.	Serve cold in sandwiches or on crackers.
Mortadella	Made of beef, pork, and fat; contains garlic. Refrigerate.	Use cold in sandwiches or heat and serve with a sauce.
Pastrami	Smoked, dried, beef sausage seasoned with garlic, cumin, and other spices. Refrigerate.	Serve hot or cold in sandwiches.
Pepperoni	Made of pork and sometimes beef, seasoned with pepper. Sold in large links. Keep refrigerated.	Slice thinly and use in Italian dishes, especially pizza.
Polish sausage	Cooked and smoked pork and beef sausage seasoned with garlic and coriander. Keep refrigerated.	Fry and serve for breakfast.
Smoked thuringer	A cooked and smoked, pork and beef sausage found primarily in the Midwest. Keep refrigerated.	Grill and serve in buns.
Summer sausage	Made of beef, beef heart, and pork. Mildly seasoned and dried. Keep refrigerated.	Serve as snack, in sandwiches, or cooked with cabbage.
Vienna sausage	Mild, tiny, canned sausage links that are lightly smoked.	Serve as a cocktail snack or in casseroles.
Weisswurst	A mildly seasoned, pork and veal sausage characterized by its light color. Keep refrigerated; use promptly.	Serve fried for breakfast.

the sausage is smoked, this is done after curing. The most important step in making dry sausage is the air-drying process. This is done under specially controlled conditions of humidity and other factors. Pepperoni, salami, pastrami, summer sausage, cappicola, and other types of dry sausage can be served cold or hot.

How to store: Sausages that belong to the first four types—fresh; uncooked, smoked; cooked; and cooked, smoked—require storage in the refrigerator. Like other fresh meat, fresh sausage is highly perishable, so use it a day or two after purchase. Sausages that have been cooked and/or smoked can be kept longer.

Although uncut dry sausages will keep in any cool, dry storage place, refrigeration is recommended for long periods of storage. After the sausage is cut, it definitely needs to be refrigerated.

Because freezing affects the flavor of the fat in sausage, freezer storage is not recommended for sausages.

How to use: Italian sausage pizza, sausage patties and scrambled eggs, frankfurters in buns, sausage casseroles, apples and sausage links, sausage and sauerkraut, bologna sandwiches, and salami and cheese are only a few examples of popular uses for sausage. Quite naturally, the wide selection of sausages that are available has led to the development of numerous uses for sausage. Not only is it easy to use your favorite kind of sausage in several different ways, but it is also easy to acquaint your family with a wide selection of sausages served in a variety of ways. (See also *Pork.*)

Snapperoni Franks

Cover 6 frankfurters with cold water; bring to boiling. Simmer 5 minutes. In saucepan slightly mash one 21-ounce can pork and beans in tomato sauce with a fork. Blend in ½ cup diced pepperoni, ¼ cup catsup, and 2 tablespoons sweet pickle relish. Cook and stir until mixture is heated through. Split and toast 6 frankfurter buns. Place franks in buns; spoon pepperoni-bean mixture over franks. Serves 6.

Easy Italian Chicken

   ¼ cup all-purpose flour
   ½ teaspoon paprika
   ½ teaspoon dried oregano leaves, crushed
   ¼ teaspoon garlic salt
   1 2½- to 3-pound ready-to-cook broiler-fryer chicken, cut up
   ½ pound link sausages, sliced
   1 16-ounce can tomatoes, cut up

Combine first 4 ingredients and 2 teaspoons salt; coat chicken pieces with flour mixture. Brown sausage in large, shallow baking pan at 400° about 15 minutes. Remove pan from oven; pour off excess fat. Stir in *half* of the tomatoes. Place chicken, skin side down, in a single layer in pan. Bake at 400° for 30 minutes. Turn the chicken. Add remaining tomatoes and bake until browned, 45 minutes longer. Spoon sauce over the chicken. Makes 4 servings.

Frank Triangles

   8 frankfurters
      Butter or margarine
   8 slices bread, crusts removed
   ¼ cup grated Parmesan cheese
   3 tablespoons prepared mustard
   3 tablespoons finely chopped onion
  16 pimiento-stuffed green olives

Place frankfurters in cold water; bring to boiling and simmer 5 minutes. Drain.

Butter one side of bread; dip buttered side in cheese. Spread other side with mustard. Sprinkle each mustard-spread side with about 1 teaspoon onion. Place a frank diagonally across each slice. Fasten two opposite corners of each slice, cheese side out, with wooden picks. Place on side on broiler rack. Broil 3 inches from heat 2 to 3 minutes. Turn triangles over. Broil 2 to 3 minutes more. Trim with olives on wooden picks. Makes 8 servings.

Hearty meal-on-a-platter

Fluffy whipped potatoes surround the other →
foods—weinkraut, sausages, boiled beef, and pig's knuckles—that make up Hausplatte.

Individual Sausage and Muffin Bake casseroles combine English muffins, a sausage mixture, and tomato (see *Pork* for recipe).

Sausage in Biscuits

Convenience foods give you a head start—

> 1 8-ounce package refrigerated
>   biscuits (10)
>   Prepared mustard
> 1 4-ounce can Vienna sausages
>   • • •
> 1 10-ounce package frozen peas
>   in cream sauce

Pat out *seven* biscuits lengthwise*; spread lightly with mustard. Roll each Vienna sausage in a biscuit; seal edges with fingers. Place biscuits, seam side down, on small baking sheet; bake at 425° for about 10 minutes.

Prepare frozen peas in cream sauce following package directions. Spoon the cooked peas over the biscuits. Makes 7 sausage rolls.

*If desired, bake remaining biscuits.

Sausage Kabobs

Alternate brown-and-serve sausages, canned peach halves with a maraschino cherry in center, and mushroom caps on skewers. Brush generously with melted butter. Broil the kabobs 4 to 5 inches from coals till heated through, about 5 minutes on each side.

Hausplatte

> Precooked bratwurst
> Knackwurst
> Duchess Potatoes
> Weinkraut
> Corned Pig's Knuckles
> Boiled Beef
> Mustard
> Horseradish

Grill bratwurst and heat knackwurst briefly in boiling water. On a large, oval, seasoned plank, make a border with Duchess Potatoes. Fill center with Weinkraut. Top with these: Corned Pig's Knuckles, Boiled Beef, grilled bratwurst, and cooked knackwurst. Baste the meats with Burgundy gravy from Boiled Beef. Broil 5 to 8 minutes to brown the potatoes lightly. Pass mustard and horseradish.

Duchess Potatoes: Combine 4 cups hot mashed potatoes, 1 tablespoon butter, and 2 beaten egg yolks; season with salt and pepper. Mix well. Using No. 7 or No. 9 star tip, pipe the hot mixture around the rim of the plank; drizzle with 2 tablespoons melted butter.

Corned Pig's Knuckles: In saucepan cover corned pig's knuckles with fresh water. Add 1 small onion, halved, a few peppercorns, and a few bay leaves. Simmer till tender, about 2½ to 3 hours; remove meat from water.

Weinkraut: Finely chop 1 small onion; cook in ¼ cup butter or margarine till onion is just tender. Add 2 tablespoons brown sugar and let melt. Add ½ teaspoon salt; 1 teaspoon vinegar; 1½ cups dry white wine; 1 cup chicken broth; 1 small potato, grated; and 4 cups sauerkraut, drained. Cook, uncovered, for 30 minutes. Add 2 green apples, peeled and diced, and the cooked Corned Pig's Knuckles. Cover and simmer 30 minutes more. Drain the sauerkraut and remove the Pig's Knuckles.

Boiled Beef: Rub 4 pounds fresh lean beef short ribs with 1½ teaspoons salt; place in pot and cover with boiling water. Bring quickly back to boil; cook 10 minutes. Skim top.

Add 2 or 3 sprigs parsley; 4 peppercorns; and ½ teaspoon dried thyme leaves, crushed. Cover; cook slowly 3 hours. Last half hour add 2 onions, 2 carrots, 1 parsnip, 1 turnip, and 1 bay leaf. Lift out chunks of meat. Boil stock until reduced to rich gravy. Add about ¼ cup Burgundy to ¾ cup stock. Spoon some gravy over meats before broiling. Pass remainder.

Bologna Baskets

    6 or 8 slices bologna
    2 tablespoons shortening
    1 16-ounce can German-style
        potato salad
    Paprika

In stacks of 2 slices each, heat bologna in hot shortening in skillet until meat forms cups. Heat potato salad. Fill bologna cups with potato salad. Sprinkle with paprika. Serve individually or as a garnish. Serves 3 or 4.

SAUTÉ *(sō tā′, sô-)*—To cook quickly in a very small amount of fat. Since sautéing is done rapidly, the food cooked in this way must be thin in order to cook thoroughly. Vegetables such as onions are often sautéed before using them.

SAUTERNE, SAUTERNES *(sō tûrń, sô-)*—**1.** A very rich and sweet, golden-hued wine that is made in the Sauternes region of France. In this context, the name of the wine is properly spelled sauternes. **2.** The generic name for a category of dry to sweet white wines that are produced in the United States. The final *s* is left off when denoting a United States wine.

Sauternes of France: Five townships in southern France legally comprise the area in which French sauternes are made. Even though a wine producer just outside this region produces wine from the same type of grapes and in the same manner, he cannot call it wine sauterne.

According to legend, the first French sauternes was developed accidentally at the Yquem château. Reportedly, the grapes at that château reached the peak of their maturity while the owner was away. When he returned, the grapes were overmature, shriveled, and covered with a mold. The owner harvested the grapes anyway and processed them into wine. What resulted was a uniquely rich, sweet wine that is now known as sauternes.

Today, scientists understand what changes the grapes undergo during the ripening. As the three varieties grown in this region—Semillon, Sauvignon blanc,

and Muscadelle—pass their peak of ripeness, the sun causes the grapes to shrivel and dehydrate. This increases the concentration of sugar in the grapes. At the same time, a specific mold, *Botrytis cinerea,* which gives the wine its unusual and characteristic aroma, develops on and penetrates through the fruit skins. These changes are called the noble rot.

The high sugar content and the yeast produced by noble rot are a hindrance in making dry wine, but they are essential if a natural sweet wine is desired. To make sauternes, therefore, harvesting the grapes just at this noble rot stage is of utmost importance. Oftentimes, the grapes must be picked one by one in a series of harvests. The grapes are picked only when the sun is high in the sky so that any dew on the grapes has evaporated. Fermentation and bottling of sauternes are similar to other wines.

Uses of French sauternes: Because of the intense sweetness, sauternes is categorized as a dessert wine. When used as a dessert beverage, it should be served at cool room temperature, 60° to 70°. Sauternes is also used as an ingredient in desserts, particularly fruit-flavored ones.

Sauterne of the United States: A wine designated as sauterne (without the *s*) by a United States winery has quite different specifications than those of a French sauternes. Although golden in color, these sauternes are, in general, dry to semisweet table wines. There are a few sweet, American-produced sauternes.

Unlike French sauternes, there are no set grape varieties that must be used in the production of a United States sauterne. Any variety that produces a wine within the American defined limits of the sauterne category can be used. Some of the better United States-produced sauternes are made from one or more of the traditional varieties. Under federal law, if the wine contains over 51 percent of this varietal grape, it may be given that varietal name, such as Semillon.

Three names—dry sauterne, sauterne, and sweet, haut, or château sauterne—are applied to United States-produced

wines to indicate the relative dryness or sweetness of the wines. What determines the name used on the sauterne label is not legally defined in this country. Instead, each vintner determines his own specifications for the three types.

Sauterne as produced in the United States parallels that of other wines. Harvesting is carried out in one session. A very few premium sauternes are produced from grapes to which *Botrytis cinerea* usually must be induced artificially. These wines, quite naturally, command higher prices at the stores.

Uses of United States-produced sauterne: In order to determine how to use a sauterne that has been produced in the United States, it is essential that you know whether the wine is dry or sweet.

The drier sauterne types are used as entree accompaniments or ingredients. Poultry, fish, shellfish, veal, and cheese complement the delicate flavor of sauterne. When served as the beverage of the meal, the wine should be 45° to 50°.

Sweeter sauternes should be used in a dessert fashion as are the French sauternes. (See also *Wines and Spirits.*)

Sauterne Sauce

    ¼ cup dry sauterne
    1 tablespoon instant minced onion
            •   •   •
    ¾ cup mayonnaise or salad
        dressing
    2 tablespoons snipped parsley
    1 tablespoon lemon juice

In small saucepan combine sauterne and instant minced onion; let stand about 10 minutes. Add mayonnaise or salad dressing, snipped parsley, and lemon juice. Heat, stirring constantly, over low heat. Makes 1 cup sauce.

Dessert elegance

← Decoratively mound sweetened whipped cream in the center of the cake as the finishing touch to delicious Savarin Chantilly.

Wine-Broiled Chicken

Combine ¼ cup dry sauterne; ¼ cup salad oil; ¼ cup chopped onion; 2 teaspoons bottled steak sauce; 2 teaspoons lemon juice; 1 teaspoon dry mustard; 1 teaspoon salt; ⅛ teaspoon dried thyme leaves, crushed; ⅛ teaspoon dried marjoram leaves, crushed; ⅛ teaspoon dried rosemary leaves, crushed; and dash pepper. Mix well; cover and let stand several hours at room temperature or overnight in refrigerator to blend flavors.

Brush two 2- to 2½-pound ready-to-cook broiler-fryer chickens, split in halves lengthwise or in quarters, with wine mixture. Place, skin side down, in broiler pan (without rack). Broil the chicken 5 to 7 inches from heat till lightly browned, about 20 minutes. Brush occasionally with the wine mixture. Turn; broil till done, about 15 to 20 minutes longer, brushing occasionally with mixture. Serves 4.

Herbed Chicken Bake

A company special main dish—

Prepare one 6-ounce package long-grain, wild rice mix according to package directions. Bone 3 large chicken breasts; halve lengthwise. Season with salt and pepper.

In skillet slowly brown boned chicken in ¼ cup butter or margarine. Spoon cooked rice into 1½-quart casserole; top with chicken pieces, skin side up. Add one 10½-ounce can condensed cream of chicken soup to skillet; slowly add ¾ cup dry sauterne, stirring till smooth. Stir in ½ cup sliced celery; one 3-ounce can sliced mushrooms, drained; and 2 tablespoons chopped, canned pimiento. Bring soup mixture to boil; pour over chicken. Cover; bake at 350° for 25 minutes. Uncover; bake till chicken is tender, 20 minutes. Serves 6.

SAVARIN *(sav′uh rin)*—A rich, yeast cake baked in a ring mold, then steeped in a sugar syrup flavored with rum, another liquor, or fruit juice. A savarin is often glazed, decorated, and served with whipped cream. The mold in which this cake is baked is also called a savarin.

A baba is similar to a savarin, but it is traditionally baked in a flared mold.

Savarin Chantilly

  1 package active dry yeast
  2 cups sifted all-purpose flour
  ¾ cup milk
  6 tablespoons butter or margarine
  ¼ cup sugar
  1 egg
    Savarin Syrup
    Apricot Glaze
    Blanched almonds
    Candied cherries
    Creme Chantilly

In large mixer bowl combine yeast and *1½ cups* flour. Heat milk, butter or margarine, sugar, and ½ teaspoon salt just till warm, stirring occasionally to melt butter. Add to dry mixture in mixer bowl; add egg. Beat at low speed of electric mixer for ½ minute, scraping sides of bowl constantly. Beat 3 minutes at high speed. By hand stir in remaining flour.

Cover; let rise in warm place till double, about 1¼ hours. Stir down batter; spoon into a well-greased 6½-cup ring mold. Cover; let rise till almost double, about 45 minutes.

Bake at 350° till top is browned, about 35 minutes. Cool 5 minutes, then remove from mold; place on rack on baking sheet. With a meat fork, prick top of ring in several places. Gradually drizzle Savarin Syrup, a small amount at a time, over ring, till all syrup is absorbed. Let stand about 30 minutes. Then, drizzle on Apricot Glaze. Trim top with blanched almonds and candied cherries. At serving time, fill center with Creme Chantilly. Serves 14.

Savarin Syrup: Combine ¾ cup sugar and 1½ cups water; bring to boil. Cool to lukewarm. Stir in ½ cup cognac, rum, *or* kirsch.

Apricot Glaze: In small saucepan cook and stir one 12-ounce jar apricot preserves (about 1¼ cups) over low heat till melted; sieve.

Creme Chantilly: In mixing bowl whip 2 cups whipping cream with 2 tablespoons confectioners' sugar and 2 teaspoons vanilla.

SAVORY (*sā′vuh rē*) — **1.** An herb belonging to the mint family. **2.** A nonsweet tidbit served in England at the end of a meal. These savories resemble appetizers, but instead of being served at the beginning of the meal, they are served after the dessert to clear the palate.

Savory, the herb, is a native of southern Europe where it is not only used as a seasoning but also as pillow stuffing because of its pleasing fragrance.

This herb is well known in two varieties. Winter savory is a perennial bushy herb; summer savory is a somewhat-scraggly annual plant. Both varieties can be quite easily grown in herb gardens, but the dried savory available in supermarkets is the milder summer savory.

The flavor of savory leaves is aromatic and slightly resinous. This is an herb that seems purposely made for all kinds of fresh beans. In fact, its German name means bean herb. However, savory also adds a pleasingly distinctive flavor to tossed salads, sauerkraut, cabbage, peas, scrambled eggs, fish, many sauces, and poultry dishes. Savory is frequently used in stuffings, and it is an ingredient in most poultry seasoning mixtures. As with other seasonings, use only enough savory to season the food. (See also *Herb.*)

Savory Green Beans

  2 16-ounce cans green beans
  3 tablespoons butter or margarine, melted
  2 tablespoons chopped canned pimiento
  1 teaspoon dried savory leaves, crushed
  ¼ teaspoon salt
    Dash pepper

Heat beans in their liquid; drain well. Return beans to pan. Combine butter, pimiento, savory, salt, and pepper; pour over beans. Toss lightly to coat. Makes 8 servings.

SAVOY CABBAGE — A green cabbage variety, named for the Savoy region in France, that has large, curly and wrinkled leaves that form into a moderately loose head. The shape of the leaves makes them especially good for the wrappers of stuffed cabbage rolls. (See also *Cabbage.*)

SCALD — To heat a liquid to a temperature just below the boiling point.

SCALE – 1. A flat, hard plate that makes up the covering on fish. **2.** To remove this covering from a fish. **3.** A piece of equipment used for weighing foods.

To scale a fish, first wash it thoroughly. Fish are easier to scale when wet, so do not dry. If the fish was washed earlier, dip it in cold water for a few minutes. Then, place on a flat surface and scrape the scales off with a knife or scraper. Hold the instrument almost vertically, and move from the tail toward the head.

The piece of household equipment known as a scale comes in several types. One has a sliding weight like a doctor's scales. Another has a spring balance.

A scale in the home can improve accuracy in measuring and save time. Use the scale to weigh meats, vegetables, and cheeses. If these foods are placed in a dish or pan before weighing, be sure to subtract the extra weight of the container.

It's easy to halve mixtures accurately and quickly if you first weigh the total amount and then remove part of the mixture until the scale registers half of the original weight. This comes in handy when dividing cookie doughs, cake batters, candies, candied fruits, and sauces.

Follow the instruction booklet for correct use and care of equipment. Check the scale occasionally with weights, if possible, to see that it is accurate.

SCALLION *(skal' yuhn)* – Another name for the immature-bulbed green onion. There is some possibility that the name, scallion, was derived from the Palestinian seaport of Ascalon. (See also *Green Onion.*)

SCALLOP – A shellfish in a saucer-shaped, two-part shell. Except that scallops are more active, they are similar to oysters and clams. Their large muscle, sometimes called the eye, opens and closes the shell to propel them through water. This muscle, firm and delicately sweet, is the only part eaten by Americans, although Europeans eat the entire shellfish.

The nutritional value of scallops centers around their high-quality protein. The meat also contains minerals and fat. A 3½-ounce serving, steamed, has 110 calories; breaded and fried, 195 calories.

The principal types of scallops are bay, sea, and calico. Bay scallops live inshore along the New England and Gulf coasts. They are small and have a grooved or ridged shell. The creamy pink, tan, or white meat has a more tender texture and more delicate flavor than the sea scallop.

Sea scallops live along the north and middle parts of the Atlantic coast. They are larger and whiter than those from the bay, and their shells are not ridged.

Calico scallops closely resemble bay scallops. They were discovered recently along the Florida and North Carolina coasts. Calicos are expected to be available to the consumer in the future.

The boats that catch scallops also dress and pack them at sea. The shells are opened and the muscles removed. These muscles are marketed fresh or frozen. Frozen ones are cooked or breaded.

When purchasing fresh scallops, look for those with little or no liquid and a sweet odor. Keep chilled and use promptly.

Eat scallops raw like oysters and clams, or bake, broil, fry, or boil them before eating. Dishes made with scallops are served as entrées, appetizers, and salads. Use either fresh or frozen scallops in recipes; frozen ones are usually thawed before cooking. Allow ½ to ⅓ pound for each serving. (See also *Shellfish.*)

Deep-Fried Scallops

Drain scallops; dry between paper toweling. Roll in all-purpose flour seasoned with salt and pepper. Dip into mixture of 1 beaten egg and 1 tablespoon water, then fine dry bread crumbs. Fry in deep, hot fat (375°) till golden, about 2 minutes. Drain on paper toweling. Serve scallops hot; pass tartar sauce.

Broiled Scallops

Use 2 pounds fresh or frozen scallops. Thaw frozen scallops. Place in shallow baking pan. Sprinkle with salt, pepper, and paprika. Dot with butter. Broil 3 inches from heat till lightly browned, about 6 to 9 minutes. Serve with lemon wedges or tartar sauce and garnish with parsley, if desired. Serves 6.

Hot Scallop Chowder

  1 pound fresh or frozen scallops
  2 cups boiling water
  1 teaspoon salt
      •   •   •
  1 10½-ounce can condensed cream
    of chicken soup
  1 10½-ounce can condensed cream
    of potato soup
1½ cups milk
  1 cup light cream
  2 teaspoons snipped chives

Thaw frozen scallops. Rinse and chop coarsely. Place in boiling, salted water. Return to boil. Reduce heat; simmer 1 minute. Drain. Combine soups and milk in blender container or mixer bowl. Blend or beat till smooth. Pour into saucepan; stir in cream and chives. Heat just to boiling, stirring occasionally. Add scallops; heat through. Pour into soup bowls; top with snipped chives, if desired. Serves 6.

Scallops Mornay

An elegant casserole—

Combine ½ cup dry sauterne, ¾ cup water, ¼ teaspoon salt, ¼ teaspoon instant minced onion, and dash pepper in saucepan. Simmer 5 minutes. Add 8 ounces frozen scallops (halve or quarter if large) and ½ cup sliced fresh mushrooms. Cover and simmer 5 minutes. Remove scallops and mushrooms; set aside.

Cook stock in saucepan till reduced to ½ cup, about 15 minutes. Melt 1 tablespoon butter or margarine in another saucepan; stir in 1½ tablespoons all-purpose flour. Stir in fish stock and ½ cup milk; cook and stir till mixture thickens and bubbles. Add ¼ cup grated process Swiss cheese, stirring till melted. Season with salt and pepper, if desired.

Remove from heat; add scallops and mushrooms. Spoon into two individual baking dishes. Bake at 375° for 15 to 20 minutes. Trim with 1 to 2 tablespoons snipped parsley. Serves 2.

For an easy-to-prepare main dish, try Corn and Chicken Scallop. Place chicken drumsticks atop the corn and onion mixture and bake. Mushrooms and parsley, added later, complete the dish.

Scallops Tetrazzini

Thaw one 12-ounce package frozen scallops; cut scallops in halves. In saucepan combine scallops, ½ teaspoon instant minced onion, ¼ teaspoon salt, and dash pepper. Add 1 cup water. Cover; simmer 10 minutes. Drain; reserve ½ cup cooking liquid. Melt 2 tablespoons butter. Blend in 2 tablespoons all-purpose flour; ½ teaspoon paprika; 1 drop bottled hot pepper sauce; dash dried oregano leaves, crushed; and dash salt. Add the ½ cup cooking liquid and ½ cup milk. Cook and stir till thickened. Stir a little hot mixture into 1 slightly beaten egg. Return to sauce; mix well.

Add one 3-ounce can broiled, sliced mushrooms with liquid and scallops to sauce. Mix well. Spoon 4 ounces spaghetti, cooked and drained, into a 10x6x1¾-inch baking dish. Top the spaghetti with the scallop mixture; sprinkle with 2 tablespoons grated Parmesan cheese. Broil about 5 minutes. Makes 4 servings.

Scallops and Bacon

     1 pound fresh or frozen scallops
· · ·
     ¼ cup butter or margarine, melted
     2 tablespoons lemon juice
     ½ teaspoon salt
        Dash white pepper
· · ·
        Sliced bacon
        Paprika

Thaw frozen scallops. Remove any shell particles and wash. Combine butter or margarine, lemon juice, salt, and pepper. Pour mixture over scallops; let stand for 30 minutes, turning once. Drain the scallops.

Cut bacon slices in half lengthwise. In a skillet partially cook bacon until it begins to ruffle, but is still flexible. Drain on paper toweling and let cool.

Wrap each of the scallops with a piece of partially cooked bacon and hold the bacon in place with a wooden pick. Place the bacon-wrapped scallops in a wire broiler basket. Sprinkle topside with paprika.

Broil over *medium-hot* coals for 5 minutes. Turn and sprinkle with paprika. Broil second side of scallops until bacon is crisp and brown, about 5 to 7 minutes. Serve while hot.

Scallop Salad

Thaw 1½ pounds frozen scallops. Place scallops and 2 tablespoons salt in 1 quart boiling water. Cover; return to boiling. Reduce heat; simmer 3 to 4 minutes. Drain and cool; slice. Combine cooked scallops; one 10-ounce package frozen green beans, cooked and drained; 1 cup sliced celery; 2 tablespoons chopped green onion; 2 tablespoons chopped green pepper; and 2 tablespoons chopped, canned pimiento.

In screw-top jar combine ½ cup vinegar; 1 tablespoon salad oil; 1 tablespoon sugar; ¼ teaspoon salt; ¼ teaspoon dried tarragon leaves, crushed; and dash pepper. Cover and shake. Pour vinegar mixture over scallop mixture. Cover; chill at least 1 hour, stirring occasionally. Drain before serving. Spoon salad into lettuce cups. Makes 6 servings.

Scallops Elegant

     1 pound fresh or frozen scallops
     ½ cup finely chopped celery
     ¼ cup chopped onion
     1 small clove garlic, minced
     3 tablespoons butter or margarine
     ¼ cup fine saltine cracker crumbs
     1 tablespoon snipped parsley
     1 tablespoon all-purpose flour
     ¼ teaspoon paprika
     ½ cup milk
     2 tablespoons dry sherry
     ¼ cup shredded process Swiss cheese

Cook scallops; cut large scallops in half. Cook celery, onion, and garlic in *2 tablespoons* butter till tender but not brown. Stir in scallops, crumbs, and parsley. Turn into an 8-inch pie plate. Melt remaining butter. Blend in flour, paprika, and ⅛ teaspoon salt. Add milk all at once. Cook and stir till thickened and bubbly. Remove from heat; stir in sherry. Pour sauce over scallops; sprinkle cheese atop. Bake at 425° for 15 minutes. Serves 4.

SCALLOPED—Foods combined with a saucy mixture that often contains cracker or bread crumbs, then baked. Scalloped vegetables, poultry, and seafood are excellent dishes to prepare several hours ahead and keep refrigerated.

Delectable Scalloped Corn and Oysters makes a perfect vegetable accompaniment for meat dishes such as roast turkey.

Corn and Chicken Scallop

Meat and vegetable cook in one dish—

      1 17-ounce can cream-style corn
      1 cup milk
      1 egg
      1 tablespoon all-purpose flour
      6 green onions and tops, snipped
      6 to 8 chicken drumsticks
        Paprika
        Seasoned salt
     30 saltine crackers
      ¼ cup butter or margarine
      1 3-ounce can sliced mushrooms,
        drained

In a large, shallow casserole (or 13x9x2-inch baking dish), thoroughly combine cream-style corn, milk, egg, flour, and snipped onions. Generously sprinkle drumsticks with paprika; arrange over corn. Dash with seasoned salt. Crumble crackers over all. Dot with chunks of butter. Bake at 350° till chicken is tender, about 1 hour. Place mushrooms in center of casserole. Return to oven to heat. Garnish with parsley, if desired. Serves 3 or 4.

Scalloped Corn Supreme

      1 17-ounce can cream-style corn
      1 cup milk
      1 well-beaten egg
      1 cup saltine cracker crumbs
      ¼ cup finely chopped onion
      3 tablespoons chopped, canned
        pimiento
      ¾ teaspoon salt
      ½ cup buttered cracker crumbs

Heat corn and milk. Gradually stir in egg. Add next 4 ingredients and dash pepper. Mix well. Pour into greased 8-inch round baking dish. Top with buttered crumbs. Bake at 350° for 20 minutes. Makes 6 servings.

Scalloped Corn and Oysters

Combine one 17-ounce can cream-style corn; one 10½-ounce can frozen condensed oyster stew, thawed (if desired, reserve a few of the oysters from stew for garnish); 1 cup medium saltine cracker crumbs; 1 cup milk; ¼ cup finely chopped celery; 1 slightly beaten egg; 1 tablespoon finely chopped, canned pimiento; ¼ teaspoon salt, and dash pepper. Pour into greased 1½-quart casserole. Combine 2 tablespoons butter, melted, and ½ cup saltine cracker crumbs. Sprinkle over corn mixture in wreath design. Bake at 350° for 45 minutes. Garnish with reserved oysters; bake till knife inserted halfway between center and edge comes out clean, 15 minutes. Serves 6.

Scalloped Potatoes

In saucepan melt 3 tablespoons butter or margarine over low heat. Blend in 2 tablespoons all-purpose flour, 1½ teaspoons salt, and ⅛ teaspoon pepper. Add 3 cups milk all at once. Cook quickly, stirring till thickened and bubbly. Remove mixture from heat.*

Peel and thinly slice 6 medium potatoes (6 cups). Place *half* the potatoes in greased 2-quart casserole; cover with 1 tablespoon chopped onion and *half* the sauce. Repeat layers, using another tablespoon chopped onion. Cover and bake at 350° about 1 hour. Uncover; bake 30 minutes. Serves 4 to 6.

*Shredded cheese may be added to sauce.